What's
Left to
Believe?

What's Left to Believe?

J. SCHONEBERG SETZER

NASHVILLE • ABINGDON PRESS • NEW YORK

111302

WHAT'S LEFT TO BELIEVE?

Copyright © 1968 by Abingdon Press

Library of Congress Catalog Card Number: 68-11473

SET UP, PRINTED, AND BOUND BY THE
PARTHENON PRESS, AT NASHVILLE,
TENNESSEE, UNITED STATES OF AMERICA

PREFACE

It was toward the end of the hour in an unusually vital seminar session at Duke Divinity School. We all sensed from our discussion the reality of the "resurrection" appearances of Jesus, and the crucial significance of this reality. But much of the New Testament record now lay shattered about our feet, disqualified for one valid reason or another by the science of literary criticism. The action among us—mostly supplied by the Ph.D. candidates—was vigorous, until one of the senior B.D. students, who would soon be faced with the practical challenge of communicating this knowledge to a congregation, queried: "But how do I explain all this to my laymen? If I begin to tell them about all these myths and legends and mistakes in the New Testament accounts, will they not turn on me in distress and ask 'Then what is left? And are you really sure about anything?'"

At this anguished inquiry the room fell strangely silent. For the first time in my acquaintance with him our beloved professor, who was an eloquent preacher and a highly astute scholar, was speechless. He was appreciative of the fundamentalist situation into which the young man was going. In the few minutes that remained before dismissal the awkward and frustrating attempts of a number of us to say something meaningful in reply were painful testimonies to the present communication barrier that separates the scholars and a growing proportion of the younger clergymen of the church from the bulk of the lay people and the older pastors.

This book has been written with that worried seminarian and his concerned laymen in mind. Each chapter was originally a sermon; and the method that worked for me in bringing my congregation into the twentieth century theologically was to hold a Bible study class for key adult leaders, and then over a period of a year and a half to preach this series of twenty-one sermons that follows the outline of the Apostles' and Nicene creeds.

Perhaps other preachers may discover in this book useful homiletical grist for similar programs; and their hard-to-convince laymen may also find herein the additional material that they need in order even to begin to accept the new positions being expounded from the pulpit. (Unsettling new thoughts must often be heard at least twice before they can be truly comprehended; and the testimony of two men, all things being equal, is always more weighty than the testimony of one.)

The chief difficulty in any such educational program, of course, is in translating and condensing the polysyllabic terminology of libraries of scholarly research into digestible and yet intellectually respectable form. Nevertheless, as unsatisfying as any such attempts will be to us, these attempts must still be made. For, I am convinced, the contemporary church is in grave danger of losing its present great influence for spreading the kingdom of God, and is simultaneously in danger of being halved in membership, unless it can soon find effective means of enlightening the great mass of Christian laymen with the "new" scholarly knowledge that alone can make the Christian faith crucially relevant to the needs of twentieth-century man. Unless the church at large is permitted, and even forced, to go through the shattering reformation of its antiquated dogmas and outworn habits that intellectual integrity requires, the church as an ecclesiastical institution, which should be the spearhead of God's spirit-inspired program of salvation in every age, will, not too far in the future, I feel, find itself largely relegated to the innocuous position of a historical curiosity by both disappointed Christian laymen and uninterested non-Christians.

This book is predicated on a number of personal convictions: (1) that the critical findings of the scholars in many major doctrinal areas are for all practical purposes conclusively proved as true; (2) that these critical findings alone provide an interpretation of God's program of salvation in Jesus Christ which is intellectually respectable in the twentieth century and which speaks to the needs of modern man persuasively; (3) that our laymen and pastors must understand the basic outline of these findings even if they cannot handle, or are not interested in, the involved and detailed scholarly apparatus; (4) that this basic outline can be adequately communicated even at the cost of partial caricaturing through necessary oversimplification and brevity; (5) that the pulpit is still the rostrum which reaches the largest percentage of our church members; (6) that laymen are often wondering why we are waiting so long to begin a recatechization of the church, and that they will gladly listen to a limited number of long doctrinal sermons as long as both they and we understand exactly what we are trying to do; and (7) that the relatively more tradition-bound denominations, such as my own Lutheranism, will never become totally committed to the ecumenical movement in North America until a grass-roots clamor for new twentieth-century doctrinal formulations has brought our churches to the realization that all Christendom today stands together and shares together in its more humble search for a clearer apprehension of God's truth.

I am keenly aware of the presumption of attempting to be simple and straightforward in declaring what the scholars concur in. However, the absence of perfect unanimity should not discourage, I feel, such sorely needed practical attempts to make the productive efforts of the scholars useful to all. For despite the continual controversies among them, are they not frequently differing over details? The larger matters, many of which are settled, no longer challenge them. It is precisely these larger matters, on which there is more conclusive research, of which I wish to see our laymen informed. They have heard often enough the declaration that the church today needs "more faith and less dogma." What they are now anxious to study are systematic efforts to construct that smaller body of dogma which calls for a larger faith. I can only apologize to my scholar friends at those points where this practical endeavor has done violence to the canons of scholarly sophistication.

There are numerous places in these sermons where I have obviously drawn my own conclusions from scholarly data which have not yet received much attention from the bulk of theologians. I can only plead that these "plausible" hypotheses have the practical effect for deeply concerned Christians of providing a temporary "swinging bridge" arrangement for gaps in our data and in our systematizing until stronger structures can be provided to fill these gaps. Georgia Harkness' little book *What Christians Believe*[1] is a superb example of what

---

[1] (Nashville: Abingdon Press, 1965).

I have in mind. I can also appeal to what I rather presumptuously shall call "Setzer's Law"—which is this: "The probability for the accuracy of any hypothesis is in direct proportion to the decrease in the number of unknown factors relevant to that hypothesis."

No bibliography has been appended for two chief reasons: First, the average layman or pastor who reads this book would not be able to benefit from a lengthy scholarly bibliography because of the unavailability of an adequate library. Second, this book was written while I was a busy parish pastor who was temporarily separated from a major theological library and from the time essential to the preparation of a bibliography that would satisfy the average scholar.

For these reasons I refer my readers to two excellent reference sets that every pastor and congregation should own: *The Interpreter's Dictionary of the Bible*[2] and *The Interpreter's Bible*.[3] Mention should also be made of two monumental volumes written at the request of the Society for Religion in Higher Education. These college introductory texts are *Understanding the Old Testament* by B. W. Anderson (2nd ed.; Englewood Cliffs: Prentice-Hall, 1966) and *Understanding the New Testament* by H. C. Kee, F. W. Young, and K. Froehlich (2nd ed.; Englewood Cliffs: Prentice Hall, 1965). A third work, *Invitation to the New Testament* by W. D. Davies (Garden City: Doubleday, 1966), provides a fine balance to what, I feel, is the occasionally excessive skepticism of Kee *et al.* Intelligent use of these works will yield further information and selected bibliographies that are quite adequate for initiating any independent research.

Let me also be quite candid here about my techniques in order that no reader will be misled as to my purposes.

I shall frequently disagree with the literal intention of certain sections of the Apostles' Creed and the Nicene Creed. My continual effort to find positive value in each creedal section, however, is not motivated by a desire to imply that the framers of these ancient creeds were intending the modern interpretations that I apply to their efforts. For I am persuaded that, from a literal point of view, a large proportion of these two creeds must be rejected today as definitely inadequate and erroneous. Nevertheless, my investigation has convinced me that each section of these creeds contains in figurative form a vital truth that must still be affirmed and proclaimed by the Christian church. For the

[2] (4 vols.; Nashville: Abingdon Press, 1962).
[3] (12 vols.; Nashville: Abingdon Press, 1951-57).

often embarrassing myths and legends, as well as the more abstract interpretations, preserved in these early creeds are in a powerful way testimonies to our basic Christian message about God and man.

Gratitude must be expressed to the host of patient teachers and friends who have helped me struggle through my intellectual pilgrimage in search for "what is left" and for "what we can really be sure about" on the basis of reasonable probabilities. The encouraging and long-suffering reception which the good people of Emmanuel Lutheran Church in Lincolnton, North Carolina, accorded the original sermons will always be warmly remembered. The generous financial assistance of the Lutheran Church Men of North Carolina, who helped to make my graduate studies possible, will be partly repaid, I hope, if this book proves to be of assistance to some of them. But nothing can repay my wife, who stood by me loyally and who unflinchingly urged me to preach the full truth in love to modern man, leaving the consequences to the eternal Father. Her encouragement mattered much at those times when I questioned whether I really had the courage to be straightforward about these things. This effort is dedicated to her, and to all those fellow pastors who themselves know what it means to go through the fiery furnace in bringing the church of God up to date.

J. SCHONEBERG SETZER

CONTENTS

Section V—SANCTIFICATION

Section VI—DESTINY

Appendixes

Section I: INTRODUCTION

1. Is the Bible Really the Word of God?

"From childhood you have been acquainted with the sacred writings which are able to instruct you for salvation through faith in Christ Jesus." II Timothy 3:15

For nearly two thousand years the Bible has been the Christian church's chief authority in matters of doctrine. So revered has the authority of this book been that, especially in certain Protestant denominations, the Bible has been alternately referred to as the "Word of God."

Since the Bible has historically been such a unique source book for Christian faith and practice, it is essential that I preface this entire book, which follows the structural outline of the Apostles' and Nicene creeds, with an introductory chapter on the nature of the Bible's authority. For unless the reader understands precisely how I am using the Bible, and also precisely how I am not using the Bible, and unless I can also persuade the reader that my manner of using the Bible is valid, then all the pages that follow will be wasted. Consequently, in this chapter I shall try to answer the very momentous question: "Is the Bible really the Word of God?"

I can still hear the voice of my godly old father in catechetical class as he declared to us catechumens with all the conviction at his command: "The Bible does not merely *contain* the Word of God! The

13

Bible *is* the Word of God!" In support of this conviction my father advanced two main arguments.

The first argument was the practical observation that if the Bible merely contained the word of God, then it could also contain material that was not the word of God, or material that was only the word of man. And since we could not be sure exactly which material was God's word and exactly which material was man's word, we would lose all surety about our Christian beliefs.

But more important to him was my father's scriptural argument that the Bible itself declared that it was the Word of God. He made us children memorize passages such as II Timothy 3:16: "All scripture is inspired by God"; and II Peter 1:21: "No prophecy ever came by the impulse of man, but men moved by the Holy Spirit spoke from God"; and Matthew 5:18: "Truly, I say to you, till heaven and earth pass away, not an iota, not a dot, will pass from the law until all is acccomplished"; and John 10:35: "Scripture cannot be broken"; and other verses.

In harmony with the official position of the church from the early centuries, my father believed that the spirit of God had so manipulated the minds and hands of the original Bible writers that the original Bible writings were the pure Word of God without the adulteration of a single human error. My father believed that any biblical errors that exist today had crept in later when scribes, who were not under the same divine guidance, made mistakes in producing copies of the original documents.

Naturally I accepted this conviction of my beloved father and church as my own. And while I had considerable difficulty in seminary with this theory that the original Bible was the pure Word of God, still I managed to adjust to those difficulties.

Then I went to my first parish. I was still single and had time to study my Bible exhaustively and at leisure, as I had not been able to do earlier. I benefited greatly from these three years of study. But I also began to be distressed by contradictions and inconsistencies that I found in the Bible. This sacred book that I loved so much simply did not hang together as perfectly as I wanted it to do.

It is difficult to communicate how deeply this matter disturbed me. I had promised Almighty God that I would proclaim his truth and serve his people. Nothing in life was so important to me as to be right about the things of God. I had no other passion so strong as my

14

desire to preach that which was really the truth of God, and not just human opinion. But materials which had seemed so clear when I read the Bible only in the light of the orthodox doctrinal positions of Christian history seemed so very unclear when I scrutinized the Bible as an integrated whole. Many were the times when I cried out in spiritual agony: "Lord God, how can *this* verse be true when it is directly contradicted in this *other* verse? What is the truth?"

As a result of this continual struggle, there gradually developed in me a compulsion to go to graduate school, as my seminary professors had earlier urged me to do, and there to settle for myself once and for all the status of the Bible as the Word of God. In the graduate school of religion at Duke University, I believe that God led me to a true understanding.

There I discovered a world of biblical scholarship that I had hardly more than tasted before. Brilliant scholars for a hundred and fifty years had been studying the Bible according to principles of scientific literary criticism. Libraries of research material had been written on the biblical languages—Hebrew, Aramaic, Greek, and a host of neighboring languages—because of large new finds of ancient literature. Libraries of material had also been written on the history and customs and beliefs of antiquity in the light of dozens of fruitful archaeological expeditions. And every one of these scientific biblical investigations seemed to substantiate the modern discovery that the Bible was very much a *human* book.

Christians have always been mystified, for instance, by the disconcerting manner in which prophets, such as Isaiah, jump from one subject to another for no apparent reason at all. But modern biblical scholars, by analyzing the vocabulary and grammar of the prophets, have discovered that Isaiah is not a continuous book in which God had mysteriously jumped from one subject to another as he magically guided the hand of a single prophet. Rather, it is now known that Isaiah is actually a scrapbook of the collected writings of several prophets over a period of two hundred years.

Modern biblical scholars have also learned how the traditional belief developed which held that the writing of the Scriptures was divinely controlled in every detail. Frequently, they explain, when the prophets spoke for God they were so aroused as to appear possessed and moved totally by God. Also, some of the prophets, such as Moses, reported that they were told to write down all the words that God had spoken to them.

The logical conclusion that had been drawn from these facts was that, if the perfect God had possessed the prophets totally, and also had demanded that these men write down his words, then their words must have been perfectly the words of God. But the old Hebrew fathers who had arrived at this opinion were not modern literary scholars who are persuaded by examining the evidence in the books themselves. Rather, the old Hebrew fathers were simply pious men of God who, by this opinion that God himself had written the Bible by the instrumentality of men, were operating by their faith that wanted to give glory to God, and not by actual knowledge of the Bible's beginnings.

This concern of the ancients to give glory to God produced some fantastic fables. There is the tale, for instance, about the manner in which the Greek translation of the Hebrew Old Testament was supposedly carried out. This translation, which dates from about 250 B.C., was believed by many people in Jesus' day to have been translated by seventy Holy Spirit–inspired scholars who, working independently of each other, in seventy days produced seventy identical copies of the Old Testament in Greek. As a result of this fiction, the translation has always been known as the Septuagint, which is the Greek word for "seventy."

As I studied, I learned facts like this. I also learned that the apostles very likely shared the general conviction of their day that God had magically guided the writing of the Old Testament. I learned that the sayings of Jesus had been collected and organized in such a fashion that sometimes it is impossible to know exactly what he meant by words such as those in Matthew 5:18 that not an iota or dot would pass from the law until all was accomplished. I learned that an adequate analysis of Jesus' speeches seems to challenge the magical biblical interpretation of his day. For instance, where Jesus says in John 10:35, "Scripture cannot be broken," he is in the middle of an argument with the scribes in which he is showing them that on their magical view of Scripture they are faced with a contradiction in which God causes his own Messiah to break the fourth commandment concerning honor for parents. I learned enough that finally I was forced to abandon the traditional belief of the Christian church in a magically inspired Bible. It simply did not fit the facts.

But then the practical problems began. The biblical scholars knew that they were discovering truth. They knew that in the process they were making some mistakes and were working with unfinished theories. For in every scientific endeavor the progress of knowledge is from a vague theory drawn out of some data to a clearer theory drawn out of more data. But the most acute problem that faced the scholars was—and still is—How do you inform the Christian layman about these scientific critical findings when the Christian layman for nearly two thousand years has been taught that the Bible is indeed the perfect Word of God?

Among American Christian scholars, furthermore, there is an extremist element composed of out-of-date, reactionary thinkers who are abysmally ignorant of the reasons why biblical literary and theological criticism is necessary, and who are continually urging that all Christians return to what they consider the still true "fundamentals" of the faith. These often self-styled "fundamentalists" have as their key doctrine the traditional belief in the divine perfection of the Bible's inspiration. They believe that the original Bible was "infallible" and "inerrant" —which means that it was absolutely free from human mistakes and misunderstandings.

The fundamentalists base their argument upon a narrow interpretation of those passages in which the Scriptures testify to their own inspiration. "Inspiration," the fundamentalists insist, must mean "perfect dictation of God's revelation," a concept of inspiration that impartial examination of the Bible simply does not support.

The fundamentalists declare that since the Bible, according to their interpretation, claims that it is a perfectly inspired book, we must humbly accept this testimony at face value and not challenge it. But, logicians point out, thus accepting the claim of anyone as true simply because he says it is true is to commit the logical fallacy called "begging the question," or "arguing in a circle."

Because the fundamentalists invalidly assume that their peculiarly interpreted proof passages are also the inspired Word of God, they are guilty of such arguing in a circle which assumes what must be proved in order to set about proving it.

For at least fifty-seven years these fundamentalists have been boldly labeling the biblical scholars and educated clergymen in every denomination, who are more careful about their biblical interpretation and their logic, "liberal heretics" and even "apostates." As a consequence, many of our better educated young clergymen are going into teaching fields, where the fundamentalists cannot make their livelihood insecure by arousing well-meaning but ignorant people in their congregations against a pastor who, they think, is merely propagating his own "new-fangled ideas" rather than the pure Word of God. Several of my classmates at Duke told me quite bluntly when they heard that I was returning to the parish ministry: "Frankly, I just don't have the guts. I don't want to be crucified. My denomination is too far back in the dark ages to take it yet."

But I was reared to believe that God's people deserve honest and adult treatment, and that they thrive on truth rather than on falsehood. Consequently I decided at graduate school to take this problem by the horns and to spend the third year writing my dissertation on this very subject. My dissertation ended up a four hundred and fifty page book with the jawbreaking title: *A Critique of the Fundamentalist Doctrine of the Inerrancy of the Biblical Autographs in Historical, Philosophical, Exegetical, and Hermeneutical Perspective.*

I share this biographical information with the reader in order to explain why I feel that we must be perfectly straightforward about the findings of modern scientific biblical research as we consider the question "Is the Bible really the Word of God?" An honorable frankness and openness to facts is the only clear path to truth.

Let me now propose that this question about the nature of biblical authority requires a triplex answer: No, Yes, and Perhaps. *No,* the Bible is not the Word of God. *Yes,* the Bible is the Word of God. And *perhaps* the Bible is the Word of God.

First the No. No, the Bible is not the Word of God. It is one hundred percent the word of man. Literary experts, as already explained, have discovered that the Bible bears every mark of totally human authorship. It contains old traditions that were passed down by word of mouth for hundreds of years before being recorded. And these traditions received some changes and embellishments—or decorative additions—as they were passed on. The Bible writers also make some historical mistakes and occasionally contradict themselves.

First Samuel, for instance, states that David was both known to Saul (16:21) and unknown to Saul (17:58) before David killed Goliath. The Gospel writers differ on whether Jesus healed blind Bartimaeus before he entered Jericho (Luke 18:35) or after he left

Jericho (Mark 10:46). The editor of Exodus fits together contradictory traditions on whether men have ever seen God's face (33:23 versus 24:11).

Occasionally some of the things which the Old Testament writers report that God commanded or said are so unworthy of God as to be quite obviously human interpretations that over the generations became intermixed and confused with God's own words (Num. 31:17). Sometimes the Gospel writers did not clearly understand what Jesus had meant, judging by the vastly different settings that they assign to his darker sayings (Matt. 17:20; Luke 17:56). It seems obvious that all the Gospel writers, with the possible exception of John, misunderstood what Jesus meant by the second coming of the Son of man (John 14:18 ff.). And Christianity has been embarrassed for two thousand years about Jesus' reported declaration that before the first disciples would all die he would return in power and glory (Mark 13:20). Sometimes it seems that Paul picks up some of his opinions from Jewish theologians of his own day and also out of his own very creative intellect, as well as from Jesus himself (Rom. 8). Paul also corrects himself as he writes (I Cor. 1:14 ff.) and cuts himself off in the middle of sentences (Eph. 3:1), as any unmanipulated human being would do.

No matter where we turn in Scripture, the human element is there, testifying that God refused to overrule the weaknesses of men when he revealed himself and testifying that God honored man who is created in his own image by refusing to take from man his own independent willpower in a fashion that would denigrate man by reducing him to a divinely operated writing machine.

But, lest this knowledge of the humanity of the Bible which deals honestly with its failings should overly distress us, let us remember that in our daily conversations we stumbling human beings are still usually able to get our main point across quite well whenever we wish to communicate with each other. None of us is perfect in communication. But despite this fact, humanity seems to do quite well in going about its business.

We do not expect the presence of occasional errors to upset the general trustworthiness of our passing on of information. In fact, if the stories of witnesses in a court trial agree in every single detail, the case is likely to be lost because of suspected collusion—or previous agreement—between the witnesses. For it is generally known that the observations and memories of the most honest men fail in many details.

Why, therefore, should we become greatly alarmed just because the writers of the Bible are also fallible mortals who are trying to report and interpret the words and deeds of God as best they can? If God himself, who certainly knows what is in man, has decided that men are capable of receiving and transmitting his revelation of himself and has therefore proceeded to reveal himself to men, then we must confidently assume that God knows what he is doing and that men are indeed capable of preserving enough of that revelation for God to achieve his purposes.

Furthermore, historical study is continually substantiating this judgment. Despite the errors in the Bible, the Bible is amazingly correct in its data, and generally its accuracy excels any other ancient history. Historical research has many times more evidence for the life of Jesus than it has for the life of Julius Caesar. And even secular historians cannot come up with an explanation for the explosive evangelistic beginning of the Christian church that is as plausible as the proclamation of Jesus' resurrection that the New Testament reports.

So let us have no fear! Good men may indeed make mistakes. But good men are also basically reliable and trustworthy. The fact that the Bible is first the word of man, and not directly the Word of God, does not need to distress us.

So much for the No. Now for the Yes. Yes, the Bible is the Word of God! When I was a boy of ten, I would sometimes return home from school to hear my older sister say: "Daddy told me to tell you to cut the yard before you do anything else." Now I know that while those were the words of my sister, and while she often said it a bit differently than my father and sometimes even made mistakes, nevertheless—unless I wanted some "peachtree tea" when my father returned —I had better acknowledge that those were indirectly, or by a messenger, truly the words of my father, and get outside and cut the grass. If my father were away from home, it did no good to question somebody else to whom he had not spoken about his orders or to try extrasensory perception in order to figure out his wishes. For the only person to whom he had given his word was my sister, regardless of the shape that word was in when I received it.

So it is with the Bible. Christians believe that through the history of one people only—the people of Israel—God has brought the full knowledge of himself and of man to the world. And while his messengers worked with faulty understandings and faulty memories and faulty documents and faulty alertness, nevertheless, they are the only ones to whom he has entrusted this essential knowledge. And we ignore or despise their reports at peril of eternal loss.

The prophets and patriarchs and apostles were men who had been confronted by God. He had spoken to them. And they had seen his mighty acts. He had sent them forth to speak for him and to testify about him to the rest of mankind. And while their reports of these encounters are one hundred percent in their own words, nevertheless, since they pass on to us the message of God himself, their words are in a very deep sense also the Word of God.

It is impossible thus far—and may always be impossible—for the most pious and learned of scholars to separate some parts of the biblical message of God from its human additions and errors. But the Word of God is still there in the book. And there is no doubt about the central points of his message. Yes, in a very real sense the Bible is indeed the Word of God.

So much for the No and the Yes. Now for the Perhaps. Perhaps the Bible is the Word of God.

The chief problem for most of us believers is not whether the Bible in itself is, or is not, the perfect Word of God. It makes little difference whether we have been among those who believe God caused every word to be written, or whether we have been among those who realize that this book is the Word of God through the words of men. We are usually all in the same boat when it comes to the fact that, in whatever sense the Bible is the Word of God, *we seldom read it*. And we seldom try to learn more about it.

Radio, television, newspapers, journals come first; the Word of God sits on a shelf gathering dust. Business, housework, schoolwork, hobbies come first; the Word of God sits on a shelf gathering dust. The most up-to-date and instructive Sunday school course on the Bible in all Christian history may presently be offered to us. But we do not read the textbook materials. And the Word of God sits on a shelf still gathering dust. Many days go by when even the average pastor does not spend much time with his Bible.

So the question "Is the Bible really the Word of God?" is more precisely phrased "Is the Bible really the Word of God *for me?*" And the answer is determined by whether we will permit the Bible to be the Word of God for us by reading it, so that these men of old can relate to us their marvelous news. Yes, perhaps the Bible is the Word of God. Perhaps the Bible is the Word of God because perhaps we read it, and perhaps we do not read it.

These then are the three answers to our question: No, Yes, and Perhaps. The No helps us to be intelligent. The Yes helps us to be respectful. The Perhaps helps us to be responsible. For in the end each of us must answer this question for himself. Although Paul declares strongly, "From childhood you have been acquainted with the sacred writings which are able to instruct you for salvation through faith in Christ Jesus" (II Tim. 3:15), nevertheless, each of us must search primarily in his own soul and ask "Is the Bible really the Word of God —for me?"

2. Why Have Creeds?

"I believe. . . ." The Apostles' and Nicene Creeds [1]

"If you confess with your lips that Jesus is Lord, and believe in your heart that God raised him from the dead, you will be saved." Romans 10:9

It is significant that both the Apostles' Creed and the Nicene Creed begin with the words "I believe." For what we believe determines everything that we are and everything that we do as distinctively human beings. This is why Paul is concerned here in our text with the beliefs of our heart and with the declaration of those beliefs in the first Christian creed—"Jesus Kyrios!"—which was a two-word creed affirming that "Jesus is Lord!"

The Christian church has had such official creeds almost from the very beginning of the Christian era because the church desires to proclaim its faith and to ensure that its members have an official formula of that faith which can guide them into being and doing that which is good and true. The early creed "Jesus is Lord!" received its "official" authority from its acceptance by apostles such as Paul. This creed gave a necessary organizational identity to the first generation church and provided a stirring evangelism theme. The later, and much longer, official creeds that the churches have constructed at various times

[1] Contained in appendixes A and B, pp. 225 and 227.

23

through the centuries, even in the present era, have come into existence to serve these same vital needs.

But no sooner have the first words of any official creed been emitted from our mouths than we hear objections from at least four groups of persons whom we may designate "anticreedalists," that is, people who are opposed to official creeds. These four groups are the biblicists, the activists, the sentimentalists, and the false scientists. None of these groups believes that the Christian church is greatly benefited by official creeds.

First, let us hear the objections of the biblicists. These people, among whom we number our Baptist friends, are committed Christians who protest "We don't believe in creeds. The creeds of the churches have been written by men. And men make mistakes. So when a church insists that Christians believe the creeds of that church without reservation, then men are making their words as important as the Word of God itself. This insistence, furthermore, has led to the persecution of minorities who have interpreted some parts of the Scriptures differently from the majority. We believe only in the Bible, since it is the pure Word of God and not the fallible words of men. Let Christians just agree to accept the Bible as their creed."

This opinion is officially held by perhaps less than one out of ten of the world's Christians. But there is a certain amount of truth in it. Let us proceed with a part-by-part examination.

First, in a sense, the biblicists are incorrect when they declare "We don't believe in creeds." The word "creed" comes from the first Latin word of the early Christian creeds. This word is *credo,* which means simply "I believe." Our creed, therefore, is merely what we believe. The statement "We don't believe in creeds" is thus literally the same as saying "We don't believe in having beliefs." But, of course, these people do very much believe in having beliefs.

What the biblicists actually mean is that they do not believe Christian denominations should have official creeds which they force all their congregations to acknowledge and adhere to. These anticreedalists insist that they want only a belief in the Bible and freedom in its interpretation.

Second, the denominations of the biblicists do not actually practice this claim of creedlessness themselves. They cling strongly to an *unwritten* official creed that all their members and congregations must confess. The first part of this creed, of course, is that there must be no *written* creed. Then they will insist upon believer's baptism, upon immersion, upon foot washing, upon refraining from cosmetics, smoking, drinking, upon not robing the ministers and choirs, upon not having crosses and altars in the sanctuary, and so forth. Different anti-creedal denominations have different unwritten creeds. But they must have at least an unwritten creed for their congregations to follow if they are to have any denominational unity of belief or action.

Third, all Christians agree that the Bible contains the Word of God. For all Christians are biblical Christians. They are just not all biblicistic Christians. Furthermore, many of these biblical Christians insist that the Bible cannot take the place of creeds because they believe that the Bible has never been able to take the place of creeds.

The position of the biblicists is built upon the belief that the Bible is the perfect Word of God, without any errors, and that the Bible is perfectly clear about every matter of belief. But, as the previous chapter explained, modern scientific literary research has shown us that this ancient understanding of the Bible is not correct. The Bible is a marvelous record by and about men who had encountered God in a unique history of revelation. But occasionally these men and their editors have misunderstood or forgotten or poorly explained something. As a result, it is very difficult to interpret and evaluate some parts of the Bible.

This is the reason that the Christian church was forced to hammer out its historical creeds in the first place. Christians in the early centuries were disagreeing sharply on the meaning and importance of different parts of the scriptures. Consequently, conventions—or synods —of the church were held in which votes were taken on the mooted matters of faith. New creeds were formulated or existing creeds were officially adopted at these conventions. The Nicene Creed, which is a prime example, is the theological consensus of the majority of the church leaders in the fourth century after Christ. The Apostles' Creed, which was not written by the apostles but developed gradually in the early church, is the legislated opinion of the majority of the church leaders in the sixth century after Christ. This second creed was developed and accepted in a much more gradual manner which was less dramatic than the workings of the great Council of Nicaea. Thus we see that an element of uncertainty in the interpretation of the Bible has required official interpretations in the form of creeds from the beginning of Christian history.

Fourth, the biblicists are quite right when they declare that the official creeds of the Christian churches are only the words of men and that men can make mistakes even in these ancient interpretations of the Bible. We Lutherans, for instance, have always been quite willing to acknowledge that the creeds of the Christian churches have contained errors and misinterpretations. We have pointed out what we have felt were the errors in the creeds of the Roman Catholic, Eastern Orthodox, and the other Protestant churches, whether these creeds were written or unwritten. We have even been willing sometimes to admit that we Lutherans may have a few mistakes in our special denominational creeds, which we call our "confessions." But until the present century we have usually drawn a line at about the seventh century after Christ and have insisted that all the official church creeds before that time, namely the Nicene, Apostles', and Athanasian creeds, were as purely truth as the very Word of God itself. In this century, however, we have begun to realize as a denomination that we cannot draw a line between fallible and infallible creeds anywhere in history. We must admit that even the Apostles' and Nicene and Athanasian creeds can contain errors and that even these creeds require periodically to be reexamined by the theologians of the church. Modern research, therefore, has embarrassed not only the anti-creedalists. It has equally embarrassed creedalists such as the Lutherans, Catholics, Methodists, and Presbyterians.

Fifth, despite the imperfections of any official church creed, the Christian churches still need to have official church creeds. For such creeds are useful in maintaining good order, in providing a rallying flag, and in expressing our faith in a devotionally stirring manner. A church completely without a creed would be a church whose members would not know what it stood for. The result would be chaos. Our creeds inform both Christians and non-Christians why the Christian church exists and what it stands for. Furthermore, the official creed is a rallying flag. All of us gather together behind it in order to give a united testimony of our Christian faith to the world and in order to recognize one another for mutual encouragement. And finally, the official creed is a helpful element in our worship service by which we devotionally review and declare our faith before Almighty God in a great unsung hymn of praise.

So much do the Christian churches need their official creeds that the anticreedal position of the biblicists appears gradually to be losing out. The denominations that are merging to form new denominations are writing new creeds for their members that reflect our modern Christian scholarship. The splendid *Statement of Faith* that the United Church of Christ adopted in 1959 is an outstanding example,[2] as is also the United Presbyterian Church's *Confession of 1967*. It will indeed be a momentous and glorious day when all Christendom can stand and with one voice united in the same words of faith and love declare "I believe."

Now let us hear briefly the objection of the second group of anti-creedalists. These are the activists, who protest "It's not your creed but your deed that counts. Forget all this business of creeds and just live a life full of good deeds."

Many well-meaning Christians hold this position without being aware how much this position is itself an ambitious creed. Although this outlook has certain limited uses, it is still a very shallow creed because all our actions in life are the fruit of our beliefs. Everything we do has a conscious or subconscious belief behind it.

We look both ways before we cross the street because we *believe* that moving vehicles can kill or crush us. We fish with live minnows in the mouth of a creek because we *believe* that the bass will take them there. We pay our taxes because we *believe* that this is the only way to have a good government and peace with the powers that be. We serve and obey God in all his demands because we *believe* that it is to our benefit and the good of everybody here and hereafter to do so. Or we murder our neighbor because we *believe* that no God exists to punish us and because we *believe* that the police are not crafty enough to catch us.

Yes, behind every act is a belief. Behind every deed is a creed. Creedalist Christians are concerned about having a truly good creed because they are aware that this is the only way man can perform a truly good deed. The activist who wants us to forget about creeds and to think only about deeds does not realize how much everything we do in life is shouting to the world "I believe!"

Now let us hear from the third group of anticreedalists—the sentimentalists. The sentimentalist says "It doesn't make any difference

[2] Contained in Appendix C, p. 229.

what you believe, just so long as you really believe it. For we are judged for the sincerity in our heart, not for the information in our head."

Once more an anticreedalist wants to discard all emphasis on creeds except his emphasis on his own creed which says that creeds are not important. And once more I feel that the anticreedalist position is shallow. For the sentimentalist does not dare to operate by his own creed in any area of his life except in the religious area. He will not drink from bottles labeled "poison," for instance, because he knows that it makes no difference how much he tries to believe that it is really sugar water. If it is poison, it is going to kill him, whatever he may try to imagine that it is.

Any man who would attempt to live completely by the sentimentalist code would not be long for this world. Whether a man really believes it or not, tigers are not teddy bears; rattlesnakes are not ropes; an open manhole is not a black paint spot on the street; a falling rock is not a big brown marshmallow. Life is filled with facts. And it is important that we believe the right thing about these facts if we desire to stay around very long.

Furthermore, why should people expect the situation to be greatly different in the religious area? If the sentimentalist position does not work anywhere else in life, why should it work in the church? I am highly suspicious of a philosophy of life that cannot be applied in every area of life. And, judging by the unhappiness that those nations and individuals who have believed that there are no definite religious facts seem to have brought upon themselves, I suspect that it is highly important in our religious life not only to feel strongly about a matter but to feel strongly about the matter in the right way.

It is simply not true that "It doesn't make any difference what you believe, as long as you really believe it." Realistic Christians have always abhorred this belief of the quasi sentimentalists in their midst. And this is why concerned churchmen have always struggled to put the truths about God into creeds that begin "I believe."

Finally, let us consider the objection of the fourth group of anticreedalists—the false scientists. The false scientist protests "I am not interested in mere belief. I want factual surety. This is an age of science. So don't speak to me of faith; speak to me of knowledge. Don't hand me a creedal formula; hand me a data report."

Yet once again someone who claims not to believe in creeds is denying all creeds but his own. He believes—it is his creed that—scientific investigation makes belief unnecessary. But the false scientist does not realize the difference between faith and credulity, and so does not appreciate that the whole scientific enterprise is built upon a veritable mountain of faith assumptions. Let me list four of them.

Scientists believe that their senses of sight, hearing, touch, and smell, which tell them there is a real world outside them, can be trusted. Unless scientists believe that the world is really "out there," they will not bother to investigate it.

Scientists believe that there is some connection between the way the world outside them is put together and the way their minds work. Unless scientists believe that there is some connection between mind and matter, they will not bother to try to "crack" the mysteries of matter with their minds.

Scientists believe that the whole universe, from protons to planets, is established and controlled by one great complex rational force that can be depended upon. Unless scientists can believe that one rational force controls everywhere always, they will not bother to predict even the rising of the sun or to call the force of gravity a law.

Scientists believe that it is best for all scientists to be honest and truthful. Unless scientists can trust other scientists, the scientific enterprise, which is largely a group effort, will collapse. Yes, the whole world of science that deals with hard matter is still a faith world.

Furthermore, the physical sciences cannot subject God to the same tests to which gold is subjected. God cannot be crammed into a test tube and analyzed, placed upon a scale and weighed, tested for temperature, color, shape, or any other quality, by the measuring instruments of the physical sciences.

And not only is this true for God. The same is the case for truth, beauty, and goodness considered apart from God. The physical scientist, like anyone else, recognizes and values these spiritual qualities. But he cannot perform physical tests which tell us anything about them. The laboratory proof of the physical sciences simply cannot be applied to the spiritual truths and to the relationship between God and man. Spiritual realities are proved to us and for us only in the realm of personal experience. God, for instance, speaks to one man. Then another man listens to the experience of that man and must decide whether to believe it enough to try to experience contact with God himself.

Thus man's only connection with the heavenly Father, who refuses to show himself physically, is a faith connection, encouraged by historical testimony, that must rely finally upon spiritual experience for proof. Consequently, only the false scientists, who do not realize the limitations of the measuring instruments used in the physical sciences, want to have spiritual fact without faith. The true scientists, many of whom are Christians, realize that when the scientist talks about religious facts he must stand with all the rest of mankind and declare "I believe" on the basis of the same faith experiments and experiences. His life is benefited just as much by adequate religious creeds as are the lives of the rest of us.

Yes, the Christian faith that invariably forms creeds must be appreciated for what it is. The biblicists should recognize that the church needs its creeds for the sake of good order, for rallying flags, and for devotional helps, despite the human shortcomings of these formulations. The activists should recognize that worthy creeds are the foundations of worthy deeds. The sentimentalists should recognize that not only sincerity but also truth is essential. The false scientists should recognize that the most important knowledge of all comes to us through spiritual faith experience.

Christians believe that God has revealed himself in the history of Israel. Christians believe that God has shown his face, given us the laws of life, and proved to us in the life, death, and resurrection of Jesus Christ that eternal life may be ours. Christians believe they can demonstrate that God has blessed the human race with every physical and spiritual blessing by pointing to situations where Jesus Christ has been sincerely and joyfully proclaimed as Lord. It is to express clearly this vital faith that the Christian church has been a creed-writing body.

Paul is declaring the value of such creeds when he exhorts: "If you confess with your lips that Jesus is Lord and believe in your heart that God raised him from the dead, you will be saved."

3. Is There Really a God?

"I believe in God." The Apostles' Creed

"I know whom I have believed." II Timothy 1:12

"I believe in God." So most Christians state weekly in the familiar ecumenical creeds of Christendom. But why do we believe in God?

Today the world is demanding that Christians give sharper and more relevant answers than we have been giving to this question. Have we seen God or heard him or touched or tasted or smelled him? Or do we believe in God only because our parents did? Have we simply accepted uncritically the opinions of our elders, or do we have better reasons?

It is imperative that we become able to explain to the modern man in a persuasive, up-to-date manner exactly why we believe in God. For all around us today unbelievers are challenging us with the disturbing claim of the pessimistic German philosopher Nietzsche that "God is dead." And for many people today it is indeed true that God is dead, because they believe that the modern world has grown up and come of age. They believe that finally men really know what makes the world go round, and therefore that we need not pay attention any longer to the childish and superstitious "religious fables" of our prescientific grandfathers.

"Consider our weather forecasting," the atheist remarks. "The weatherman on television does not call rain an act of God. Rather, he points to his maps and charts and calls rain a result of the interaction of certain principles of temperature and moisture and air pressure. Consider also the physician. He does not speak of a typhoid epidemic as a mysterious act of God. Instead, he speaks of the typhoid epidemic as a natural phenomenon, as a very understandable disease caused by a particular germ and various unwholesome conditions. In this modern age," the atheist concludes, "simple cause-and-effect, as measured by physical science, is sufficient to explain the world and everything that happens in it. And as for God being a cause of things: we simply have no need for that hypothesis. We can get along perfectly well without that theory."

This is the message that is coming to our Christian youth in so many different forms in our high schools and colleges and universities. And, since they have not developed the critical faculties to challenge this position and have not been given the data to contest it, an alarming percentage of them are succumbing, consciously or subconsciously, to such modern atheism.

This is one reason why so many of our Christian youth fifteen years of age and over are not to be found in the worship services and schools of the church. Their faith has been shattered by doubt, often with them hardly realizing it. And since their elders seldom mention, or reasonably criticize, this modern unbelief, many of our Christian young people can only conclude that their elders are harmless old foggies who do not know what is going on in the world of knowledge and who should not be bothered with it.

But increasingly the Christian church is realizing that it must be more open to the doubts of its young people—and of its older people as well. When our youth doubt some aspect of the faith of their parents, we must not cloud up darkly and hiss "Shame! Shame!" at them, while internally we quake in our boots. Rather, we should realize that doubt is a growing pain of faith. For in a real sense faith is a spiritual muscle which can be strengthened and enlarged only by exercise. And the weights that exercise the muscle of faith are doubt and trouble and opportunity.

This is why I believe that every pastor should announce to all the young people in his congregation that he will not shame them or become angry with them whenever they begin to express doubt about their Christian faith. Rather, he should tell them that he almost welcomes their doubt because it is a sign that they are beginning to stretch spiritually.

In fact, I believe that the pastor himself is the person who should first arouse their doubts, in order to teach them how to handle the matter when later it is brought up by an unsympathetic person. For this reason I periodically badgered my catechetical classes until they were painfully distressed. I would not permit them to rest with their belief in God until I could take the part of the atheist and the agnostic and they could give me a good rebuttal. If they do not remember a single point that I taught them along the way for refuting these non-Christian positions, they will at least remember that the first time they tangled with atheism and agnosticism the church had a satisfying answer.

Taking the part of the disbelievers in God is not an artificial or strange activity for me either. For at one time in my youth I was an atheist. And for a longer period of time I was an agnostic. But today I can declare confidently in the words of our creeds that "I believe in God."

But *why* do I believe in God, after having once fallen away from the faith? Let me give you five reasons. Every one of these reasons has been the subject of numerous books. Every one of these reasons also is couched in the terms of personal experience. For, at the core, belief in God is always an intensely personal affair. And arguments for the existence of God are simply an intellectual form of personal testimony. This is the reason that I do not apologize for continual use of the personal pronoun "I" throughout this chapter.

Before I begin, let me assure you that atheism is not a new problem for Christendom. Back in the thirteenth century, when Thomas Aquinas was defending the Christian faith with powerful arguments that have been given weighty labels such as "the ontological, cosmological, and teleological arguments for the existence of God," even Thomas' arguments were so old that they "had beards." Most of the modern arguments against Christianity and most of the modern Christian retorts were stated in essence near the beginning of the Christian era. And even long before Jesus' day the inadequacy of the atheistic position was noted by the wise men of Israel in their terse proverb: "The fool says in his heart, 'There is no God'" (Ps. 14:1). Furthermore, this problem of atheism is so perennial that a recognized area in systematic theology is devoted to it, an area that is called "apologetics" or "eristics." I cite these facts so that no reader will imagine that the

33

Christian church is just today emerging from the intellectual dark ages and facing its detractors for the first time.

Here are my five reasons for belief in God:

First, *I believe in God because the order that I see in the physical world does not make sense to me unless God exists.* The modern atheists claim that this orderly universe is the result solely of a blind and unguided evolutionary urge. They claim that over a period of unknown billions of years a great chaotic madhouse of energy particles *arranged themselves* into this beautiful, orderly, stable, serene universe that we see around us. They claim that even the human mind evolved without supernatural help out of this original total chaos.

But this theory I must challenge because to me it violates one of the cardinal principles of logic. Every one of us knows that "out of nothing, nothing comes." This is why the order we see around us, and why our own minds, could not have come out of an original *total* chaos. For if there had not been some eternal organizing force that took those electrical particles and set them in an orderly pattern, then there still would be no universe and no us. There would be only a great cauldron of energy particles seething about wildly in space.

To assert that this orderly world came forth purely by chance out of total chaos appears in essence to be as ludicrous as claiming that our unabridged dictionaries are the result of an explosion in a printing factory or that watches just coagulate naturally out in iron ore fields. For a total chaos by definition cannot contain any principle that arranges energy in an orderly fashion. Pure chaos, on its own, can only remain forever pure chaos. And for the atheist to admit that chaos somewhere had within it the seeds of order, so that in five billion years "chaos" became cosmos—or the universe—is for the atheist to admit that in some sense rational power was present from the very beginning.

Even if the atheist agrees that the cosmic order originated out of a "predisposition toward organization" inherent in the energy particles themselves, he has still made room for at least a minimal naturalistic God, and perhaps for much more. So if the atheist is willing to admit this much, why should he not go ahead and call this rational power and predisposition toward organization "God," as we Christians do?

Furthermore, despite the arguments that have been raised in the last hundred years against this so-called cosmological argument for the existence of God, anyone who accepts the contemporary theory of comprehensive cosmic evolution must remain open to the possibility of rational divine causation. For the theory of evolution leaves room not only for an eternal Creator guiding the process from the beginning but also for an evolved "finite" God who after evolving from the basic, eternal, organization-prone energy particles himself, became the self-conscious free agent of the continuing evolutionary process.

Yes, I believe in God because the order that I see in the physical universe does not make sense to me unless God exists.

Second, *I believe in God because the order that I see in the moral world does not make sense to me, and does not last, unless God exists.* Nearly every thinker on earth would admit that all men have a sense of right and wrong—or a conscience. Nearly every thinker would admit also that our conscience depends upon some external authority to teach it what is right and wrong, because our conscience gives us back primarily the same sense of values that we put into it. If we are taught in childhood that it is wrong to kill flies, for instance, our conscience will hurt us whenever we kill a fly. But if we are taught in childhood that it is wrong to permit flies to live around us, then our conscience will commend us every time we kill a fly. Thus the conscience is in many respects a neutral mechanism that operates according to what it is taught.

Many atheists, who may also call themselves pragmatists, believe that the human conscience does not need God, or any other mysterious depth of reality, to inform it of what is good and bad for mankind. These pragmatistic atheists believe that the individual man can always do what is good simply by trying to do what is best for the sake of the whole human race. "Man can see and do what is best for his own species without God," the pragmatistic atheist claims. "And man has invented the moral nature of God, just as he has invented the creator-ship of God, in order to put into effect what he has become convinced is best for him."

I must strongly disagree. This kind of atheist with his pragmatistic moral code has drunk deeply from the well of Christianity without knowing it! He is arguing against Christianity from a half-Christian viewpoint and is not aware of it. The pragmatistic atheist says that man can do what is good for the whole human race without God. But why should an atheist be concerned about the human race at all? If there is no God, and if the universe contains nothing but a blind evolutionary force at work, and if we are each just an animal living out one brief life in one minute of evolutionary time, from where comes

35

this great moral concern for the race of human animals? If there is no God, and hence no one to establish absolute moral law and to punish evil and reward good, then the moral codes of men are just human conveniences with no absolute value. And any moralizing that commands us to be good to the human race has no absolute authority.

But many pragmatistic atheists in Western lands are still genuinely concerned for the whole human race. And they are often not aware that they have inconsistently borrowed their concern from the Christian atmosphere of Western Civilization. These people who are sure that every man feels the urge to love mankind are often too lightly assuming that every man has by nature the concern for all mankind that Christianity teaches. Any good world history book or anthropology book, however, should disabuse them of this moralistic myth. For cannibalism and mass extermination have been equally "natural" moral options for mankind.

Let us consider for a moment a man named Adolf Hitler. Hitler was a *consistent* atheist. He was not a halfway Christian like the pragmatistic and humanitarian atheists with whom we frequently deal. Perhaps Hitler was a consistent atheist because he did not inherit their "gentle hormones." But whatever the cause, he reasoned like this: If there is no God, and hence no absolute right and wrong—for only an eternal being above us could establish absolute moral principles—then only might makes right. The man with power can make the laws that he desires. He can even commit murder, as long as he has the power to get by with it. And Hitler had the power to get by with it—almost. He declared that the evolutionary process had made the Caucasian peoples of northwestern Europe superior to all the other races of mankind. And therefore, for the sake of the human race, this best element should subjugate and eventually wipe out the inferior elements, in order to assure the highest evolution of the human race. How frighteningly consistent Hitler was with the moral principles of atheism!

Consider another man named Joseph Stalin. This tyrant set about destroying all the millions of people who were not members of the working classes. And why not? He believed that there was no God, and hence no one to establish and maintain absolute right and wrong. He believed that we are all merely animals with one life to live. Why not, therefore, kill off those human animals that economically did not "part their hair" as he wanted it, if he had the power and felt like using it?

Furthermore, such moral monsterism does not happen only halfway around the world from us. It happens every day right here in America on a much smaller scale. And, I am convinced, it will multiply until it fills our streets with rivers of blood if the Christianity that resists it should ever die. We have all known individuals who have caused us to shudder as we contemplated the possibility of their moral bankruptcy becoming the order of the day. I still wince at the savagery of my university professor who declared in class: "To hell with the human race! Because there is no God and no future life, I am going to look out just for myself in this one short life that I have. And I am going to use you in any way that I wish, or even cut your throat, if I need to or want to do so."

We should notice also that human society has been preserved from the tyranny of these moral frankensteins only where God has been strongly believed in and worshiped, and only where his decree of absolute love with its functional principles of right and wrong have been acknowledged. It is ironic that the atheist himself is safest in a Christian society that publicly repudiates the atheist's philosophy of life.

I must point out, however, that I am presuming to place those profound atheistic humanists who have a strong sense of the deep and awesome mystery in all that exists in the category of theists—that is, of those who believe in God. These thinkers actually have, I believe, a great sensitivity to the reality of God, despite their reluctance to use the traditional term "God." What they lack seems to be some crucial element in their experience of the mystery of life that would convince them that they are involved therein in a type of person-to-person contact. If this missing element were supplied, they would accept as valid the claims of person-to-person contact with God that individuals have made down through history, especially in the Judeo-Christian religious history.

However, this "godly" type of humanism still has not proved that, without the help of committed theists, it is able to produce social good on a large scale in a manner that prevents the majority from being oppressive and that stirs up the populace to sacrificial good deeds on behalf of all humanity. It has also not yet proved that it can account for its own coming into existence, or even its ability to survive, in separation from the great theistic cultures which have believed that God exists and that he has revealed himself to man.

Yes, I believe in God because the order that I see in the moral world does not make sense to me, and does not last, unless God exists.

Third, *I believe in God because the most fulfilled people I have known have believed in God and have claimed to be fulfilling themselves by his power and guidance.* It is true that we can all survive without electricity or indoor plumbing or machines or cloth or a complex economy or music or art or formal education or houses or maybe even fire. But after we have all become used to these blessings of civilization, I doubt that many of us would be willing to call such survival "living." It would be only a very impoverished existence.

So it is in this matter of living with and without God. It seems that one can usually survive without any conscious dependence upon God's guidance and protection and encouragement and strengthening and comforting and love. It seems that one can usually survive without the warm fellowship of God's family on earth that brings men great joy and delight and help. But I doubt that one can really "live" in such a deprived way of life. I cannot bring myself to call it more than a very impoverished "subsistence."

I have seen too many bitter, shallow, bored, beaten, and aimlessly drifting atheists to think otherwise. And I have seen too many joyful, deep, interested, victorious, and purposeful children of God—many of them cripples with all the "breaks" against them—to think otherwise.

Yes, I believe in God because the most fulfilled people I have known have believed in God and have claimed to be fulfilling themselves by his power and guidance.

Fourth, *I believe in God because I have received miraculous answers to prayer.* There are times when God answers our petitions with the "no" of a loving father who refuses our request because he knows what is best for us. There are times when God answers our petitions with the "maybe" or the "wait awhile" of a loving father, for the same reason. But there are also those many occasions when God says "yes" and grants us our request.

The atheist, however, scoffs at this. He retorts: "When you imagine that God is saying 'yes' and helping you, what is actually taking place is simply the coincidental meeting of natural forces in a manner that happens to please you."

We must acknowledge that it is true that many answered prayers could possibly be explained away in this fashion. But many answered prayers contain such extraordinary elements that the probability that the answers were mere chance is so low as to be insignificant. I, for instance, can tell of my experience as a lonely young man when I prayed to God at a crisis point in my life, pleading with him to reveal to me who my wife would be, and how I was answered in that same hour from six hundred miles away. I can tell of my experience as a young bellhop in a Swiss hotel, when I received the twenty dollars I had prayed for in the last few seconds before I had to use it. The chances that the answers to these two prayers—and many others in my life—were the mere working out of chance are so astronomically small that I can easily dismiss them.

Yes, I believe in God because I have received miraculous answers to prayer.

Fifth, and most importantly, *I believe in God because I frequently experience contact with the supernatural realm which in the light of my thoughts and experiences I can only define as the "Presence of God."* The atheist, however, in a sometimes brash manner denies the reality of my spiritual experience. He asserts that it is only my subjective emotions and imagination conjuring up a fantasy of the divine. But I know better. It is *my* experience and not his. For this reason I feel justified in calling him a presumptuous person whenever he insists that the *richness* of my experience must have its value determined by the *poverty* of his experience. To me such a determined atheist is a type of blind man who is insisting that all seeing is an illusion because he cannot see, and a type of deaf man who is insisting that all hearing is an illusion because he cannot hear, and a type of misanthrope who is insisting that all love is an illusion because he has never known love.

It is quite natural, of course, for the atheist, since he has never had any experience with God, to doubt the value of my contact with God. It is quite proper, too. For neither he nor I should make assertions about reality beyond our experience. He has no choice—on the basis of his experience to this point—but to attempt to interpret my experience of God in terms of something that he, too, has experienced. Since he has not walked the path of life in fellowship with God—loving, obeying, learning, praying, receiving, growing, sowing—his normal first reaction is that I have a grand talent for fooling myself.

But it behooves the atheist to have the scientific humility to acknowledge that it is equally possible that I do know God, and that I am correct when I charge that his position seems to me to be built upon a bleak poverty of experience. It behooves the atheist to acknowledge that he may not know God because he has not searched for God in the right spirit and manner. Rather, by remaining content merely to defend his position with doubtful data and challengeable logic, he may be fooling himself.

Now what kinds of experiences are these in which I have experienced the Presence of God. One kind is individual, the other corporate; and most Christians seem, like me, to have come to God through a dialectic process that alternates between both kinds of experience.

The way into God's presence through our experiences as an *individual* seems to be through the door of humility. For the greatest barrier to contact with God for many men seems to be their intellectual pride.

My impression has been that atheists are generally men who are over-balanced in their concentration on the self-conscious, this-worldly aspects of the intellectual life. They are men with a bias against prayer, men who are hesitant to be humble enough to take the child's leap of faith and pray when they are not sure God is there listening, men who are unwilling to have "blind faith" in the existence of a highest possible being in order to gain "seeing faith" in him.

I am persuaded that no man has ever known God who has not first surrendered up his life to God—including in that surrender the sovereignty of his intellect. "He that loses his life shall find it," Jesus declared so profoundly. The pride of intellect which will not attempt to believe until it can see with certainty is the idol which holds back many an intellectual from fellowship with God.

The man who declares to himself that he is not going to acknowledge God until God clearly comes to him is deciding to make God do obeisance to the sovereignty of his puny human mentality. All things must first kneel and be recognized before such a man's enthroned rationality before he will acknowledge them. This "intellectual integrity" as he labels it in self-defense is actually in a sense the highest and most subtle form of self-deification. God is going to come to him on his terms, or else not be recognized. But God refuses to reveal himself except to those humble, childlike souls who will accept his divine sovereignty totally. And I suspect that deep inside themselves many atheists really believe in God but are peeved at him for not meeting their royal rules of recognition.

Our human intellect is a type of data computer that must become self-centered from infancy in the process of acquiring self-consciousness. For our intellect reaches out with its tentacle-like means of perception to encompass and assimilate to itself everything that exists. In knowing things, to a certain extent, it conquers them and submits them to itself. Our intellect wants to handle God in the same way. "Come here and let me touch you with my mind; then I'll fit you into my understanding of the scheme of things."

But God will not be so handled. He will remain God! Only when we are willing to be assimilated to his intellect does he give us knowledge of himself. Only when we come before him humbly, intellectual hat in hand, acknowledging that we believe without real evidence that he is "out there" or "in there" and that we want to know him, have our intellects truly done fitting obeisance before him as God.

Furthermore, is this not the most intellectually respectable way to go about our quest for God? Is not our concept of intellectual integrity ultimately the end result of pragmatic testing? We discipline our intellectual investigations in certain ways because we have discovered by trial and error that only a particular method produces valid results. Consequently, if God really exists—in all the fullness of what the Christian conception of God implies—then surely here too the path of true intellectual integrity is the path that produces valid results. Intellectual principles that may apply elsewhere may here be quite disreputable.

This was the conclusion that I finally reached when I was an atheist. Either I got off my prideful intellectual "high horse" and came to God in the appropriate childlike surrender to my true sovereign, or else I was going to spend the rest of my life on the outside of the most vital things, unsuccessfully looking in.

It has been my experience that a man seems to have primarily himself to blame—as a rule—if he does not know God. He seems to have been unwilling to meet the conditions of finding God. The time comes when a sincere seeker must cease merely thinking and begin to pray. Like the father of the epileptic boy in the Gospel story, he must cry out "Lord, I believe; help my unbelief!" He must swallow his pride and begin praying with all his heart into the emptiness where there may or may not be a God, to the God that in the depths of his heart he hopes is there. This is the point that Augustine was making when he said that he believed in order to understand, rather than understanding in order to believe. And as the proof of the pudding is in the eating, and as the proof of the lover is in the loving, even so the proof that God has truly met a man is given only to the individual who has the experience.

41

The way into God's presence through our *corporate* experiences seems to be through the door of Christian brotherly love. The Christian gospel proclaims that God is perfect and complete love—that is, holy love; that God desires to live in relationships of holy love with every man; and that God desires everyman, as well, to live in relationships of holy love with every fellowman.

This amounts to an immense claim of togetherness and community of God and man within the relationship of holy love. And the claim is vindicated whenever a love-impoverished person enters into heart-felt fellowship with that society called the church which God has created to dwell in him, to reflect him, and to mediate him to the world.

In the brotherly love that is expressed in the formal worship and informal friendship activities within the church, the searching soul begins to sense that there is something greater than mere gregariousness or herd feeling involved. He begins to feel that the whole of indwelling spiritual reality which is present in this community is infinitely more than the sum of the visible human parts. In, with, and under the loving—although quite imperfect—Christian fellowship, the living God who is unperceived by the senses inexplicably but undeniably manifests himself, and faith begins to develop in the seeker.

That this is the chief sphere where divine activity is located should be no great surprise to us. For there is a proper place in which to search for anything. Gold, for instance, is sought for not in granite but in quartz. Also, deeper contact with personalities is not sought for in a boiling test tube or in an appreciative session with the setting sun. Rather, we search for deeper contact with personalities within the sphere of our personal relationships.

Even so, if God is indeed the original and greatest of persons, as Christians testify, and if his greatest interest in man is personal, then he too will most likely be found in the sphere of personal relationships. And if man is to enter into contact with God, man must search out those golden relationships between man and God, and between men in God, that are found as veins in the quartz of the totality of human relationships.

The experience of the Christian church has been that God is a historical, self-revealing God who himself initiates contact with man; that God wants to be found, or else man would not find him; and that he will be found only where he wishes to be found. We do not claim that he can be found only in the Christian church. We only claim that in the church is where we have felt ourselves found in him.

We believe, furthermore, that one of the chief reasons that many men have not yet found God is that they have not been searching in the right places. And we view the impassioned altruistic search for total human community that is carried out by atheists such as Erich Fromm, Albert Camus, and Julian Huxley as a rationally confused but truly instinctive longing for the God of holy love who is essential for the total fulfillment of our need for personal relationships.

Yes, I believe in God because the order that I see in the physical universe does not make sense to me unless God exists. I believe in God because the order that I see in the moral universe does not make sense to me, and does not last, unless God exists. I believe in God because the most fulfilled people I have known have believed in God and have claimed to be fulfilling themselves by his power and guidance. I believe in God because I have received miraculous answers to prayer. I believe in God because in individual and corporate circumstances I frequently experience contact with the supernatural realm, which in the light of my thoughts and experiences I can only define as the "Presence of God."

Consequently, I, an ex-atheist and ex-agnostic, in company with the whole Christian church, staunchly affirm in the words of our ecclesiastical creeds that "I believe in God." "For," as Paul declares, "I know whom I have believed."

Section II: GOD

4. What Is God Like?

"I believe in God the Father." The Apostles' Creed

"For the Father himself loves you." John 16:27

"I believe in God the Father." So declare the great church creeds from the fourth and sixth centuries after Christ. But in reality it is only in the nineteenth and twentieth centuries that Christians have really begun to appreciate in all its fullness the concept of the Fatherhood of God which Jesus proclaimed.

For more than one hundred years the biblical scholars of the Christian churches have been "peeling back" the later theological, and partially legendary, layers of the New Testament in order to get to the core, which is Jesus' life and message. The scholars have come almost unanimously to the conclusion that none of the four Gospels was written directly by an apostle. All the Gospels were probably written between A.D. 60 and A.D. 90 by the apostles' disciples who, after the death of the apostles, gathered and organized and interpreted their materials as best they could.

The earliest materials, and also those that give the most reliable accounts of Jesus' acts and words, are the greatest portion of the earliest Gospel, which is Mark, plus large portions of Matthew, Luke, Acts, and the epistles of Paul to the Romans, the Corinthians, the Galatians, and the Thessalonians. These earliest parts of the New Testament speak not at all of the Holy Trinity, or of Jesus as God, or of his death as a payment for sin. These particular doctrines, rather, are later doctrines that were developed by pious Christians who were trying to interpret the significance of Jesus in terms of their Jewish traditions and Hellenistic—that is, primarily Greek—philosophy, rather than in terms of what Jesus himself had said and done.

Unfortunately, much of the truth that has been uncovered by these studies has been resisted until fairly recently by conservative elements in nearly every denomination. For few Christians have been happy to learn that some of the most cherished and bravely defended doctrines of orthodox Christianity since the fourth century of the Christian era are apparently foreign to Jesus' own beliefs and intentions. However, the progressive new Sunday church school materials that many denominations are presently enjoying are finally the beginning of a general acceptance of the inevitable. Even in the Southern "Bible Belt" and in the Lutheran Church Missouri Synod and in the Roman Catholic Church, the new enlightenment is steadily making its way.

The earlier resistance of distressed Christians to what was mislabeled "theological liberalism" is gradually being erased. And in most of the churches the leaders and scholars are aware that the entire Christian church is passing through an essential period of theological readjustment that in some respects is even more sweeping than the Protestant Reformation of the sixteenth century. In fact, so momentous is this Christendom-wide doctrinal readjustment that, quite accurately, it is being called "a new reformation." In this new reformation the Christian church is trying to go back to Jesus himself, insofar as this is possible, by de-emphasizing the latest portions of the New Testament and emphasizing the earliest portions.

This modern "back to Jesus" reformation has recognized that to a decisive degree Jesus of Nazareth was different from the other men of his age, in that he was someone with a unique outlook on divine and earthly matters. The leaders of this new reformation, unlike some of the New Testament writers, refrain from interpreting what Jesus says and does in terms of the old Jewish traditions that he was sent forth to supersede and discard. The leaders of this new reformation, again unlike some of the New Testament writers, refrain from interpreting what Jesus says and does in terms of the Greek logos philosophy that became so popular among many early Christian leaders. Rather, the leaders of this new reformation insist that Jesus the Christ is a distinc-

45

tive historical person and that his mission from God must be interpreted in terms purely of what *he* said and did.

Now this new movement which tries to go behind the later theological opinions of the New Testament writers to Jesus himself, is very important to our present subject. For this new reformation has made it possible to recover the delight and the dynamite that resulted from Jesus' introducing into history the doctrine of the Fatherhood of God.

When we turn back to look at Jesus in the light of our modern and more proper perspectives, we discover that the main new doctrine which he taught was the Fatherhood of God. Jesus directly refers to God as Father, or addresses him as Father, nearly two hundred and fifty times in the four Gospels.

But exactly how Jesus' novel emphasis on the Fatherhood of God changes and brings to perfection the religion of Israel can be appreciated only if we are aware of the stages through which Israel's idea of God had progressed. Very roughly, we can distinguish three main stages. And the stage that Jesus inaugurates is the final, and highest, stage.

In the first theological stage Israel viewed God as the divine Lord of one tribe who dwelled among many other divine lords, each of whom had one tribe. Israel was in the first stage of its understanding of God from the time of the patriarch Abraham, on through the Egyptian bondage and Moses' leadership. This stage began to phase out about the time of David's kingship, although it was not fully superseded until after the exile into Babylon. This stage saw God as little more than a tribal deity, as no greater than the protector of one little clan.

Such a first stage was necessary because God began this program of revelation among mankind during a polytheistic era. Polytheists, of course, are people who believe that many gods exist. A polytheist may believe that there is a god for the sun, a god for the moon, a god for the rain, the wheat, the trees, the mountains, the plains, the seas, a god for each city of the Philistines, a god for each group of Egyptians, for the Ammonites, the Edomites, and so forth. Even the Israelites when they first heard of the true God were polytheists. Consequently, in the beginning they naturally viewed all information about this new God in terms of their basic polytheistic outlook.

For instance, when Moses told them that God had sent him to be their leader out of slavery, the Israelites wanted to know the name of this new God (Exod. 3:13). They wanted to know the name of this new God so that they could call him by name in their prayers, in order that he would know that their prayers were intended for him and not for some other God lounging around in the heavens. Thus Moses' message meant to the Israelites that one of the many invisible gods who existed had for some strange reason taken a liking to them and would see to it that they escaped from the Egyptians. The Israelites doubted Moses at first because, until the plagues were completed and the Reed Sea was crossed, they were not sure that this new God, who had intervened in the affairs of Egypt, was powerful enough to protect them from the native Egyptian gods. Later, standing on the other side of the Reed Sea and watching the drowned Egyptians washing in to shore, the delivered Israelites could sing "Who is like you, O Lord, among the gods?"

In the wilderness and in the invasion of the Promised Land the Israelites learned to be totally confident of the power of their new God. But they were not monotheists during this period. Their theological development had not progressed this far. They only understood that their God was stronger than any other god and that he absolutely and jealously refused to permit them to have anything to do with any other god. "You shall have no other gods before me," he demanded (Exod. 20:3). When they even so much as threw a dry bone—religiously speaking—to another god, their new God punished them. This theological viewpoint of God as the strongest among the many gods (which is technically known as "henotheism") lasted in some measure until the Jewish exiles returned from captivity in Babylon.

This view of God was not sufficient. It was only the beginning. God was not big enough in this view. The Israelites believed that he was only the God of the clans of Israel, that he loved no one else but them, that he had ordered the complete extermination of their enemies, that he loved their friends and hated their enemies. God was little more than their powerful tribal patriarch in the sky who shared all their narrow loves and prejudices.

Yet in this period God established confidence in his power and his promises. He established obedience to his moral demands and utter loyalty to himself. It was a fruitful stage.

In the second theological stage Israel viewed God as the Holy Creator and August Sustainer of the universe. Around the time of King David the theology of Israel progressed to this second stage. The Israelites

47

began to realize that God was bigger than their forefathers had thought. Consequently, they began to appreciate God as the God of all men.

It seems that the day came under David when the Israelites had conquered their enemies on every border so thoroughly that they began to despise the gods of their enemies, not only as weaker gods than their God but as no gods at all. The Israelites had seen the power of their God come in answer to their prayers, as the Lord had swept in with hail and lightning storms and arranged other events in nature to help his people win battles and end famines and plagues (Judg. 5:4; I Kings 18:41 ff.). Their unseen God came in to help with the power of the earthquake and the thunderstorm (Ps. 18:7 ff.). And he was equally overpowering on Israelite soil and on the home grounds of other gods (I Sam. 5:1 ff.). The wooden and metal gods of the surrounding nations could not even keep themselves from getting captured by the Israelites and burned or melted down (Isa. 44:9 ff.; 46:1-2). So it was only a matter of time until the Israelites realized that, wherever they looked about them, only one God really appeared to have any power (Ps. 47). It was quite easy, then, for the people of Israel to agree with their prophets who in their personal experiences with God had been carried inexorably to the conclusion that he must be the only God.

This second stage was the golden age of Old Testament religion. The prophets in this age spoke in exalted language of God's universal dominion. Isaiah proclaims: "Thus says the Lord: 'Heaven is my throne, and the earth is my footstool'" (66:1). "I am the Lord, who made all things" (44:24). "Besides me there is no God" (45:5). This is the stage from which the Genesis 1 story of creation comes. This is the stage in which the beautiful Temple of Solomon was built, and when continual sacrifices were first offered up to pay for the sins of men against the august, awesome King of the whole earth. This is the stage when God was transformed in the eyes of his people from a little family god, whom they alone worshiped and obeyed, to a great worldwide deity so awesome that they could only fall on their faces before him in holy terror and praise him in the most sublime words that they could stutter forth.

Isaiah perfectly exemplifies for us this new understanding of God as the Holy Creator and August Sustainer of the universe when he relates his famous Temple vision:

48

In the year that King Uzziah died I saw the Lord sitting upon a throne, high and lifted up, and his train filled the temple. Above him stood the seraphim, each had six wings: with two he covered his face, and with two he covered his feet, and with two he flew. And one called to the others and said: "Holy, holy, holy is the Lord of hosts; the whole earth is full of His Glory." And the foundations of the thresholds shook at the voice of him who called, and the house was filled with smoke. And I said: "Woe is me! For I am lost; for I am a man of unclean lips, and I dwell in the midst of a people of unclean lips; for my eyes have seen the King, the Lord of hosts!" (6:1-5.)

This second stage, which adjudged the awesomeness and holiness of God as primary, extended from about the time of David until the time of Jesus. It was the basis of much of the temple worship and of much of the nationalistic fanaticism of the Pharisees. Furthermore, this second stage of theological development was also a good stage. For it greatly increased the desire of men to render due praise and honor to God. It contained much more truth about God than the first stage had contained.

But this second stage was also not sufficient. God's revelation of himself was still unfinished. And it is finished only in the third and final stage.

The Old Testament does provide glimpses, however, of the third stage as present in embryo in the first stage. It is present in Abraham's call (Gen. 12:3) and in God's concern for a degraded people in Egypt (Exod. 3:7) and in God's mercy toward a foreign prostitute and a foreign widow (Josh. 6:25; I Kings 17:8 ff.). The third stage is also present in embryo in the second stage. It may be spied biding its time in the many passages in the psalms and prophets that speak of God's mercy and compassion and in the dozen passages that speak of God's care for Israel as the care of a loving Father (Exod. 4:22; Deut. 14:1; 32:19; Ps. 68:5; 89:26; 103:13; Prov. 3:12; Isa. 12; 63:16; 64:8; Jer. 3:4, 19; 31:9, 26; 35:6 ff.; Hos. 1:10; 11:1; Mal. 1:6; 2:10). But nowhere in the Old Testament does the Fatherhood of God become a close and familiar relationship. The "distance of deity" is maintained throughout. And, very importantly, in the Old Testament the concept of the Fatherhood of God is not extended specifically to cover anyone except the Israelites.

In the third theological stage Israel viewed God as the loving Father of all men. It remained the mission of Jesus to raise Israel's understand-

49

ing of God to this third and final stage. Christians believe that Jesus was sent forth by God during that "fullness of time" when the Western world under unified Roman rule was in need of a better spiritual principle of unity than a shallow and confusing nationalistic polytheism. Jesus was sent forth by God to preach the kingdom of God as a royal family in which the King of Kings is above all else the loving, close Father, and in which we are all his sons and brothers of each other.

Thus Jesus introduces a new way of understanding God. God is still the Protector of Israel as in the first stage. God is still the awesome and glorious Majesty as in the second stage. But now God is also someone close and comfortable to be with, as a child is close and comfortable with a loving father.

Jesus declared that God is the Father of all men. He drew attention to overlooked Old Testament illustrations that show how God had been merciful to people of other nations—such as the widow who cared for Elijah (Luke 4:26). He declared that a father's family-wide care is shown in the way God sends rain and sun on the evil and on the good (Matt. 5:45). He reached down to the despised and downtrodden classes of society (Matt. 15:24; Luke 5:30). He reached out to Greeks and Samaritans and others who were not Israelites (Mark 7:26; Luke 9:52; John 12:26). He made sinners and foreigners our neighbors and brothers (Luke 10:33; John 4:7). And thus Jesus rejected the narrow nationalistic Jewish tradition which taught that God considered only law-abiding Jews to be his sons.

In his prayers, furthermore, Jesus did not approach God with the awe of Isaiah who panicked at his vision of the Divine Majesty. Jesus prayed with a fitting reverence. But he never appeared to be afraid of God (Matt. 11:25). He approached God easily and confidently and joyfully, without strain or fear (John 11:42-43). He simply walked into God's presence as a son and began to talk by saying "Father."

The very Aramaic word for "father" which he used disclosed Jesus' real intimacy with God. For Jesus called God *"Abba"* (Mark 14:36), which carries with it the connotation of familiarity that is borne by the equivalent English word "Daddy." Jesus' disciples, who were reared to acknowledge an awesome and fearsome God, were amazed at Jesus' easy yet reverent closeness to God and desired him to teach them to pray with the same confidence (Luke 11:1). In reply Jesus said simply and fearlessly: "When you pray, say: 'Father, hallowed be thy name.'"

Jesus' belief in the Fatherhood of God is possibly the chief reason why Jesus is never mentioned as participating in the Temple sacrifices. In Jesus' eyes God was not an offended sovereign—an angry emperor in the skies—who had to be bought off with a price. Rather, to Jesus, God was a kindly Father who forgave his children purely out of divine love. To Jesus, God was not a distant deity who could be reached only by the blast of rams' horns and the odor of burnt offerings and the shouts of priests and Levites. Rather, to Jesus, God was a loving Father who is nearer to us than we are to ourselves and who is eager to hear the weakest whisper of his child's heart. This central belief is probably the reason why the Temple seems to have been valued by him purely as a house of prayer (Luke 19:46).

Everything that our Lord Jesus said and did had the effect of establishing the loving Fatherhood of God and the consequent brotherhood of all men. He spoke of how God the Father rules (Matt. 11:25), provides for (Matt. 6:8, 11, 26), guards (Matt. 6:13; 26:53), heals (Matt. 4:23; John 5:36), teaches (John 8:28), punishes (Luke 10:10 ff.; John 15:1, 2, 6), retrieves (Matt. 18:12), forgives (Matt. 6:12; Luke 6:36), encourages (Luke 11:13; 12:32; John 14:1, 2, 10, 11), delights (John 16:24; 17:13), and communes with his children (Luke 19:46).

Furthermore, Jesus never permitted his concept of God's Fatherhood to degenerate into a frequent twentieth-century American concept of fatherhood which views the father figure in the family as an indulgent, spineless sentimentalist who cannot bear to discipline or direct his children. Jesus' heavenly Father was always the powerful realist who not only permitted his Messiah son to drink the cup of Calvary's suffering but also steeled him for this demanding task (Luke 22:42-43).

Thus nearly everything that Jesus did and said further communicated his message that God is a strong loving Father. Christians consequently believe that they are not living in the first stage of God's revelation of himself. For Christians do not believe that they have an exclusive, clannish claim on God by virtue of which he will bless only them and will curse all non-Christians. God is the Father of the non-Christians too, and will deal with them as beloved children with an often weaker spiritual light should be dealt with.

Christians also believe that they are not living in the second stage of God's revelation of himself. For Christians do not believe that they have in God an awesome emperor before whom they are to fall with fear and trembling, even though he is still to them the Lord of all and is still due their deepest reverence and obedience.

Rather, Christians believe that they are living in the third and final stage of God's revelation of himself. For Christians believe that they have a Father who has gently and eloquently and eternally called them and all men to him through the ministry of his son, their leader and elder brother, Jesus the Christ. Christians believe that they can come close to the Almighty Creator and Sustainer in the fearless and intimate confidence of little children approaching an affectionate parent. For Jesus has revealed that "the Father himself loves you."

5. Does Man Have Free Will?

"I believe in God the Father Almighty." The Apostles' Creed

"When Abram was ninety-nine years old the Lord appeared to Abram, and said to him, 'I am God Almighty, walk before me, and be blameless.' " Genesis 17:1

The Apostles' Creed and the Nicene Creed both declare belief in God "the Father Almighty," that is, in God "the Father Omnipotent," or God "the Father All-Powerful." This word "almighty" has been a mixed source of spiritual joy and theological sorrow throughout Christian history. For the whole argument of whether man has the free will to choose his spiritual destiny or whether God predestines man to his spiritual state here and hereafter is involved with the word "almighty."

The question is this: Is God's almightiness *literal and absolute* or is God's almightiness only *figurative and comparative?* If God's almightiness is literal and absolute, then God predestines and brings to pass everything that happens in the entire universe, even our thoughts and our salvation. But if God's almightiness is figurative and comparative, then God's almightiness is only a poetic way of saying that God is so inexpressibly more powerful than we are that our freedom of will and the power at our disposal are quite insignificant by comparison.

One of the tragedies of Christian history is that Christians have often separated from each other in bitterness over this issue. Just before and during the Protestant Reformation the argument probably reached its blackest depths. Most of the "mainline" reformers believed in God's absolute almightiness and his absolute predestination of man. Most of the "left-wing" reformers believed in God's figurative almightiness and in human freedom of will. Traditionally the chief difference between the mainline Lutherans and Calvinists has been that Lutheran churches have held to a less harsh but also less logically consistent doctrine of "single-barreled" predestination, which teaches that God chooses only those who will be saved, while the Presbyterian and Reformed churches have held to a harsher but also more logically consistent doctrine of "double-barreled" predestination, which teaches that God chooses both who will be saved and who will be damned. Lutherans have also been more willing to permit freedom of will to man in matters that do not pertain to the soul's salvation, which is equally as inconsistent and also is quite insignificant, since God predetermines all the important matters.

But modern theological progress is finally laying this unfortunate problem to rest. Today the doctrine of divine predestination is being discarded, or at the least is being reinterpreted. For it is now known that the literal and absolute form of this doctrine is based on a serious misunderstanding of the almightiness of God. Consequently few Lutheran or Reformed pastors ever bring up the subject today. And when they do, they usually support only the figurative and comparative form of it. But many laymen, who have been confused by what they have heard and read about the subject, are often eager for someone to explain lucidly what is taking place.

In order to keep the matter as simple as possible, we shall follow the historical approach that was used in dealing with the fatherhood of God. The preceding chapter was concerned with the fact that in the Bible, Israel's concept of God progresses through three obvious stages. The first stage, which lasted through the early kings, understood God as exclusively interested in one tribe, and as something of a jealous patriarch in the sky. The second stage, which lasted until the time of Jesus, understood God as the universal Creator-Lord before whom men should fall prostrate in holy awe and terror. The third and final stage, which was inaugurated by Jesus, understood God as the universal Father of all men, who may be approached with childlike confidence and courage, as well as with awe.

The problem of how to view God's almightiness is closely connected with these three stages of Israel's theological development. For Israel's concept of God's almightiness, since it is always an integral part of the total picture of God, has gone through the same three stages.

In the beginning of the first stage, which viewed God as a tribal deity, the people of Israel doubted that the God about whom Moses informed them could deliver them from the Egyptians and their gods. But God did deliver them. And he cared for them in the wilderness and destroyed their enemies before them as they invaded their Promised Land. The people of Israel observed that God could overpower any other people's gods, that he could command the weather and smite the earth with storms and blow back the sea. Very early, therefore, the Israelites began to sing their admiration of this mightiest of gods. One of their oldest songs is the Song of Moses which is sung on the eastern shore of the Reed Sea:

I will sing to the Lord. For he has triumphed gloriously. The horse and his rider he has thrown into the sea. . . . Your right hand, O Lord, glorious in power . . . shatters the enemy. At the blast of your nostrils the waters pile up. . . . The enemy said: I will pursue. I will overtake. . . . You blew with your wind. The sea covered them. . . . Who is like you among the gods, O Lord, . . . terrible in glorious deeds, doing wonders? (Exod. 15:1 ff.)

Another ancient song, which comes somewhat later in the days of the judges, is the Song of Deborah and Barak after the overthrow of the Midianite oppressors:

Lord, when you went forth from [mount] Seir, . . . the earth trembled, and the skies dropped. Yes, the skies dropped water. The mountains quaked before the Lord, . . . the God of Israel. . . . The kings came. They fought. . . . They did not get spoils of silver. From the sky the stars fought against [their general] Sisera. The River Kishon swept them away. . . . March on, my soul, with might! (Judg. 5:2 ff.)

Psalm 18, coming still later, is a poetic picture of the power of the greatest God:

In my distress I called upon the Lord. . . . From his temple he heard my voice. . . . Then the earth reeled and rocked. The foundations also of the mountains trembled and quaked, because he was angry. He bowed the

heavens and came down. He came swiftly on the wings of the wind. . . .
The Lord also thundered in the heavens. And the Most High uttered his
voice, hailstones and coals of fire. He sent out his arrows and scattered
[my enemies]. He flashed forth lightnings and routed them. (6 ff.)

Another hymn attributed to David praises the power of God in the
wind, which he sees blowing the trees of the wilderness. This wind
David called the "voice of the Lord."

The voice of the Lord is powerful and full of majesty. The voice of the Lord
breaks the cedars. The voice of the Lord makes the oaks to whirl and
strips the forests bare. The voice of the Lord shakes the wilderness. He
makes the [wooded hills of] Lebanon to skip like a calf. (Psalm 29.)[1]

On and on go the biblical hymns to God's power and might from
the first stage of Israel's theological development. Each hymn is filled
with poetic imagery. Each hymn speaks of God having the power to
do anything that he desires. *But these hymns never speak of God taking away from man the power to decide his own destiny or even to
resist God himself.* In fact, the tragedy of Israel during much of its
history is that God's special people *do* turn their backs on their Savior.
And although God has the power to punish and even to destroy his un-
faithful people, he does not appear to have the power, or else the desire,
to take from them their ability to be persons with free will. The history
of Israel demonstrates quite adequately that the stiff-necked Hebrews
were not robots manipulated by God but true persons who often used
their free will to exasperate and sadden him. Isaiah speaks for God:

> Sons have I reared and brought up,
> but they have rebelled against me. . . .
> they have despised the Holy One of Israel. (1:2, 4.)

Thus in this period God was only poetically and comparatively the Almighty God, and man was truly a free person. For God's election of
Israel was no absolute predestination of them to be his people, since
his election was conditioned by Israel's free response.

Then comes the second stage of Israel's theological development,
when God becomes the only God, who is the Holy Creator of all things.
This seems to be the period in which the belief in absolute predestina-

---

[1] These excerpts are partially paraphrased.

tion arose. And three main ingredients appear to compose this belief.

The first ingredient in absolute predestination was the new understanding of God as the only, and eternal, God who is everywhere and who has a total and amazing power over all things. This realization that God was not just one tribal god among many gods was a great step forward. But the greatness of God tended to be overemphasized. It was a temptation to emphasize God's glory and might by speaking disparagingly of man. It was a temptation to make God everything and man nothing at all. (See Job 14, 40, 42.) This emphasis on God's power made it rather easy to overlook man's inherent spiritual dignity as a real person who is created by God to have freedom of will.

The second ingredient in absolute predestination was a misunderstanding of God's election of Israel. Israel was always aware that the one thing that distinguished it from other nations was the fact that God had elected Israel out of all the nations of the earth. The equally true fact that God had elected them in order to bring the blessing of his revelation of himself to all nations seems usually to have been overlooked by the Hebrews. They easily assumed that God played favorites, as Isaac did when he chose Esau over Jacob in a measure exceeding the ancient custom of primogeniture. And they saw nothing wrong with God's rejecting ninety-five percent of the humanity he had created, if God so desired. "You only have I known of all the families of the earth," Amos has the Almighty say (3:2). And the psalmist exhorts the Israelites to rejoice that they, the sons of Jacob, are "his chosen ones" (105:6). Thus God's mercy upon an enslaved people and his program of revelation are unfortunately viewed as an arbitrary divine favoritism.

The third ingredient in absolute predestination was the matter of spirit possession. All the great leaders and prophets in the Bible are men with whom God dealt in a rational way. When God spoke to Moses and Elijah and Isaiah, these men appear to have been in full possession of their mental faculties, including their willpower. But the rational prophets had to compete with a strain of prophets known as "ecstatic prophets," or "possessed prophets." These prophets would seemingly lose control of their bodies and minds to some divine spirit, or to God himself, who would cause the affected prophets to rave and rant almost as though drunk or demented. The religions of the peoples around Israel were often organized around these possessed prophets.

Most of the writing prophets were struggling in their day against the ecstatic prophets whom they decried as false. There is a minor theme in the Old Testament, however, of temporary divine possession of the true prophets that includes the ecstasy. The writers of the books of Judges and I Samuel, for instance, report that the Spirit of the Lord came upon Samson and gave him miraculous power (Judg. 14:6) and that the spirit of God came upon Saul so that he prophesied naked all night (I Sam. 19:24).

Close examination of such passages, however, reveals that the divine spirit possession of the Old Testament prophets and heroes probably did not deprive them of their free will or rationality. Or, if it did deprive them to some extent, the possession was only temporary. It would be one thing for God temporarily to possess a man and then to turn him loose again. It would be another thing for God permanently to control a man's mind. It would be one thing for God periodically to give a man new thoughts and promises in an ecstatic experience so that afterward that man of his own free will would become afire with a message of new hope. It would be another thing for God to have created a man so that he would be always a robot whose willpower is God's own willpower.

But unfortunately in this second stage of Israel's theological development the people's understanding of God's almightiness changed from comparative-poetic almightiness to absolute mechanical almightiness. They reasoned something like this: "If God is powerful enough to create and sustain all things, and if God elects and rejects whom he chooses, and if God in ecstatic experiences can overpower a man's mind and body, then ultimately all power must be God's. God must cause everything to happen that happens—even our thoughts and desires. Therefore we are all merely puppets whose strings are pulled by the Spirit of God." (See Proverbs 21:1.)

This belief that man's willpower is a helpless pawn in God's hands can be noted in a number of passages. The editor of the Genesis stories, for instance, reports that God hardened Pharaoh's heart against Moses' demands. Yet the editor also reports that Pharaoh hardened his own heart (Exod. 10:27 versus 8:15). The early tellers of this story, who belonged to the first stage of Israel's theological development, must have meant that their tribal God affected Pharaoh's decision through external elements is the situation, such as the impressive magical prowess of his own magicians. But the Genesis 1 editor, who belonged to the

58

second stage of Israel's theological development, interpreted the story to mean that the universal God affected Pharaoh's decisions internally by working directly on the ruler's soul. Consequently, he could interpret the report that Pharaoh hardened his heart as a way of referring to the outward actions of Pharaoh that were caused by God's internal interference. (See also I Sam. 2:25.)

There is also David's famous prayer:

> *Create* in me a clean heart, O God,
>   and *put* a new and right spirit within me.
>   (Ps. 51:10, italics added.)

David may have meant this symbolically and poetically. But later generations took him literally and believed that God changed men's hearts as he pleased. Again, Isaiah proclaims to Israel:

> The Lord has poured out upon you
> a spirit of deep sleep. (29:10.)

Later generations interpreted this to mean that God simply shut off the minds of people whenever he so willed.

By the time of Christ the Jews, working along this line, had developed a quite hard-shell doctrine of absolute predestination. They believed that God had arbitrarily chosen a few Jews to be saved and had decreed that the rest of mankind was to be destroyed. With this doctrine God could be loved only if you were fortunate enough to have been among the chosen ones, and only if you were as narrow in your sympathies as you understood God to be, so as not to be horrified by such favoritism.

The third stage of Israel's concept of God's almighty power was initiated by Jesus, whose conception of the fatherhood of God demolishes any idea of predestination which is based on a literalistic and absolutistic understanding of God's power, election, and inspiration. In the Synoptic Gospels—Matthew, Mark, and Luke—we find the earliest and most reliable accounts of what Jesus said and did. In these documents Jesus presents God as a Father—not as a celestial manipulator of robots. Only twice is predestination espoused in the Synoptics. And these seem to be rather obvious interpolations, that is, subsequent additions to the text (Matt. 11:25 ff.; 13:10 ff.).

Jesus never magnifies the power of God so highly that God is pic-

59

tured as ceasing to respect the dignity of man's God-given willpower. In the Sermon on the Mount, for example, Jesus teaches his disciples how to live and how to believe without indicating that he has any hesitation about the ability of their free wills to follow his recommendations if they so desire. In this sermon Jesus rejects the old Jewish favoritism by revealing how God's love extends to both the wicked and the righteous (Matt. 5:43 ff.). Jesus also does not say on that "occasion" that God has arbitrarily closed his heart to most of mankind. The concept of God as the concerned Father of all men simply makes impossible any notion that God coldly hardens any man's heart so that he cannot believe. The very idea of God as a Father, therefore, must put a crucial limit on God's almightiness.

On many occasions Jesus rebukes his disciples for their little faith (Matt. 8:26). And he informs those who desire to be healed that he can heal them only if they have faith (Matt. 9:28-29). But Jesus does not indicate that God is responsible for installing this faith in men. Rather, Jesus exhorts his listeners to create within themselves the necessary faith, as though they are men who have the willpower to decide to believe and to act on that belief. "Have faith in God," he exhorts (Mark 11:22). And when his disciples ask him "Lord, increase our faith" (Luke 17:5) Jesus does not pray for some miraculous power from the Almighty God to strike into their puppet hearts. Rather, he simply encourages them to want to have faith by telling them what marvelous things can happen for them and for others if they choose to believe. And he urges them to increase in faith—or in God-confidence —by putting the small measure of faith that they already have to work so as to grow in faith by the additional experience.

Furthermore, Jesus does not condone the sins of the hypocrites around him with the excuse that, since God has not put it into their hearts to be sincere, they cannot be blamed for their insincerity. Rather, Jesus continually scalds them verbally for their own wickedness, as though they alone are responsible for it (Matt. 15:1 ff.). And, even though Jesus rebukes the Sadducees for not knowing the mighty power of God, he always recognizes that God has given man a large enough measure of independent power to resist God if man chooses. "O Jerusalem, Jerusalem," Jesus laments. "How often I would have gathered your children together as a hen gathers her brood under her wings, and you *would not!*" (Luke 13:34).

This real human spiritual freedom is also the reason Jesus declares that there is joy in heaven over one sinner who repents. There is joy not because God has mechanically manipulated a man's will but because a lost soul, of his own free will, has turned back to his God (Luke 15:10).

Jesus does recognize demon possession, however. And demon possession by definition involves the overwhelming of a man's own willpower. But there is every indication that Jesus treated demon possession as a spiritual condition that occurred only when people were mentally ill and hence were unable to keep control of their mental faculties. After Jesus healed the Gerasene demoniac, Mark reports, the man put his clothes on and sat down "in his right mind" (5:15).

Yes, the Gospels reveal that Jesus was thoroughly in favor of people having control of their own minds and wills. In everything he was and did he stirred up people to give their hearts to their heavenly Father and to their brother man as though the responsibility and ability were entirely theirs. For Jesus, as for the earliest Hebrews, God's almightiness was figurative, comparative, poetic, and limited.

Unfortunately, however, from its beginning the church almost covered up Jesus' correction of late Hebrew theological extremes. And we are only beginning to appreciate this fact in the twentieth century.

Saul of Tarsus, or Paul, as we usually name him, despite the wonderful truths in his letters, is one of the main causes of the trouble. Paul was educated to be a strict predestinarian Pharisee under Gamaliel. He was not educated under Jesus as one of the Lord's personal disciples. Paul's not knowing Jesus' true position was probably the reason Paul retained to the end his Pharisaic, second-stage doctrine of absolute predestination. Evidently Paul never realized how basically the favoritism and the robotism of Pharisaic predestination conflicted with the universal fatherhood of God that Jesus taught. And if Paul did see the conflict, he still failed to indicate to his readers that the predestinarian terminology he used was to be interpreted in a figurative manner.

Apparently, Paul believed that in Jesus the Christ, God had expanded his election considerably to take in many Gentiles as well as Jews (Rom. 11:11 ff.), and also that God had given the necessary faith to these souls whom he had chosen and had hardened the souls of those whom he had not chosen (Rom. 9:17 ff.; 11:7-8, 26). Paul was confident, in addition, that God had made his choices before the creation of the world (Eph. 1:4). And Paul viewed the chosen people of God as essentially a society of righteous robots who "have been destined and appointed to live for the praise of his glory" (Eph. 1:12). However, Paul is not fully consistent on this doctrine in the New Testament, or else his eloquent and valuable exhortations to be responsible in belief and ethics would never have been written.

Judging from Romans 9, we find that Paul evidently received some criticism of his position from objectors who claimed that such an arbitrarily "choosey" God would be a malicious and unjust God. But Paul retorts that God is not limited to man's principles of right and wrong. He insists that God has the right to harden the heart of whomever he wills and to have mercy upon whomever he wills because we are all simply clay and God is the potter. Any potter, of course, has the right to do whatever he wishes with his own clay pots. But Paul fails to see that the metaphor of man as a spiritless clay pot and God as a potter is so inadequate as to be subchristian. God, Jesus taught, is a Father who loves and is tender to his children. God is not a potter who makes mindless, unfeeling clay-pot people and then takes delight in arbitrarily smashing a certain percentage of them. God is a Father who obviously has more moral responsibilities toward his children than a potter has toward his clay pots.

Paul, however, is not the only New Testament writer who favors absolute predestination. The editor of the Gospel of John (who may be distinguished from the author) also accepts this doctrine. He believes with the Pharisees that all men are governed by God or by the devil and that either God or the devil supplies and controls the thoughts and desires in man's mind. While in the three Synoptic Gospels, Jesus strongly rebukes the wicked for their own sins, in the Gospel of John, Jesus is reported as merely telling the wicked unbelievers that they are unable to believe because the Father has chosen not to put belief into their hearts. The Father about whom Jesus talks in the Fourth Gospel is often the arbitrary, choosey, favoritism-showing Father of Paul, and not the universally loving Father of the other Gospels who calls to all men and holds all men responsible for their own decisions. Christian scholars have noted the late date of John and the diverse strands of interpretation within it. The largest consensus of scholarly opinion, consequently, is that this Gospel's form is due to at least one second-generation Christian editor who had partially misunderstood the words of Jesus that were transmitted to him by the apostle John, either directly or through the liturgies of the early church. The scholars are generally convinced that the universal fatherhood of God position in the three earlier Gospels is the true position of Jesus.

So perceptive Christians today usually are convinced that the almightiness of God is only comparative and poetic. Compared to us, God is indeed almighty, even more than the ocean's tide is almighty in comparison with the fall of a single raindrop. But because God is a Father who wants children who are true persons, he has given us a small amount of independent power in our self-conscious free wills. And he does not violate our tiny willpower with his mighty willpower. For if he were to do so, we would immediately cease to be true persons. God is all mighty at the same time that we are a little mighty.

Let me use an illustration here. Practically speaking, I have the same relationship with my tropical fish that God has with man. I have total power and responsibility over them in their fragile aquariums. I see to it that they get water, food, heat, light, medicine, plants, aeration, and sanitation. I can permit them to swim about, or I can catch them in a net and transfer them to another aquarium. My fish are completely in my power. Thus, from their "fishes' eye" point of view, I am, comparatively speaking, their almighty god.

But even these little fish have a type of free will, a power to cooperate or not to cooperate with me. Within the confines of their glass walls they can swim wherever they wish, run from me or toward me, fight each other or love each other, and so forth. They can, and usually do, flick their tails at me and hide behind a rock or a plant when they see me approaching with a net. In the same fashion, man is insignificant in God's sight when we compare our might to his. But we are still independent persons who can resist the Almighty Creator himself if we so wish.

By now it should be quite clear what free will means for the daily life of Christians. Free will means that we can lay only part of the blame upon God—if even that much—for our vices, attitudes, fears, doubts, lusts, decisions, words, or deeds. Free will means that even God himself may not know yet just when or how our life will end. Free will means that, since our fickle purposes and sudden desires as well as God's eternal purposes are involved, life may be cut shorter than our biological time clock allows us. Free will means that, since not even God can predict how a free will will decide, our life is an exciting parental adventure even for God.

Free will means that God must set up the world with an element of chance and uncertainty in it, so that even though he will protect and guide us as he sees best, we must be prepared to take the consequences of our free actions and the free actions of others. Free will means that God will not live our lives for us or make our decisions for us. Free will means that we must hear the voice of God and decide our own destiny. Free will means that every man is on his own and frequently has no one but himself to blame if he fouls up his life. Free will means that life is exciting and filled with opportunity, but also frightening and filled with danger.

Oh, yes! Christians believe that God has all might and that man has the small might of free will. They believe that this is why God said to Abraham both "I am God Almighty" and "Walk before me and be blameless."

6. Where Does Everything Come From?

"I believe in God the Father Almighty, Maker of heaven and earth."
The Apostles' Creed

Thus says the Lord, your Redeemer,
   who formed you from the womb:
"I am the Lord, who made all things,
   who stretched out the heavens alone,
   who spread out the earth—Who was with me?" Isaiah 44:24

For at least 2,500 years the people of God have believed that he is the Creator and Sustainer of the entire universe. The great ecumenical creeds of Christendom together express this faith thus: "I believe in God the Father Almighty, Maker of Heaven and Earth, and of all things visible and invisible."

But in our modern scientific age how fares our Christian belief that the universe is the creation of Almighty God? Its reception is a mixed one. Periodically, for instance, we hear disgruntled reactions from a rather limited brand of scientist who refuses to ask the ultimate "hows" and "whys" about the area of the universe that he is investigating, either in his capacity as a scientist or in his capacity as a human being. "A God?" he queries. "I can do without that hypothesis in my work. Why, I'm not even interested in it at any time! I'm interested only in dissecting and counting and comprehending things that have physical properties. I'm not interested in matters that may be beyond the scope of valid laboratory techniques. The only things that are real to me are the things that I can get to through my five senses." But not all scientists are of this narrow and sense-bound type. There are thousands of profound scientists whose questing spirits cannot avoid the ultimate "hows" and "whys" that are constantly jabbing at them for attention as they study the physical universe.

They look up into the macrocosmic, or telescopic, end of the universe, and their spirits faint at the impossibility of taking in how magnificent its largeness is. For the size and number and distance of the heavenly bodies are indeed awesome. Our sun is one and one-half million times larger than the earth. And our sun is only one rather small middle-sized star in a universe that contains unknown billions of burning stars, perhaps a goodly proportion of them providing light and heat for life-bearing planets like our earth. The expanse of the space in which these tremendous heavenly bodies are located is also awesome. The distances are so great that astronomers must use an immensely long imaginary measuring tape called the "light year." A light year is the distance that a beam of light, traveling at light's constant speed of 186,000-plus miles per second, can travel in one full year—a tremendous distance!

With this measuring tape the ninety-two and one-half million miles from the sun to the earth is reduced to a mere eight light minutes. Then the astronomer looks through his telescope and, using this light year scale, reports that the sun, around which we circle, is part of a family, or galaxy, of thirty billion suns that are all gathered into a slowly whirling dish-shaped collection that from top to bottom is ten thousand to twenty thousand light years thick, and that across the broad face of the dish is from one hundred thousand to two hundred thousand light years in diameter.

But even while his mind swoons at the size of our galaxy, the astronomer must report further that the universe on out beyond our galaxy appears to be divided into gigantic cubes that are three million light years apart—gigantic cubes that contain from dozens to a thousand huge galaxies like our own. The astronomer can pick out fifteen of these gigantic cubes of galaxies before he reaches the limits of his largest present telescope, which is the Mount Palomar telescope that peers into space two billion light years. The splendid organization of all this macrocosmic matter is enough to make a sizable proportion of our astral scientists see a divine Mind and Hand behind it all, which, of course, is to believe in a Creator.

But scientists also look down into the microcosmic, or microscopic, end of the universe. And their spirits faint here also, but now at the impossibility of taking in how magnificent its smallness is.

Biochemists look into the living cell and discover ever more diminutive and intricate chemical activities therein. Geneticists are just now breaking the genetic codes in the amazing strings of tiny chemical dabs that are gathered up in the chromosomes of each cell. In the future they anticipate being able to alter the inheritance factors of plants and animals at will. Other biochemists are just on the threshold of creating biological life in the laboratory, now that they have almost learned how to duplicate the complicated conditions that existed when life first began on earth.

Even further down the scale of smallness, atomic physicists still find themselves awed by the now familiar discovery that all the apparently hard matter scattered through space is really energy that is trapped in fancy electrical patterns called atoms. Furthermore, these atoms, since they are made up of electrons circling around protons, are also mostly empty space. If the proton nucleus of a hydrogen atom, for instance, were the size of a pea held in a man's hand, its single electron would be the size of a mosquito circling it from a half mile away. Then, even further, we note that the numerous parts of the atom are so very tiny that the physicist cannot plot both the location and the speed of a particular particle from a smashed atom. The light rays that do the photographic work knock about the tiny atomic particles, so that the physicist must settle for learning either its speed or its location, but never both. All this, plus the fact that the equations needed to report happenings in this subatomic world are so intricate and mathematically beautiful, is sufficient to cause thousands of scientists to see a divine mind and hand behind it all, which, of course, is to believe in a Creator.

But why do the complex order and organization that scientists observe through the telescope and the microscope cause many of them to conclude that there must be a Creator? This conclusion is certainly not a judgment proper to physical science itself. The scientist is going beyond the limitations of his laboratory procedures when he says that there must be a Creator behind it all. For, from a strictly scientific standpoint, his instruments can tell him exactly nothing of the Creator. He is permitted from a professional point of view to say only that the universe is the result of a long process in which "simple energy" has undergone a conversion into increasingly complex patterns.

Nevertheless, the scientist is just as entitled as any of us to go beyond his laboratory findings and to make for himself the commonsense religious judgment that there is a Creator. He has every right to feel that it is highly doubtful that "simple energy" could have evolved into this complex universe without the guidance and power of a Creator. Thus the scientist who believes in the Creator still does so by an act of reasonable faith, just like all other believers. And his scientific study which produces his religious awe cannot prove or disprove his act of faith. Still it does encourage Christians that so many modern scientists must conclude for themselves that there is indeed a Creator.

But, as comforting as the religious judgments of thousands of profound scientists may be, the Christian belief in God the Creator is based primarily on something that Christians believe is considerably more solid than cosmic awe. Our Christian belief is based primarily not on the experience of God's people in their meditations about the physical universe, but on the historical experience of God's people Israel with the Creator himself.

In the beginning of God's dealings with Israel, however, God was not recognized as the Creator of all things. For in the first stage of Israel's theological development, Israel knew God only as tribal redeemer. He had delivered his people out of slavery in Egypt and had led them with "his mighty hand and his outstretched arm" into their Promised Land.

The children of Israel could have come by several ways to their eventual conviction that this God—their Deliverer, Protector, and Provider—was also their Creator. Perhaps Israel's thinkers arrived at the idea by logical reasoning. They had experienced in their deliverance that God controlled the wind and the rain and the sun. He could cause earthquakes and heal diseases and, in general, could manipulate nature at will. It was only logical for them to conclude that God had this power and authority over the world because he owned it, and that he owned it because he had made it. For even as the Israelite who dug a well owned and controlled that well because he had made it, and even as the Israelite who built a rock wall owned and controlled that wall because he had made it, so God must own and control the whole world because he has made it. The writings of the prophets seem to contain this thought as an implicit assumption (Deutero-Isaiah—that is, the later portion of Isaiah, sometimes called Second Isaiah; Job 38, 39).

Again, the idea of God's creation of the world may have received some impetus from the ancient creation myths of the pagan nations that bordered Israel. Men have always wondered where the world came from. And numerous ancient peoples believed that this orderly world came forth out of a gigantic struggle between the forces of order and chaos. In Babylonian mythology, for instance, Marduk, the god of order, was supposed to have battled victoriously with Tiamat, the fishlike monster-goddess of chaos. According to the story, Marduk slew Tiamat and out of her body made the earth and the seas. In a few places the Old Testament psalms and prophets refer poetically, and perhaps even literally, to this battle (Isa. 50:9-10; Ps. 89:10; 74:13-14), calling the monster of chaos who was slain by God "Rahab," or "Leviathan."

But the greater theologians of Israel turned away from these ancient myths about order battling chaos, since this primordial conflict did not accurately reflect their nation's experience of the almightiness of God, in which they had observed that he seemed to be able to manipulate nature in their behalf with great ease and flexibility. Consequently, they preferred to picture the world as a creation of the Almighty God who had worked with his material without getting any resistance from it.

Whatever method God may have used to reveal to his people Israel that he was the Creator of the cosmos, we can find three basically concurring types of creation account in the Old Testament: the *instructional* type, the *dramatic-poetic* type, and the *devotional* type. All three types of biblical creation story agree in their testimony that God's material has responded to him in an orderly and totally submissive manner.

The first and most important type of creation story is the *instructional* creation account. The oldest such narrative is in the second and third chapters of Genesis (2:4b–3:24), which the biblical scholars date in the tenth century before Christ. This oldest account is the attempt of ancient theologians to express the crucial truths in God's creation of man through the literary form of a parable. The scene opens with the barren, newly created earth watered by a mist. The first object that God creates to inhabit this raw earth, surprisingly, is a single man. After the man, God creates a garden of fruit trees called Eden, including the tree of the knowledge of good and evil. In the garden God creates the animals and presents them to the man for him to name. The end of God's creation is the making of a woman from the man's rib in order that the man may have a suitable companion. Finally the sin of eating from the forbidden tree occurs, and the punishment of expulsion from the garden is meted out.

This story communicates at least these five theological truths: (1) That God created man; (2) that God placed his creature man under certain obligations; (3) that man is to be the master of the physical world; (4) that woman is to be subordinate to man, and yet that man is to cherish her; and (5) that all our troubles are the result of man's failure to obey God.

Now the original purpose of this oldest creation story was almost certainly not to reveal the order in which God created the furniture of earth. Rather, chapters 2 and 3 of Genesis should be interpreted not as literal history but as sacred parable. The continuing use of this parable in Christian marriage ceremonies is a testimony to its essentially practical purpose.

The second, and the younger, of the instructional creation accounts is in the first chapter of Genesis (1:1–2:4a). This account is placed by the biblical scholars in the sixth century before Christ. Our present version was probably the end result of a long oral tradition that was written down by a priest-scholar in the period of the Babylon exile, or later.

Once more we are not dealing with a literal account of creation but with an ancient religious parable. This account shows the results of considerable logical thought. Here man is not created before the trees and the grass and the other animals are created. Instead, everything appears in the necessary sequence. Man appears after the animals that he lives on. And they appear after the grass that they feed on. And the grass appears after the earth and the sun that it feeds on, and so forth. Since this creation parable comes late in Israel's history, scholars are usually convinced that its seven-day scheme of creation was simply a literary device that the writer of the parable used in order to fit creation into the seven-day Hebrew week of that time.

This second parable proclaims at least seven theological truths: (1) that God created everything, (2) that God was in complete and unresisted control of the operation, (3) that God used an orderly and developmental process, (4) that we have been created in his likeness,

70

(5) that we are the ruling creatures of the earth, (6) that we are to observe a day of rest, and (7) that the universe is perfectly good because God made it.

When Christians thus understand that these two creation stories are essentially ancient parables in which God's people once passed on to their children the spiritual truths of creation, then Christians are not duty bound to interpret these instructional narratives literally. We are not required to defend the six days of creation as scientific knowledge that was divinely revealed three thousand years before modern science developed.

Most of the battle between Christians and evolutionists—highlighted by the "Scopes Monkey Trial" in Tennessee in 1925 that pitted William Jennings Bryan against Clarence Darrow—has been an unnecessary tragedy. For it has usually sprung from a fundamentalistic misinterpretation of the first three chapters of Genesis.

The scientific theory of evolution merely says that the entire universe began very simply and that it gradually "evolved," or developed, into its present complexity over a great span of time. Biological life was one stage along the way in this process. And from very simple one-celled forms biological life developed into creatures as complex as man. For humility's sake, scientists still formally refer to the process of evolution as a theory. But from a practical point of view the evolutionary process in nature is so well documented by hundreds of scientific studies that we may accept it as an established fact.

But this fact of evolution does not disturb the scientist who is a Christian. Rather, he delights in it. "Only the eternal God," he insists worshipfully, "could handle a process of development requiring some five billions of years. And here in the first chapter of Genesis, written 2,500 years ago, is the first evolutionary treatise in human history. A child of God with his parable of six days of creation has been the first person to describe how life has gone through an orderly process of development."

The only kind of evolutionist that Christians need combat is the atheistic evolutionist who believes that the universe has developed from the most simple energy particles to the self-conscious human spirit purely through a process determined by blind chance. To this man the scientifically sophisticated Christian replies: "Sir, you are speaking beyond your laboratory data. We are not objecting that you teach the physical aspects of evolution in your biology class. We know that you must teach about the basic process. But we are objecting that you are not doing so in a religiously neutral manner, or at least in a fair manner. For when you teach that the process of evolution blindly guides itself without acknowledging that this is only your personal religion of atheism giving testimony, you are giving the false impression that your scientific data includes your religious judgment. We will resist you as a bad teacher of science if you do not candidly admit that your laboratory data on the physical universe is religiously neutral."

So Christians have no cause to fight the "fact" of evolution. Evolution is the technique that God has used in his creating. And in this matter the physical sciences have done us the service of helping us properly to interpret our ancient Scriptures.

This is not the first time, either, that physical science has assisted Christian biblical interpretation. Several hundred years ago everyone, including Christians, thought that the earth was flat and had four corners. They believed this because the Bible spoke of the "four corners of the earth" (Isa. 11:12). But when Captain Magellan sailed around the globe, Christendom realized that the phrase "four corners of the earth" must originally have been only a figurative way for the ancient Israelites to say "the farthest parts of the earth." For convenience' sake these men of old had assigned the earth four corners—making it just like their blankets. So here is an instance where scientific discovery long ago helped us properly to interpret a portion of Scripture. The creation stories are cases of precisely the same kind.

The second type of creation account is the *dramatic-poetic* type. These accounts were written about the same time as the first chapter of Genesis. One of them is in the eighth chapter of Proverbs (vss. 22-31), where Wisdom is given credit for being the master craftsman who did God's work of creation. Another of these accounts is in Job 38 (4 ff.), where from the whirlwind God reminds the suffering man of his majestic creational works. Numerous brief dramatic-poetic creation accounts are sprinkled through the golden age prophets who remind faithless and frightened Israel of the glory of the Creator God in order to restore the people to faithfulness and courage (e.g., Isa. 42:5; 43:1; 44:2, 24; 45:5 ff.; Jer. 31:34). These accounts agree with the instructional accounts. But the figurative aspect must be even more carefully observed.

The third type of creation stories, which also comes from about the same time as the first chapter of Genesis, is the *devotional* type. These accounts are to be found primarily in the book of Psalms, especially in the beautiful Psalms 104 and 136. These songs were a high point in the golden age of Israel's Old Testament history and were used in majestic and uplifting worship services. They constitute a reverent recital of God's many creative acts in which he provided man with this wonderful environment of earth. The mountains, the valleys, the seas, the springs, the grass, the herbs and trees, the animals, the sun, the moon, the stars—all are listed and worshipfully credited to God's fecundity. The same orderly progression of creation from the simple to the complex, which is contained in the instructional narratives, may be noted in these devotional exercises as well. Thus, while these psalms are basically devotional, they have a considerable instructional effect also.

These three types of creation account are the primary source of our Christian belief that God is the Creator of all things. For we believe that whatever thought processes may have been involved, God himself was the primal source through whom his special people Israel came to this understanding of the beginning of the universe. Our doctrine of creation, we believe, is ultimately founded upon historical revelation, rather than upon natural speculation.

If we Christians are correct that the Hebrew belief in divine creation is the product of special divine revelation, then our lives are blessed with some wonderful knowledge. First, divine creation means that *life has meaning.* If we were instead the end result of a process of blind evolution, life would have no transcendent meaning for us poor human animals. But the Creator God has made us, and has made us like himself, because he has a special purpose for us. Thus life has a real meaning for us only in our Creator.

Second, divine creation means that *we are God's possession.* We often live as though we own ourselves. But as a boy owns a whistle that he whittles out of wood, even so our Creator owns us. He has the right to tell us how our life is to be lived. We exist under perpetual obligation to him.

Third, divine creation means that *God is love.* God cannot bear to live selfishly locked up within himself, enjoying himself in the mirror of his divine thoughts. God is love! He must get out of himself and give of himself. He must create others to whom he may give himself,

73

others for whom he may care, others with whom he may share his glorious eternal life.

Fourth, divine creation means that *we can live in security and confidence*. The God of love has poured out his energy for billions of years to make this world and us to live in it. After going to all this effort in order to produce this creation, he is going to be painfully particular, we may be assured, in his care of it.

Yes, Christians believe that it is a great blessing to be able to declare with confidence: "I believe in God the Father Almighty, Maker of Heaven and Earth." And Christian hearts expand with wonder, love, and praise to read words such as those of Isaiah:

> Thus says the Lord, your Redeemer,
>   who formed you from the womb:
> "I am the Lord, who made all things,
>   who stretched out the heavens alone,
>   who spread out the earth—Who was with me?"

Section III: CHRIST

7. Is Jesus the Son of God Because He Is a Man?

"And in Jesus Christ his . . . Son." The Apostles' Creed

"So God created man in his own image." Genesis 1:27
"For all who are led by the Spirit of God are sons of God."
Romans 8:14

One of the most crucial and distinctive doctrines of the Christian church, and a doctrine that is central in all Christian creeds, is that Jesus of Nazareth was and is the Son of God. Consequently, one of the greatest theological needs of the Christian church today is to come to a clear understanding of what we mean when we say that Jesus of Nazareth is the Son of God.

The same problem did not exist two hundred years ago. Back then theologians simply assumed that, since the Bible had been dictated by God himself, all the passages that dealt with Jesus Christ were harmonious and supplementary; or, in a sense, that all the passages about Jesus were only different sparkling facets of the same diamond of christological truth. And how natural it is sometimes to wish for those less complicated days when we lacked much of the information that we now have!

But the discoveries of biblical research have made it impossible for us ever to return to any simple interpretation of the New Testament passages that speak of Jesus. Since we now realize that the Bible is a very human book written by unmanipulated men about their marvelous experiences with God, we are forced to examine each contributing author's work separately. We are also forced to break down each author's work into the originally independent traditions which he has sometimes fitted rather uncomfortably together, in order to see how each of these diverse traditions understood the divine sonship of Jesus. In such an investigation we discover that the New Testament editors and the reporters from whom they gathered their materials present quite different interpretations of what it means to say that Jesus of Nazareth is the Son of God. We find also that with the passage of time after Jesus' resurrection the church had a general tendency to develop increasingly glorious and awesome interpretations of Jesus' divine sonship.

Jesus was crucified in approximately A.D. 30. The Gospel of Mark was written about A.D. 65, Luke-Acts about A.D. 80, Matthew about A.D. 85, and John about A.D. 95. None of these works, it is believed today, was written directly by first-generation disciples of Jesus. All were written, rather, by second-generation Christians. Each of these Gospels is in essence a rope woven together out of a number of originally independent strands of oral tradition. When we unravel these literary ropes as best we can and when we analyze along with them the writings of Paul that date from A.D. 50 to A.D. 67, we find at least five different meanings to the affirmation that Jesus is the Son of God: (1) Jesus is the Son of God because he is a human being created in God's image. (2) Jesus is the Son of God because he became like God. (3) Jesus is the Son of God because he was adopted to be the Messiah. (4) Jesus is the Son of God because he was physically conceived by God. (5) Jesus is the Son of God because he is the eternally outgoing part of God.

But how many of these interpretations are correct? How did the early church arrive at them? And how many of them would Jesus himself acknowledge? Modern scholars unanimously concur that Jesus would agree to the first two kinds of sonship. Most of them are convinced, in addition, that Jesus would also claim the unique third kind of divine sonship. But most scholars seem to doubt that Jesus would support a modern literal interpretation of the fourth and fifth interpretations of his divine sonship. The scholars can accept the story of the miraculous conception of Jesus, as a rule, only if it is understood very symbolically. They can accept the idea of the eternal partnership with the

Father only if it is understood within what may be its original and very special philosophical framework.

This is the first in a section of four chapters on "How Is Jesus the Son of God?" In this first chapter we shall consider the first two biblical meanings of Jesus' divine sonship. Neither of these types of sonship is in any way a unique, "only-begotten" kind of divine sonship. But we must appreciate the more general kinds of such sonship before we can appreciate the particular kind of "only-begotten" sonship that applies to Jesus alone.

Now to understand these two most basic and early meanings of divine sonship should be very simple for us because they parallel exactly the relationships between an earthly father and his son. In a physical sense every male infant *is born* a son of his father. But in a spiritual sense every infant *must become* a true son of his father by taking on his father's knowledge and attitudes and beliefs and habit patterns.

In the first sense we look through the hospital nursery window and say "Yes, you can tell that is Frank's son by his nose." In the second sense we look at an honest, hardworking teenager and say "Yes, you can tell that is Frank's son by his sterling character."

Jesus, therefore, is the son of his heavenly Father in the physical sense because he was born with all the basic personality equipment that was necessary to give him the potential to become spiritually like his heavenly Father as he grew up. And Jesus is the son of his heavenly Father in the spiritual sense because he actualized his potential and became for us the perfect image of the divine, self-giving love.

Now that we appreciate how simple and supplementary these two kinds of divine sonship are, let us locate them in the Bible. We will depend upon the writings of the prophets of Israel's golden age, upon the letters of Paul, and upon a strand of the Gospels that is called "Jesus' ethical teachings"—the earliest strand of all which, unfortunately, is often confusedly altered by the interpretations of the early church. We will discover in these biblical portions that both these kinds of divine sonship are attributed in some degree to other human beings long before the time of Jesus, and that the New Testament writers expect all Jesus' disciples to share with Jesus these two kinds of sonship.

First, let us consider the biblical basis of the doctrine that Jesus is the Son of God because he is a human being. This idea that every human being is a child of God is one of the high-water marks reached by Old Testament Hebrew religion during Israel's second stage of theological development. The Hebrews began, you remember, as a nation of slaves delivered from bondage who believed, because of their deliverance and the destruction of their enemies by God, that they alone were the beloved children of God. "For you are a people holy to the Lord your God," Moses announces to them. "The Lord your God has chosen you to be a people for his own possession, out of all the peoples that are on the face of the earth." (Deut. 7:6.) And Amos voices the same belief when he quotes God as saying "You only have I known of all the families of the earth" (3:2).

But by the golden age of Israel's religion (which is the second stage of Israel's theological development) the outlook of the nation had changed. The outstanding example of this change is the first chapter of Genesis which was written by a priestly writer some four hundred years before Christ. In the creation story all mankind is recognized to be but one species—and this is the religious species—in which everyone was capable of divine-human fellowship.

The Genesis writer declares this great truth by having God say to his spirit family in heaven on the sixth day of creation: "Let us make man in our image, after our likeness" (1:26). This story that mankind had been created in God's image was an early parabolic way of noting that the entire human race—not just the children of Israel—were self-conscious spiritual beings with the ability to set values on things and freely to determine their destiny. This story is an incipient recognition also of the Fatherhood of God, because if man has been modeled on his Creator by his Creator, the end result is nothing less than being given birth by his Creator. Then, because it implies that all nations of men have sprung from this fatherly act of creation-birth, this story is an incipient recognition, as well, of the brotherhood of man.

Israel's new awareness of the unity of mankind bursts forth in the golden age eighty-sixth psalm: "All the nations you have made shall come and bow down before you, O Lord, and shall glorify your name! For you are great and do wondrous things! You alone are God!" (vss. 9-10, paraphrased). This great vision of all men as subjects of God shines forth also in that prophecy of the Isaiah school which foretold a day when all the nations of the earth would go up to Jerusalem to worship the one true God: "Come," the nations all will say.

> Let us go up to the mountain of the Lord,
> to the house of the God of Jacob;

> that he may teach us his ways
> and that we may walk in his paths. . . .
> He shall judge between the nations,
> and shall decide for many peoples; . . .
> Nation shall not lift up sword against nation. (Isa. 2:3-4.)

The grand universalism to which the golden age seers were led by God was explicitly only a political universalism. The unity of mankind to them was the unity of all men as subjects under the universal Sovereign, the King of Kings and Lord of Lords. The concept of a family unity of mankind under a heavenly Father never quite came into focus, despite the implications leading on to it and despite the occasional use of the metaphor of God as the Father of Israel.

Unfortunately, after the division, decline, and destruction of the Hebrew nation and the deportation to Babylon, Israel's religion around the fifth century before Christ took a step backward to the old narrow nationalism of the early tribes, who believed that they alone were beloved of God. The Jews under Ezra and Nehemiah separated themselves and refused any social contact with the other nations, as though these people, by not sharing in their Jewish religious traditions, were somehow less than human (Ezra 9:10 ff.; 10:10 ff.).

But the universalism of the golden age prophets, which had trembled at the edge of a recognition of the universal Fatherhood of God and brotherhood of man, did not die. It lay dormant for hundreds of years in the sacred writings of the Hebrew people and in the hearts of a compassionate minority among them (Luke 2:32; 7:1-5). And finally the vision broke out completed and with great glory and compelling power in the ministry of Jesus of Nazareth. Jesus successfully brought forth this truth of God when the dominant spirit among his people was fiercely nationalistic. The people of other nations were, in Jesus' day, officially considered outcasts from the compassion of God and were threatened with death if they dared to enter the interior of his temple in Jerusalem (Acts 21:28; 22:22).

Jesus was reared in the town of Nazareth that lay in the northern province of Galilee, about one hundred miles from Jerusalem. This area was a crossroads of the ancient world. In his boyhood Jesus had seen the camel caravans coming and going from East and West and from North and South. He had some contact with these traders of all nations, a number of whom had settled in the bustling cities on the western shore of Lake Galilee. He was aware of the several Roman garrisons nearby which were composed of men from all over the sprawling empire. He had met some of the Greeks from the eastern shore of Lake Galilee where lay the western end of the Greek colony known as the Decapolis. He had probably been overland twenty-five miles to the coast of the Mediterranean Sea where lay the port of Ptolemais, and there seen the hundreds of ships of all nations busily coming and going.

In short, Jesus grew up in a great cosmopolitan environment that was more like a suburb of New York City than like an isolated rural town in midwestern America. Galilee was practically a Hebrew island in a great sea of Gentiles. So Jesus had surely met many people of these other nations and races. And undoubtedly he had seen that they were just as human as he, and just as much interested in the things of the Spirit as his own people were (Matt. 8:11). This healthy international contact is probably the reason that the young boy Jesus was so strongly attracted to the writings of the great prophets of Israel's golden age during his years of study in the synagogue school at Nazareth (Luke 4:17-22). It is also likely that the reason this Galilean boy of twelve so amazed the theologians in the Temple in Jerusalem with his understanding and answers was that already in his youth he had absorbed the truth of the old Isaiah school with its profound view of the unity of all men under God, while the Temple theologians in all-Jewish Judea had not progressed this far. It was probably no accident that God's revelation to Israel that reached a high point in the golden age prophets should be revived and raised to perfection in a man coming from cosmopolitan, mongrelized Galilee.

The qualitatively new ingredient that Jesus introduced was the truth that God was not merely the holy Creator-Lord but also a loving Father. This new ingredient could have come only out of Jesus' own experience with God—perhaps during meditation upon some of the poetic imagery of the Old Testament. But just how Jesus was led to the recognition of God's fatherhood we are nowhere informed in the New Testament.

But we want to note that Jesus must have made a very early connection between his new knowledge of God as Father and the human unity under God which had been impressed upon him in his childhood through study of the seers of Israel's golden age. For in the earliest and most reliable Gospel materials, Jesus never speaks of divine sonship as something that applies only to him. Rather, he always speaks of the Fatherhood of God as a reality which equally includes all men as sons and makes them all brothers.

Jesus appears on the scene as a man who is entirely without national or racial prejudice, as a man who opens his arms of ministry to Galileans, Jews, Greeks, Romans, and Samaritans. He exhorts his disciples to be perfect, or complete, in their love, as their heavenly Father is complete, by loving their enemies also (Matt. 6:48). He admonishes them to "Call no man your father on earth, for you have one Father, who is in heaven" (Matt. 23:9). He teaches his disciples to pray by addressing God as "Father" (Luke 11:2). But in none of these very early materials does Jesus imply that the divine sonship which is the basis for his close relationship with the Father is any different from the divine sonship of the rest of the human race. Rather, this Galilean rabbi, who has drunk deeply of the universalist springs of the golden age prophets, always stands among his listeners as one of them in this most essential kind of sonship.

But so revolutionary was Jesus' concept of God as Father and of all men as brothers, and so impressive was his charismatic healing power, that it was easy for those who listened to him and for those who later tried to tell of him to look only for types of divine sonship which would raise him to deity and make him unique among men. Such special sonship would erase the apparent scandal of his breaching the barrier of holiness that traditionally separated the Israelite from his God.

It is quite difficult for us to appreciate the shock that it must have been to Jesus' contemporaries to hear a mortal man referring to the Holy God as "Father" and to all men, including the ritually unclean Gentile world, as brothers. We are so accustomed to hearing God addressed as "Father" and all our fellowmen as our "brothers" that it is no easy matter for us to imagine the startling response such a thought of intimacy with holy deity and family unity with all men must have evoked from his hearers.

Jesus probably had spoken of the Fatherhood of God many times and had probably prayed to God addressing him as "Father" many times, before even his converts had the fortitude to launch out likewise into such spiritual intimacy. Because the most unique thing about Jesus' teachings was the divine Fatherhood and human sonship, the most constant report of him, furthermore, must have been that he had the audacity to call God his Father. Consequently, since respect for the holiness and distance of God was so ingrained in the people of

Israel, it would be natural for many of his listeners, who were more impressed by his personal image than they were understanding of his teachings, to raise him in their imaginations to a special level of divinity and to separate him from themselves, rather than for them to convert to thinking of God in Jesus' own familiar terms. This seems actually to have been part of the motivation behind the virgin birth story and the literal interpretation of Jesus as the eternal logos.

But we must remember that an examination of the earliest and most reliable Gospel materials reveals that Jesus spoke of divine sonship as a reality equally shared by all men. This recognition of universal divine sonship was the climactic third stage of God's program of revelation to Israel. This universal sonship which we all share with Jesus is also the source of the dynamism in his world revolution. For Christianity is primarily the result of men living out the truth of the Fatherhood of God and the brotherhood of man. We will discover as we proceed that all the other types of divine sonship which are ascribed to Jesus have the function only of establishing his divine authority to assert the truths of the universal Fatherhood of God and brotherhood of man. The most basic sense, therefore, in which Christians can speak of the divine sonship of Jesus is that Jesus of Nazareth is the Son of God because he, as well as every other human being, has been created with the potentiality to enter into fellowship with God.

Now let us turn briefly to the second biblical sense in which Jesus is the Son of God, and in which we also are the sons of God. By virtue of our creation as human beings in God's personal image we are already, in a sense, God's sons from birth. But, in a deeper sense, we are only potentially God's sons until we become like him in spirit. We are only potentially God's sons until we begin to think as God thinks and to want what God wants and to do what God does and to do it as God does it. Only then can people look at us spiritually and say "He is truly his heavenly Father's son."

Both the Old Testament and the New Testament recognize that divine sonship is a spiritual possibility as much as it is a "physical" factuality. Continually God's people are urged in the Bible to be truly his children, to be and to become more what they are created to be. "You are sons of the Lord your God," Moses reminds the Israelites. "You shall not [do thus and thus and thus]. . . . For you are a people holy to the Lord your God" (Deut. 14:1-2).

Yet distressingly often, Israel failed to achieve spiritual sonship. And the heavenly Father was heartbroken over it.

> When Israel was a child, I loved him,
>   and out of Egypt I called my son.
> The more I called them,
>   the more they went from me. (Hos. 11:1.)

"Return, O faithless sons." (Jer. 3:22.) Frequently it required punishment from the Father to make his sons become true sons. Yet punishment was only the Father's love flaring up in righteous indignation (Prov. 3:12). And his mercy and pity were always ready for a repentant son (Jer. 31:20; Deut. 8:5; Isa. 43:6-7; 45:11; Hos. 1:10; Mal. 2:10; 1:6; 3:17).

Jesus, too, takes up this theme that the physical sons of God must also become his spiritual sons. Jesus' entire sermon on the mount in Matthew and his sermon on the plain in Luke are preached, he says, in order "that you *may be* sons of your Father who is in heaven" (Matt. 5:45). The true spiritual sons of God are to achieve this sonship by becoming humble, hungry for righteousness and heaven, merciful, loving to enemies, pure in heart, peaceful, sacrificial, evangelistic, loyal, reverent, generous, patient, forgiving, confident of the Father's care, single-minded, just, self-critical, prayerful, alert for religious impostors, and hardworking in doing good.

John is speaking of this responsible and deliberately chosen divine sonship when he declares that those who believed in Jesus were given the "power to *become* children of God . . . born . . . of God" (John 1:12-13). Paul is speaking of this same obligation to become a son of God when he exhorts the Philippian Christians to "*be* blameless and innocent, children of God without blemish" (2:15). (See also Eph. 1:5; I John 3:1-2.) Paul is speaking again of this kind of sonship when he explains to the Roman Christians that "all who are *led by* the Spirit of God are sons of God" (8:14).

Thus divine sonship in the second biblical sense involves knowing who and what the heavenly Father is, and then conforming our lives to the Father's perfect, self-giving love. That Jesus grew in, and attained perfectly, this divine sonship is attested by all his writing followers (Luke 2:52). Even the pagan centurion at his cross, who watched the loving and righteous way in which Jesus offered up his soul to his spiritual Father, was thinking of this kind of divine sonship when he exclaimed: "Truly this man was a son of God!" (Mark 15:39).

Yes, according to the New Testament, Jesus is the Son of God; first, because he is a human being like the rest of us, and second, because he became perfectly like God in whose image he was created. And the significance of this subject for the life of each Christian is that frequently we have been underestimating what God has given to us as a potentiality in this life and what he expects out of us as an actuality in this life. Too often we imagine that Jesus was to be the only Son of God on earth. Consequently we permit ourselves to be satisfied with a level of personal godliness and holiness and love that falls far below his.

But this is not supposed to be the case. We are each one born into this world as a physical son of God who has magnificent possibilities. And we are each one expected, because of Jesus, to grow up and become an essentially complete spiritual son of God, like Jesus. It is all *our* responsibility. "For," as Paul explains, "all who are led by the Spirit of God are sons of God."

8. Is Jesus the Son of God Because He Is the Messiah?

"The only-begotten Son of God." The Nicene Creed

"And we bring you the good news that what God promised to the fathers, this he has fulfilled to us their children by raising Jesus; as also it is written in the second psalm,

'Thou art my Son,
today I have begotten thee.'" Acts 13:32-33

In the first chapter of this section on "How Is Jesus the Son of God?" we dealt with the two most basic biblical senses in which Jesus is considered to be God's son. First, we read that Jesus is the Son of God because he is a human being, born with all the personality (or spiritual) equipment that is necessary in order to give him the potentiality of becoming like his heavenly Father. Second, we read that Jesus is the Son of God because he became like God, by actualizing his spiritual potential until he became for us the perfect image of the Father's self-giving love. It was explained, furthermore, that we do, or may, share with Jesus these two types of divine sonship, first, by virtue of being human, and second, by virtue of following Jesus' example.

But in this chapter we shall consider a third kind of divine sonship that Jesus had which we do not share. This third kind of sonship is so distinctive that it sets him aside as a unique and crucial individual in the history of mankind. This is the special sonship to which the Apostles' Creed and the Nicene Creed probably should be referring—although they are not—when they call Jesus the "only Son of God," or the "only-begotten Son of God." We can most accurately state this third kind of divine sonship by saying that *Jesus of Nazareth is the only-born Son of God because he alone was adopted to be the Messiah.*

Increasingly, biblical scholars are coming to the conclusion that this sonship by messianic adoption is the oldest New Testament understanding of Jesus' divine sonship that sets him apart from the rest of us as sons of God. Increasingly, biblical scholars are coming to the conclusion that this understanding of Jesus' divine sonship should be considered the true historical core around which the later concepts of his unique sonship developed.

This third kind of divine sonship amounts to declaring that Jesus is a man who has been given a special divine commission to represent and advance God's loving interests among mankind. This sonship by messianic adoption is designated even in Jesus' name. For the word "Christ" is a Greek word meaning "Messiah." And "Messiah" is a Hebrew and Aramaic word meaning "anointed one." So the name "Jesus Christ" means literally "Jesus the anointed one." But, in order to trace for you Jesus' third kind of divine sonship, we must trace its beginnings in the Old Testament.

When we examine the meaning of divine sonship in the Old Testament, we discover that this sonship is often connected with God's giving of a divine commission. Adopting a particular man—or even a whole people—as his son is God's way of declaring to all men that this man—or this people—has a special responsibility and authority and mission from him. Sometimes, in order to emphasize that this man—or people—has first position among men, including any other men who may also consider themselves to be God's adopted sons, God adds "firstborn son." For the firstborn son in that patriarchal age was second in command in the household and was the one who received the bulk of the father's inheritance. Thus to say that a son was his "firstborn son" was simply God's way of emphasizing the authority and responsibility which he was bestowing upon a certain man—or people.

A very outstanding example of Old Testament adoption is found in God's words to Pharaoh. "Thus says the Lord, Israel is my firstborn son, and I say to you, 'Let my son go, that he may serve me,' if you refuse to let him go, behold, I will slay your first-born son" (Exod. 4:22-23). Israel was God's chosen people which was to be the vessel to carry his revelation of himself to the nations (Gen. 12:3; Exod. 19:6). And for the success of this mission which God was assigning to them, God gives them the favored position of the firstborn son in his divine care.

Another outstanding example of Old Testament adoption is God's adoption of Solomon. King David desired to build God a temple for worship, but God forbade it, explaining: "You may not build a house for my name, for you are a warrior and have shed blood." Yet God relieves David's concern by going on to promise him: "It is Solomon your son who shall build my house and my courts, *for I have chosen him to be my son,* and I will be his father. I will establish his kingdom for ever if he continues resolute in keeping my commandments . . . as he is today" (I Chron. 28:3, 6-7; II Sam. 7:17; I Chron. 22:10).

Again, in Psalm 89:26-27, Ethan the psalmist is singing of God's promise to continue the royal line of David for ever. The song is a messianic song, written in the midst of Israel's military defeat and occupation—a messianic song of longing for the everlasting reign of God among his people, which the psalmist understands was supposed to have begun with David. In this lament the singer, by repeating God's words, reminds God how God has promised to exalt David's line for ever:

> He shall cry to me, "Thou art my Father,
>   my God, and the Rock of my salvation."
> And I will make him the first-born,
>   the highest of the kings of the earth.
> My steadfast love I will keep for him for ever.

Certainly the most significant of all the divine adoption passages is the second psalm. Here the psalmist describes how all the nations that are subjected to Judah are conspiring "against the Lord and his anointed [one]," in order to rebel and overthrow the control of the King of Judah. But the psalmist declares that God laughs a laugh of derision at this futile attempt and informs the plotters, by punishing them with military defeat, that he has set his king on Zion—his holy hill in Jerusalem—to stay. Then in verses 7-8 the king speaks for himself concerning his position in God's favor:

> I will tell of the decree of the Lord:
> He said to me, "You are my son,
>   today I have begotten you.
> Ask of me, and I will make the nations your heritage,
>   and the ends of the earth your possession."

We want to note, also, that the words of God "You are my son, today I have begotten you" are the words of the official declaration that was made in those days when a man publicly adopted a son to share his riches and his rule. These special words play a direct part in the New Testament understanding of Jesus' sonship.

Now in the Old Testament, God indicates that a particular man is to have a special commission, not only by adoption as his son but also in other ways. Divine commissioning sometimes takes a physical form called anointing, as in the cases of the high priest Aaron and his sons and Saul and David and others. In this act oil is poured upon the head as a sign of divine appointment.

It was natural, therefore, as Israel began to develop the expectancy that God would send a deliverer to lead his people out of degradation and bondage, that they saw this deliverer in terms of anointment as well as adoption. This is why the deliverer was called the "Messiah" in the first place, since "Messiah" means "anointed one."

However, the anointment of the Messiah was evidently not expected to be performed with earthly oils. This anointment was to be by God's own Spirit descending upon the deliverer's head. Isaiah 61:1-2, for instance, is viewed by Israel as a prophecy of the proclamation that will be made by the coming deliverer. He will assert:

> The Spirit of the Lord God is upon me,
>   because the Lord has anointed me
> to bring good tidings to the afflicted;
>   he has sent me to bind up the brokenhearted,
> to proclaim liberty to the captives, . . .
> to proclaim the year of the Lord's favor, . . .
>   to comfort all who mourn.

Yet a third title for the deliverer is "servant of the Lord." All Israel is sometimes called "God's servant" (Isaiah 49:3). Godly Israelites, especially, are spoken of as "God's servants" (Isa. 65:12 ff.). But King David specifically is continually referred to as "God's servant"

(Ps. 18:1; 36:1; 67:17; Jer. 33:21; Ezek. 37:24). And because David was a foretype of the Messiah, who was to be one of his descendants, it is natural that the prophets foretell how this coming representative of God will also be God's servant. In Isaiah 52:13, for example, the prophet speaks for God: "Watch and see, my servant shall prosper, and shall be exalted and lifted up, and shall be very high" (paraphrased).

Thus at least three key Old Testament terms—"son of God," "anointed one," "servant of God"—are all bent to the single purpose of describing the deliverer whom God will raise up. In psalm two, for instance, "anointed one" (v. 2) and "son of God" (v. 7) are used closely together. (See also II Sam. 7:5.)

Now we are prepared to turn to the New Testament. By the time of Jesus the title "Messiah" was applied by every Israelite to the man of God for whom the nation was waiting. This man was expected to be God's own representative with authority to speak for God, and with the power of God backing him up. He was expected to be a political deliverer who would exalt the nation and rule the world. This man with his divine commission was the basic reality, whichever of the deliverer's names—"son of God," "anointed one," "servant of God"—the people might use to describe him and to point him out.

First, let us examine the oldest Gospel, Mark. This Gospel, as has been said, does not begin with any birth stories about Jesus, but with Jesus' baptism by John in the River Jordan (1:1-11). For Mark the meaning of John's baptism of Jesus is that this is the occasion for a spiritual experience in which Jesus receives his divine call to be God's Messiah. Mark reports that after Jesus had been baptized and had ascended the riverbank, and evidently was praying, Jesus "saw the heavens opened and the Spirit descending upon him like a dove; and a voice came from heaven, 'Thou art my beloved Son; with thee I am well pleased.'" Obviously Mark begins with this experience of Jesus because he believes that *this is the place to begin.*

If one will look carefully, one will find here in Mark both signs of God's special commissioning that occur in the second psalm. Here Jesus is anointed. And here Jesus is also adopted as the Son of God. When he stands on the riverbank and experiences the Spirit of God descending on his head as gently as a dove, Jesus is being anointed with the promised oil of God's own Spirit for his special mission. This anointing makes him literally the Messiah—"anointed one"—for whom Israel has been waiting.

The words Jesus hears in this experience are simply intended by God to reinforce the indescribable sight that Jesus sees and definitely to pin down for him the meaning of it. These words constitute essentially the same official public adoption formula that was used in the Old Testament days. The fact that the Father adds that Jesus is the "beloved son"—that is, the "most loved son"—with whom he is "pleased" is only another way of indicating that this man, after all others have been examined, is in God's good judgment the best man to have the special mission laid upon him.

Thus in our oldest Gospel this divine adoption at Jesus' anointing by the Holy Spirit is part of a single act in which God ordains Jesus to his divine mission. This act of anointment and adoption is evidently where Mark gets his idea that Jesus is the Son of God in a unique sense. His Gospel adheres to this conception of Jesus' sonship rather consistently.

We note, however, that Matthew alters Mark's idea of Jesus as the Son of God by adoption when he precedes the Jordan River ordination with a virgin birth story. Matthew does retain the story of Jesus' spiritual experience at the Jordan but so reduces it that it becomes only the public disclosure of a miraculously conceived Son of God (3:13-17).

Luke alters Mark's adoption sonship in the same manner, except that a number of very important ancient manuscripts of Luke quote psalm two so fully at Jesus' anointment that they make Jesus' riverside experience quite contradictory to the virgin birth story. One of the oldest manuscripts, for example, *Codex Bezae,* has Jesus hearing on the riverbank the entire adoption formula from the second psalm: "You are my beloved son. Today I have given birth to you." Many scholars feel that this must have been the way the disciples first heard the story from Jesus, and that most of the later editors of Matthew and Luke dropped off the key sentence "Today I have given birth to you" because it contradicted the virgin birth stories that claimed that Jesus was the special son of God from his birth.

Furthermore, in a very significant story that the Gospel of Luke alone contains, Jesus himself declares that his special relationship to the Father is indeed by anointment which, as has been said, is essentially the equivalent of divine adoption. On this occasion Jesus is handed the book of Isaiah from which to read a selection for the sabbath congregation in the synagogue at Nazareth. He turns to that messianic proclamation which we designate as Isaiah 61:1 and reads:

> The Spirit of the Lord is upon me,
> because *he has anointed me* to preach good news to the poor.
> *He has sent me* to proclaim release to the captives
> and recovering of sight to the blind,
> to set at liberty those who are oppressed,
> to proclaim the acceptable year of the Lord. (Luke 4:18-19; italics added.)

Then after a dramatic pause in which he collects the close attention of every worshiper, Jesus declares: "Today this scripture has been fulfilled in your hearing" (4:21). Thus in this only passage in the three Synoptic Gospels where Jesus himself gives us an indication of the *nature* of his divine sonship, he agrees completely with Mark's belief that he is the Son of God by adoption and that his adoption is a dramatic portion of his divine anointment to a special mission.

But Mark, we discover, is not content to mention Jesus' sonship by adoption only in the beginning of his Gospel. Mark knows that those who will read or listen to his testimony are very much concerned to be sure that this Jesus of Nazareth is not an impostor or a lunatic. For this reason Mark includes a spiritual vision that was experienced by Peter, James, and John on an occasion which the church has historically labeled the Transfiguration. On this occasion God confirms for these three disciples the significance of his ordination of Jesus after his baptism in the Jordan. Their experience, in a sense, is an extension of Jesus' own experience. Up on the mountain together, evidently during common prayer, these three disciples see Jesus change until his face and clothing shine with a heavenly glory. They see Moses, who represents the law, and Elijah, who represents the prophets, talking with him. The appearance of these two men signifies that the law and the prophets confirm and support Jesus' messiahship. Then a cloud engulfs the disciples, and they hear a voice saying: "This is my beloved son; listen to him" (Mark 9:2-8). That is, "Live under *his* command, since he now supersedes the Law and the Prophets."

Matthew and Luke report this same spiritual experience (Matt. 17:1-8; Luke 9:28-36). But Luke, very significantly, adds an ancient adoptionist phrase that is left out by Matthew and even by Mark. For Luke reports that God also said at that time: "This is my son, my

Chosen" (9:35). Now a chosen son is an adopted son rather than a natural-born son. Why Luke and his copyists kept this item in his edition of the collected reports about Jesus, we do not know. Perhaps he retained the phrase "my Chosen" because he did not realize how deeply it conflicted with his virgin birth story. Perhaps he kept this phrase simply because he was a man of integrity and knew that his job was to tell the story as he had heard it, not to make it up, even if he could not harmonize some of the details.

It is interesting to note also in the passion—that is, "Holy Week," or the last week of Jesus' life—history how, although Matthew and Luke have altered Mark's adoptionist sonship with their virgin birth stories, the adoptionist position continues to shine through in their sources. Matthew reports that the chief priests and scribes and elders, who know from their study of the Scriptures that a beloved son of God is merely a man upon whom God's favor and commission rests, significantly address Jesus only as a man and ascribe all divine action to an adoptive Father. They point out that Jesus cannot be Israel's Messiah king because he does not appear to have enough divine support to deliver even himself out of trouble, let alone to deliver the people. And they add: "He trusts in God; let God deliver him now, if he desires him; for he said, 'I am the Son of God' " (Matt. 27:41-43).

Luke is even more obviously adoptionist in his crucifixion reports. He reports that the religious leaders directly challenge only Jesus' basic messianic relationship with the Father, on the strength of which he is supposed to be able to call on, and to receive, any needed aid from Heaven: "He saved others; let him save himself, if he is the Christ [anointed one] of God, his *Chosen One"* (23:35).

Our second major source for this most ancient idea of Jesus as the Son of God by adoption is found in the stories in Acts which have been collected by Luke from very early church tradition. The only unique kind of divine sonship that these stories record Jesus having is sonship by adoption. There are at least seven of these passages.

Acts 2:22-24. Here on the day of Pentecost, Peter is preaching to the assembled multitude: "Men of Israel, hear these words: Jesus of Nazareth, a man attested to [that is, "witnessed to"] you by God with mighty works and wonders and signs which God did through him in your midst, as you yourselves know—this Jesus . . . God raised . . . up." Observe that in this speech Jesus is only a *man. God* did the things that were done *through* and *for* Jesus. Jesus did not have new life by his own power either. In Peter's christology Jesus is seen only as a very special man.

Acts 4:27. Here the church is praying after Peter and John have been released from prison: "For truly in this city there were gathered together against your holy servant Jesus, whom you *anointed,* both Herod and Pontius Pilate, with the Gentiles and the people of Israel." In this passage Jesus is declared to be a significant person purely on the basis of being the servant Messiah. He is the "holy servant" of God, and he is the one who was anointed to this work.

Acts 5:42. Here the activity of the apostles is being described: "And every day in the temple and at home they did not cease teaching and preaching Jesus as the *Christ.*" The disciples were evidently not trying to promote any divine kind of sonship for Jesus in a literal sense that would make him a superhuman creature. It satisfied them to convince God's people only that Jesus was indeed their awaited anointed one.

Acts 10:38. Here Peter is preaching in the household of the centurion Cornelius, relating "how God anointed Jesus of Nazareth with the Holy Spirit and with power; how he went about doing good and healing all that were oppressed by the devil, for God was with him." Notice here, too, that Jesus is not proclaimed as some kind of superhuman creature. He is simply a man anointed by God with his Holy Spirit and given special authority and power for a special mission. He had this power not in himself but in God's readiness to come to his aid. For "God was with him."

Acts 13:32-33. Here Paul is preaching at Antioch of Pisidia: "And we bring you the good news that what God promised to the fathers, this he has fulfilled to us their children by raising Jesus, as also it is written in the second psalm,

'Thou art my Son,
today I have begotten thee.' "

It is impossible to reconstruct Paul's presentation in full from this brief outline. But, at the least, it is definite that he insisted that the validity of Jesus' messiahship lay in the fact that Jesus had been adopted to the mission of deliverer.

Acts 17:31. Here Paul is speaking in the theater at Athens and telling the Athenians that God "has fixed a day on which he will judge the world in righteousness by a man whom he has appointed and of this he has given assurance to all men by raising him from the dead." Notice that here also Jesus is no divine creature to Paul, but an *appointed man*—a Messiah.

Acts 26:22-23. Here Paul, in making his defense before Festus and Agrippa, says: "So I stand here testifying both to small and great, saying nothing but what the prophets and Moses said would come to pass: that the Christ [anointed one] must suffer, and that, by being the first to rise from the dead, he would proclaim light both to the people and to the Gentiles." Note Paul's words "nothing but." Paul is not advocating some transcendental christology. He is simply proclaiming that God's anointed one, the Messiah, has suffered, died, and been raised again to lead all men to the truth, that is, the "light" about God.

It might also be remarked that there is an implication of the adoptive kind of sonship that Jesus had in Paul's letter to the Galatians when he speaks of adoption as sons for us as well. In Galatians 4:4-5 he declares: "But when the time had fully come, God sent forth his Son, born of a woman, born under the law, to redeem those who were under the law, so that we might receive adoption as sons." And the force of the Greek article "the" which appears in the King James Version before the word "adoption" would seem to make Paul's last phrase read "so that we too might receive the adoption as sons."

Yes, the oldest and most authoritative materials in the New Testament, and the most validly prophetic materials in the Old Testament, that pertain to the uniqueness of Jesus' divine sonship seem to be strictly adoptionist. That Jesus is the only-begotten Son of God must have meant to his earliest disciples that Jesus was a man appointed by God through a spiritual experience of anointment and adoption to carry out a special mission for the sake of all men, a man who was given the special authority and insight for his task and who was supported with special power whenever he required it.

Today Christians believe that it is the task of the Christian church to do exactly what Paul and the other first disciples did. We too must convince a world of anxious people who are looking for a sure word from God, and about God, that God has once and for all appointed a man to represent and reveal him truly, the man Jesus of Nazareth, the man for all mankind. The glory and distinction of Christianity is that it has accepted this man as God's ambassador. Through the ministry of Jesus, as it continues in the church that he established, Christians are those who have been introduced to the love of God that forgives, accepts, assists, transfigures, and delights both individuals and societies.

There is an emptiness, a vacuum, a something-that-is-lacking in the other religions of the world, I believe, despite the fact that they have gathered up many scattered rays of God's great burning sun of truth. Judaism, Islam, Hinduism, and Buddhism—all of them in large measure seem to be as much a part of man's great problem as a part of the solution to man's great problem, because they have not come to know and to accept the authoritative revelation and the redeeming organization—the church—that God has provided for mankind in Jesus of Nazareth, his Messiah.

To this end of disseminating divine revelation Paul and the other apostles declared: "We bring you the good news that what God promised to the fathers, this he has fulfilled to us their children by raising Jesus; as also it is written in the second psalm,

'Thou art my Son,
today I have begotten thee.'"

9. Is Jesus the Son of God Because He Is Born of a Virgin?

"Who was conceived by the Holy Ghost, born of the Virgin Mary."
The Apostles' Creed

"He will be great, and will be called the son of the Most High."
Luke 1:32

In the first chapter of this section on "How Is Jesus the Son of God?" we read that Jesus is the Son of God, first, because, like all of us human beings who are created in God's image, Jesus was born with all the spiritual potential that is required to become like God. Second, we read that Jesus is the Son of God because Jesus did in fact become perfectly like the heavenly Father. In the second chapter we read how Jesus was the Son of God in the unique "only-begotten" sense that God adopted him, or anointed him, after his baptism by John to be the great prophesied revealer, reconciler, and organizer who was to establish the worldwide family of God.

In this third chapter we consider a fourth way in which the New Testament speaks of Jesus as the Son of God, namely, that Jesus of Nazareth is the Son of God because God used his creative energy to cause Jesus to be conceived in the womb of his mother Mary. Jesus' sonship by divine procreation is an event that is designated in Christian tradition as the virgin birth, since, according to the tradition, Jesus' mother Mary had never had sexual relations with a man until after Jesus was born. The Apostles' Creed refers to this tradition by saying that Jesus was "conceived by the Holy Ghost, born of the Virgin Mary." The Nicene Creed declares in a shorter form that Jesus was "incarnate by the Holy Ghost of the Virgin Mary."

Few items in Christian theology need to be discussed so openly and thoroughly today as the virgin birth of Jesus. For the enemies of Christianity frequently do more damage in an intellectually unfair way to the faith of Christians, and especially of Christian students, with their attacks upon this doctrine than with nearly any other strategy. Up to a point these modern opponents of Christianity are quite sophisticated. Few of them argue any more about whether a virgin birth is biologically possible. It is now common knowledge, for instance, that among certain creatures, such as the African tsetse fly, virgin births are common. Also, it is known that unfertilized rabbit eggs can be stimulated in a salt bath to begin cellular multiplication so that female rabbits can be produced which are genetically identical twins to their virgin mothers.

But, more importantly, scientists now realize that they must not be so overbold as to claim that their research is discovering the absolute laws of the universe according to which something is possible or impossible. Rather, they realize with a fitting humility that their research simply permits them to make observations about what is happening in nature so that they can predict and manipulate nature in the future. "Possible" and "impossible" are two words, therefore, that we now know do not belong in a truly precise scientific vocabulary.

So, in view of this modern scientific humility, the contemporary skeptic does not challenge the *possibility* of the virgin birth of Jesus, but rather the *probability* of it. "Can you demonstrate with any reasonable probability that it really happened?" he demands to know. Meanwhile he is usually convinced that it did not happen because he has read a book somewhere which tells how in the ancient world any great man with unusual talents was soon rumored to be a son produced by the union of some god and an earthly woman.

The skeptic explains that this is his understanding of the story of Jesus' virgin birth. Then he asserts further that for him the "fable" of Jesus' birth is a classic illustration of the totally unreliable basis of all the Christian claims about God and his saving activity through the messianic ministry of Jesus. Sometimes the skeptic adds his personal theories of how Mary became pregnant, theories that often are scandalous and repugnant, especially since they lack any historical substantiation. Christian rebuttal, furthermore, that the virgin birth story is true merely because the Bible says so, only causes the skeptic to smirk and to reply that either this kind of statement reveals the gullibility of Christians who will believe anything their religious traditions tell them, or else this authoritarianism reveals the hidden anxiety of Christians that their religion may not be historically respectable enough to withstand systematic scientific scrutiny.

In this eight-question chapter I shall attempt to demonstrate that the virgin birth tradition is a real asset to Christianity which bolsters our claims, and that it is not a liability that leads to our refutation and dismay. But in order to see this virgin birth story as the asset that modern biblical scholars believe it to be, we will be obliged to agree with these modern scholars that the virgin birth of Jesus, as a biological fact, has only a low probability supporting it. We will not deal with the historicity of the reports that Mary and Joseph and the shepherds and the wise men had visions of angels. For there is a somewhat higher probability that these reports contain a solid historical core.

"Let us begin by asking, "What is the basis for the doctrine of the virgin birth of Jesus of Nazareth?" The report of the virgin birth of Jesus is found in the Gospel of Matthew (1:18-25) and in the Gospel of Luke (1:26-35; 3:23). Matthew reports the virgin birth only from Joseph's experience, while Luke reports the birth only from Mary's experience, thus attesting that the editors probably have drawn their information from at least two independent sources. The virgin birth, furthermore, is nowhere specifically denied in the New Testament, nor in any known writings of the first- and second-generation Christians. While the virgin birth of Jesus is denied and slandered as illegitimacy by the Jewish enemies of the early Christians, no solid evidence against the virgin birth is contained in these denials.

Second, let us ask, "According to the doctrine of the virgin birth, what actually transpired?" According to Luke, the angel Gabriel is sent to the young virgin, named Mary, to tell her that God has selected her to bear the Messiah and that the Spirit of God himself will cause her to conceive. According to Matthew, Joseph, who is Mary's fiancé, is then informed of God's miraculous act of making Mary pregnant. And he is commanded to keep Mary as though the child were his own, yet not to consummate their union physically until the infant Jesus is born.

Third, we ask, "What is the christological significance of this virgin birth tradition?" According to these birth stories themselves, it is nothing other than this miraculous conception which makes Jesus the Son of God. Gabriel, for instance, is reported as saying:

> The Holy Spirit will come upon you, . . .
> therefore the child to be born will be called . . .
> the Son of God. (Luke 1:35.)

(See also Matt. 1:20.) So God is Jesus' Father in every respect, both physically and spiritually. And Mary is Jesus' mother, both physically and spiritually.

Jesus, therefore, in the understanding of Matthew and Luke is a semidivine creature technically known as a "demigod," who in his earthly life will have many of the powers of his divine Father. This may be the understanding of any or all of those people in the Gospels of Matthew and Luke who refer to Jesus as the Son of God, from the devil who challenges him to turn stones into bread if he is the Son of God (Luke 4:3) to the demoniacs who testify at their healing that he is the Son of God (Luke 4:41) to the disciples who respond to his water-walking with "Truly you are the Son of God" (Matt. 14:33) to the crowds who shout "If you are the Son of God, come down from the cross" (Matt. 27:40) to the centurion at the cross who, when he sees the eclipse of the sun and the earthquake at the moment of Jesus' death, responds in awe, "Truly this was a son of God!" (Matt. 27:54).

Now we come to the fourth question: "What has the rest of the Bible to say about this doctrine of the virgin birth?" The story of the virgin birth is nowhere to be found in the oldest Gospel, Mark. In Mark, Jesus is never presented as more than the divinely commissioned Messiah. In fact, in Mark 3:21, 31 Jesus' family and friends—including his mother—come to take him away by force from the crowd to whom he is ministering because, Mark reports, "they said, 'He is beside himself.'" This means literally "He has gone berserk." But it is difficult to see how Mary could have been in a group that thought Jesus had gone berserk if she truly believed him to be a demigod.

The story of the virgin birth is nowhere in the youngest Gospel, John, either. John often speaks in terms of that Greek philosophy which believed in a sharp separation between flesh—or matter—and spirit.

God, as Spirit, supposedly had nothing to do with the flesh. God's children were only his children spiritually. This is why John says in 1:13 that God gave all who believed in Jesus power to become children of God, "who were born, not of blood nor of the will of the flesh nor of the will of man, but of God." Jesus also says to Nicodemus, "That which is born of the flesh is flesh, and that which is born of the Spirit is spirit" (John 3:6). This Greek-like reticence to mix spirit and matter—figurative though it might be—does not quite dovetail with Luke's virgin birth idea of God as the spiritual and physical Father of Jesus. Furthermore, in the Fourth Gospel, John the Baptizer, Jesus' cousin, says of Jesus when he appears for baptism, "I myself did not know him" (1:31) which is a puzzling statement if John's mother Elizabeth and Jesus' mother Mary, who Luke says were "kinswomen," had known the miraculous circumstances of each other's pregnancies as Luke claims (1:36). Moreover, in the Gospel of John, Joseph is referred to as Jesus' father by Nathaniel (1:45) and by a hostile crowd (6:42), and John does not indicate that this is incorrect information.

Also, we may note that neither Paul nor any of the other New Testament writers say anything about a virgin birth of Jesus. Paul seems, rather, to assume a quite natural birth for Jesus. In Romans 1:3 he speaks of Jesus as "descended from David according to the flesh." And David's line apparently ran through Joseph, not Mary. In Galatians 4:4 when Paul declares how God sent forth his Son "born of woman," he seems to indicate that the birth was in no way miraculous, by using the Greek word for "married woman" rather than the word for "virgin." Furthermore, we read that Paul had access to the disciples in Jerusalem, whom he visited on at least two occasions to double-check his information (Gal. 1:18; 2:1-2). Certainly if the original apostles had known anything about a virgin birth, Paul, who was preaching largely to people who were influenced by a Greek culture that believed in virgin births, would quickly have used the story of Jesus' virgin birth to give additional authority to his message.

In addition, Luke in his stories about the boy Jesus refers to Joseph and Mary as Jesus' "parents" five times without indicating that Joseph was only thought to be Jesus' father (2:27, 33, 41, 43, 48). This seems to indicate that even some of Luke's stories came from sources that were not aware of any virgin birth.

Then, too, the fact that Matthew speaks of the virgin birth only from Joseph's experience, as though he did not know about Mary's angelic vision, coupled with the fact that Joseph seems to have died before Jesus began his ministry, presents the question of how Matthew could have got Joseph's story. Surely Joseph would have kept secret something like this that would have endangered the reputations of both Mary and himself if it were broadcast. Surely he would have shared his vision only with Mary. How then could Matthew have known Joseph's story without also knowing Mary's story? Also, if Luke had got his story in some manner through Mary, would he not also have heard Joseph's story?

Much is sometimes made also of Isaiah 7:14, which prophesies "Behold, a young woman shall conceive and bear a son, and shall call his name Immanuel." Matthew uses this prophecy as a proof text for the virgin birth of Jesus. But we must note that in the original Hebrew text of Isaiah 7:14 the word *bethulah* is used, which is a broad term that means "young woman." Isaiah does not use the Hebrew word *almah* which is a narrow term that precisely designates a sexual virgin. When the Old Testament was translated into Greek—producing the translation known as the Septuagint—quite appropriately the more general Greek term was used, namely, the word *parthenos,* or "young woman."

The prophecy in Isaiah 7:14, furthermore, refers specifically to the days of King Ahaz and to a child who is to be born in a very few years. It is not prophesying the much later Messiah. Perhaps Matthew is referring to this prophecy in his virgin birth account only as a type, or foreshadowing, of the birth of the Messiah. But it appears more likely that he is reading a precise connotation of sexual virginity into an ambiguous Old Testament term and is seeing a definite prophecy of the Messiah where one does not exist. The Revised Standard Version translators have preserved the ambiguity of the Hebrew original, along with Matthew's apparent misunderstanding, by using the term "young woman" in Isaiah 7:14 and the term "virgin" in Matthew's quotation of Isaiah 7:14. The important point here is that Isaiah 7:14 is not a valid proof text for the virgin birth, however Matthew may intend it.

The fifth question is "If the virgin birth were not a historical fact, how could such an idea have originated among Jesus' followers?" There are Jewish preparations for, and non-Jewish sources of, the idea.

The Old Testament contains a number of conception miracles, which, however, still include the assistance of a male. God is reported to have caused a child to be born to aged and barren Sarah, Isaac's mother (Gen. 18:11 ff.) and to the barren mother of Samson (Judg. 13:3) and to the barren mother of Samuel (I Sam. 1:4 ff.). God is also said to have opened the womb of Leah, Jacob's despised wife (Gen. 29:31). Thus the Jews of Jesus' day were by tradition predisposed to think of God acting miraculously in the conception of great men.

It appears also that some of the Jews in Jesus' day did misinterpret Isaiah 7:14 as a definite prophecy of the manner of the Messiah's birth, an interpretation which probably came easily since the broad term "young woman" had gradually narrowed in meaning until it designated a sexual virgin. This is exactly what has happened over hundreds of years to our English word "virgin."

There is a possibility too that, since the disciples of John the Baptizer believed that John had been a child miraculously conceived according to divine promise by Zechariah and Elizabeth in their old age, Jesus, since he was the Messiah himself, must certainly have been conceived in a still more miraculous manner. This would leave only the option of an absolutely virgin birth.

Virgin births, furthermore, were believed to take place periodically in the ancient polytheistic world among the Greeks, Egyptians, Persians, and others. Whenever a man proved to have outstanding virtues, it was not long before the story had arisen that he was not really conceived by his earthly father but by the god who was commonly distinguished by these same virtues. Plato, Alexander the Great, Augustus, Perseus, and Hercules are outstanding examples of ancient heroes for whom virgin birth was claimed. And it was no great wonder that the popular imagination was stirred by such men. Alexander, the conqueror of the world in his twenties, had such tremendous political power, such a brilliant personality, and such fabulous achievements behind him that he could not help but put many of the superstitious people of the day into the right mind for worship.

Sometimes the stories of the conception of these demigods were bawdy popular tales of mythological adultery in which a supposed god was overcome with lust for a beautiful woman. But sometimes these stories were as chaste and pure as the New Testament virgin birth report. Plutarch, for instance, relates concerning Olympias, the mother of Alexander the Great that "it seemed to the bride before the night when her marriage with Philip was consummated, that there was a clap of thunder, that a bolt fell upon her womb, and that from the stroke a great fire was kindled, and then, breaking out in all directions into sparks, was quenched." King Philip, consequently, avoided physical contact with her until the birth of Alexander, Plutarch says, "on the ground that she belonged to one greater than he." Again, in another instance, Zeus is supposed to have descended upon Perseus' mother Danaë in a shower of gold.

Then finally, Jewish philosophers and theologians of Jesus' day, who believed that God had inspired Greek philosophy as well as Moses and the prophets, interpreted the Old Testament in such an allegorical philosophical manner that they saw the miraculous child conceptions in the Old Testament as nothing less than completely virgin births. Philo of Alexandria, for example, gives God all the credit and the husbands no credit at all, in the miraculous conceptions of Sarah, Leah, Rebekah, and Zipporah (*De Cherubim* 12-15). Thus the numerous Jewish circles in Jesus' day that were influenced by Greek thought would naturally expect a person as great as the Messiah also to be born of a virgin.

The sixth question is "In view of such a readiness on the part of both the Jews and the pagans of two thousand years ago to believe in the virgin births of outstanding men, how then did the idea of the virgin birth of Jesus most likely begin?" Most scholars seem to feel that the idea of the virgin birth of Jesus probably came out of natural reflection upon the amazing greatness of Jesus. The people who flocked to Jesus saw and heard marvelous things that surpassed anything that they had seen or heard before.

Here was a man whose every word and look burned with the love and righteousness of God. Here was a man who had the answers to their questions about matters of God and the soul, and who spoke those answers with authority. Here was a man with the power to heal in such great measure that they saw nothing less than miracles performed before them. Here was a man who prophesied of things to come like the God-inspired prophets of old. Here was a man who did not hesitate to arouse the opposition of all the ruling classes of the nation in his conviction that the Almighty Father would ultimately triumph. Here was a man who easily called God his Father and who spoke as intimately of God as a child speaks of an affectionate parent.

Here was a man who was more concerned to do good than any other person they had ever known. Here was a man who loved people so much, as he said God loved people, that he sacrificed his life to reveal God to his people and to reconcile people to their God and to organize them into the world-winning, soul-saving church. Here was a man with such glorious spiritual connections that a number of hardheaded realists joined themselves to him in a life-and-death pact. Here was a man who, although he was put to death on a cross, was seen alive in the spirit by one disciple and group of disciples after another for many weeks, and possibly years, following his interment. Here was a man whose faithful followers were frequently overcome with a spiritual power greater than themselves, which caused them to break out in strange ecstatic language and to experience a joy in God which surpassed mere physical joys.

In short, to Jesus' contemporaries he was a most marvelous and unique person. They could perceive that in him God was doing something crucial for all mankind. So it was only natural in that particular cultural milieu for many people to doubt seriously that he was merely a human being. "Surely this godlike man is at least partly divine!" people must have reasoned.

The seventh question is "If the story of Jesus' virgin birth did grow out of the marveling of the people who saw God with Jesus and in Jesus, then what significance does the virgin birth have for the Christian church today?" The significance of the virgin birth story today is that *it is a magnificent testimony to the God-ordained messiahship of Jesus.*

The virgin birth story can be viewed as a gigantic ripple on the surface of the pond which testifies that Jesus of Nazareth was a veritable boulder that was cast by God into the pond of history, and not merely an ordinary pebble. The virgin birth story is to the mission and ministry of Jesus what smoke is to fire. The smoke is not really part of the fire itself, and it comes after the act of burning. Sometimes the smoke also gets in our eyes and prevents us from seeing clearly just what is burning. But a big cloud of smoke at least bears testimony to one sure thing, namely, that somewhere nearby there is a "whale of a fire."

Thus when Matthew and Luke report the virgin birth of Jesus, they are not, in our eyes, really emphasizing the unusual fact that his mother had never intimately known a man. Rather, they are emphasizing the fact that Jesus acted so much like God and was so much in the counsel and commission of God that only God himself could be Jesus' father. Thus Matthew and Luke represent the manner in which one strain of the Christian tradition explained how the fullness of God dwelled and acted in Jesus.

Furthermore, it is significant that the story of Jesus' virgin birth stuck with convincing power for eighteen hundred years, even though Western man had universally dismissed all the pagan virgin birth stories of antiquity as so much nonsense. Jesus' story stuck because men who searched the writings of human history could find no other mortal whose godliness compared with Jesus of Nazareth's and because when men gave their hearts to God the Father through Jesus Christ they found real life for the first time. It is this recognition that causes even the scholars who point out the low probability of the virgin birth of Jesus as a biological fact to reaffirm that if any man in antiquity ever was biologically born of God himself that this man was Jesus of Nazareth.

And finally, question eight: "What are we Christians who live today to do about the doctrine of the virgin birth of Jesus?" There are a number of options.

If a Christian still wants to believe the story, he can at least claim that it has never actually been disproved. The probability for it is simply very low.

Or, if a Christian wishes to follow the insights of modern scholarship, then when he repeats the virgin birth portion of the church's creeds, he should do so figuratively, not literally. He may mean by the words "conceived by the Holy Ghost" that the wonderful spirit of Jesus was the result of the influence of God's Spirit upon Jesus from childhood. By the words "born of the virgin Mary" he may mean that Jesus' mother Mary was a young woman, in the broad sense that Isaiah's terminology intended it.

However, the Christian must appreciate that, whatever he decides, the virgin birth of Jesus is not a major concern of the New Testament or of the Christian gospel. The most prolific, and the earliest, New Testament writer, Paul, along with Mark, John, Peter, and James, did not know of the story, or else did not need it for the purposes of the kingdom of God. So even if the virgin birth story may be a pious legend produced during the period of oral tradition, nothing essential has been lost to Christianity.

The Christian must also appreciate that the virgin birth story is a tremendous testimony to Jesus' godlike impact upon the people of God, which makes the story an asset rather than a liability to the Christian proclamation. The followers who came forth with this virgin birth idea by some unknown process were declaring that in Jesus of Nazareth they saw a depth of divinity and mystery that they could explain only if he were the very child of God.

Consequently, Christians must explain to the skeptics that, even though the virgin birth may not have been a biological fact, this does not mean that they can discard the rest of Christianity as a mere fable. Rather, this tradition is a beautiful and powerful testimony which forces every man who hears of Jesus the Messiah to make a decision concerning him. For the virgin birth story presses upon us the question "What think *you* of Christ?" Christians can only say to the man who refuses to accept the church's virgin birth testimony with the proper historical appreciation and spiritual concern and who refuses to accept the church's virgin birth testimony as part of God's call to him, that he is endangering his own chance to enjoy light and life and love in God forever.

Yes, we Christians appreciate the story of Jesus' virgin birth as at least the great testimonial asset that it is whenever we read the angel's words to Mary that "he will be great, and will be called the son of the Most High."

10. Is Jesus the Son of God Because He Is an Eternal Extension of God?

"Begotten of his Father before all worlds, God of God, Light of Light. Very God of very God; Begotten, not made; Being of one substance with the Father; . . . Who for us men and for our salvation came down from heaven." The Nicene Creed

"And the Word became flesh and dwelt among us, full of grace and truth." John 1:14

How is Jesus the Son of God? We have heard that the New Testament accredits Jesus of Nazareth with at least five types of divine sonship. And in the first three chapters of this section we have considered four of these types of divine sonship.

First, we considered the claim that Jesus is the Son of God because, like all human beings who are created in God's image, Jesus was born with the spiritual potential that is required to become like God. Second, we considered the claim that Jesus is the Son of God because he actualized his potential and did in fact become perfectly like the heavenly Father. Third, we considered the claim that Jesus is the "only-begotten" Son of God in the unique sense that God adopted him, or anointed him, after his baptism by John to be the great prophesied revealer, reconciler, and organizer who was to establish the worldwide family of God. Fourth, we considered the claim that Jesus is the Son of God because his mother Mary was a virgin who was made pregnant by the Spirit of God. And it was explained that, despite the low probability that this was an actual event, the fact that the story of the virgin birth was accepted by the early church is a tremendous testimony to the god-like, authoritative impact that Jesus in his ministry made upon men.

In this final chapter on the nature of Jesus we consider the fifth type of divine sonship that the New Testament claims for Jesus, namely, that he has been the outgoing part of God—a spatial extension of God —from all eternity. Or, as the Nicene Creed of the fourth century states it: Jesus has been "begotten by his Father before all worlds," and is "God of God, Light of Light, Very God of very God; begotten, not made; being of one substance with the Father, by whom all things were made; who for us men and for our salvation came down from heaven."

In the New Testament we find the material from which this christology was constructed by the Council of Nicaea primarily in the Gospel of John and in two of "Paul's" latest letters—Colossians and Ephesians. Because of the mooted Pauline authorship of these letters and because it is likely that another man was the actual author—or at least a very freewheeling editor—we shall designate the writer of the letters to Colossae and Ephesus as "Paul B."

The key doctrine upon which the Nicene christology is based is the doctrine of the Logos. The Greek word "Logos" has been translated in our English Bibles as "Word." This is why the Gospel of John opens with the statement that "in the beginning was the Word," and continues in verse 14 to say that "the Word became flesh and dwelt among us." If we used the original Greek word, these passages would read "In the beginning was the Logos"; and "the Logos became flesh and dwelt among us." We will later consider at some length what the Logos actually is. All that John says at this point is that the Logos, in the eyes of John and his readers, is a marvelous divine being who is a part of God.

It is important that we understand that no English word can satisfactorily translate the Greek word "Logos." The meaning of the word is much more than one would ever suspect simply from reading the English New Testament. For the Gospel of John is not a simple Hebrew anthology of Jesus' speeches, as it is often believed to be. Rather, the Gospel of John is generally agreed to be a sophisticated historical and interpretative "sales talk" written by a Hebrew disciple of Jesus to a Greek audience in a Greek philosophical vocabulary and in thought forms familiar to Greeks.

In John's time the philosophical doctrine of the Logos was widely accepted by the peoples of the Roman Empire, most of whom were influenced to some extent by Greek thought. Speaking to these people in their own thought forms, therefore, John intended the chief point in his Gospel to be that the Logos, which a good proportion of his audience already believed in, had become flesh in Jesus of Nazareth. This meant that all Logos-believing citizens of the empire should accept Jesus' authority as nothing less than the authority of God himself. To demonstrate that Jesus was the enfleshed Logos is the reason John quotes Jesus making grand and sweeping statements such as "I and the Father are one" (10:30), "I am the son of God" (10:35), "I proceeded and came forth from God" (8:42), "I am from above" (8:23), "I am the bread which came down from heaven" (6:41), "I am the light of the world" (8:1), "He who sent me is with me" (8:29).

We must note, too, that these statements all appear to have been part of the primary stratum of John, which is a brilliant Hellenistic Christian body of tradition that may originally have come from a mystical Asia Minor liturgy. We shall call this earliest material "John A." But the editor of the Gospel was apparently a non-Hellenistic Jewish Christian. Most scholars seem to agree that he has added some apocalyptic christological passages of his own. (See for example, 1:51; 2:13-15; 5:27b-29; 6:39b, 44b, 62; 7:24; 9:35, 39; 12:23, 26; 13:31; 14:3, 16, 18.) This editor, whom we shall call "John B," held to a more demigod christology than did John A. He added passages that helped to harmonize the christology of John A with the apocalyptic "Son of man" passages in the Synoptic Gospels.

John B has sprinkled in at least eight short, easily spotted passages about the Son of man descending from and ascending back to heaven, about the Son of man being judge on the last day, and so forth. He has also made confusing additions to Jesus' speeches in chapters fourteen through seventeen, a section which stands as something of a catchall for "stray" words of Jesus. It is no great problem to see that the work of John B is the work of a literalistic Christian who did not truly comprehend the Hellenistic philosophical and allegorical genius of John A and who consequently does violence to John A's christology.

Paul B, in Colossians and Ephesians, without ever actually using the key term "Logos," deals with essentially the same christological terms and concepts as John A, although Paul B, like John B, takes a very literalistic perspective. According to Paul B, Jesus Christ, the beloved Son of God, "is the image of the invisible God, the first-born of all creation; for in him all things were created, in heaven and on earth, visible and invisible. . . . He is before all things, and in him all things hold together. He is the head of the body, the church. . . . For in him all the fullness of God was pleased to dwell, and through him to reconcile to himself all things." In Jesus, God was "making peace by the blood of his cross" (Col. 1:15-20). After the crucifixion Jesus was raised by God from the dead and made to sit "at his right hand in the heavenly places, far above all rule and authority and dominion." And God "has put all things under his feet, and has made him the head over all things for the church" (Eph. 1:20-22). These, quite obviously, are great claims for Jesus of Nazareth. Or, as theologians express it, this is a very "high christology."

But just where do John A and Paul B get these christological ideas? These ideas, we learn from various historical studies, were part of the common intellectual currency of the Mediterranean world long before Jesus came upon the scene. This high christology is a doctrinal rope, most of the strands of which have been drawn out of the Hellenistic—or primarily Greek—philosophical theology of their day. This is why, if we really wish to understand the high christology of John A and Paul B, we must first take a look at the Greek world which developed the basic concepts.

The idea of the eternal divine Logos, which the first Christians early identified with Jesus, began back with the old Stoic and pre-Gnostic philosophers, hundreds of years before the time of Jesus. These ancient philosophers were repelled by the pagan religions of Asia Minor with all their mythological gods who carried on much like men—sometimes better, sometimes worse.

These philosophers in their study of the universe began to see that there was Something that tied the universe together to give it a consistent and reliable unity, Something that pervaded throughout which made this a universe and not a multiverse. This unifying Something

110

the philosophers decided was Reason, since everything seemed to be reasonable. Reason was often pictured by them as a kind of vapor that permeated the whole universe, shaping it and controlling it. This Reason was called by the ancient philosophers "Logos." And these men in their religious devotions substituted this Logos for the often depraved mythological gods of the common people. For some of the ancients, therefore, the word "Logos" was simply their way of saying "God." The Spirit of God, I am convinced, had led them to a form of true monotheism.

Later on, other ancient thinkers, who were more influenced by Plato, developed a complex and very significant concept of God that was sometimes binitarian (that is, "two-part"), sometimes trinitarian (that is, "three-part"). These men believed in three or four other main eternal realities besides the Logos. First, they believed that there existed a far-removed, transcendent Realm of Ideas, which was a static, motionless realm that held every idea that could ever be thought. The second eternal reality these men believed in was the Logos. They saw the Logos as a combination of mind and energy, as a rational power which had all its ideas supplied to it by "gazing on" the realm of ideas. The third eternal reality was Chaos, which was a great ocean of unformed, seething matter out in space, an infinite cloud of something which today we would perhaps call "unorganized energy particles." The fourth eternal reality was the Cosmos, or the created universe, which was the work of the Logos. The Logos had been forever laying hold of the unformed matter in Chaos and forcing it to assume rational order, according to the Eternal Ideas which the Logos would take from the Realm of Ideas as its patterns. Some of these philosophical theologians, such as Plotinus, added a fifth reality called the Demiurge, which was positioned midway between the Logos and Chaos and which was the servant power utilized by the Logos in forming the Cosmos out of Chaos.

In this first diagram we see the first three of the eternal realities: the Realm of Ideas (drawn in dashes), the Logos mind-force, self-patterned on the Realm of Ideas (drawn in solid lines), and the realm of unformed chaotic matter. In the second diagram we see the work of creation. Here the eternal Logos, which has shaped itself according to the Eternal Ideas, has forced the eternal Chaos to assume the shape of the same Eternal Ideas. The result is the Cosmos, or the universe, which includes all of us.

111

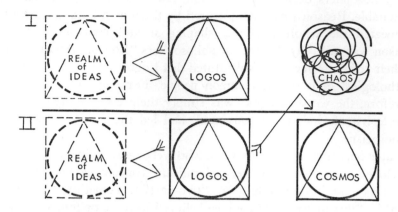

Now, considerably simplified, in the christology of John A and Paul B this divine Logos appears on earth in a powerful but minute focusing of itself in Jesus of Nazareth. The Logos appears in Jesus in order to shape the spiritual chaos which exists in deformed and unformed men according to the Eternal Ideas. However, Logos philosophical theology went through several stages before it reached the form in which John A and Paul B found it.

The first stage of Logos theology was the one we have just mentioned, namely, when the early Stoic and pre-Gnostic philosophers rejected the pagan mythological religions and developed the concept of an eternal Logos that formed eternal Chaos according to the pattern of the Eternal Ideas. The second stage was a stage of tolerance and understanding when the Logos thinkers attempted to see some good in the pagan religions which they had earlier rejected by discovering in the stories about the pagan gods allegories that portrayed the profound ideas of the philosophers. Hence, in this stage the gods of mythology became viewed as personifications of abstract ideas.

The third stage was due to man's refusal to live without a personal God. There is no comfort in an abstraction—even an eternal abstraction. Mankind seems to sense intuitively that only a God who has personality can be man's source and hence truly man's God. So in the third stage, the Realm of Eternal Ideas became personalized as God the Father. The Logos became personalized as God the Son. And in some philosophies, such as Neoplatonism, where the Demiurge stood between the Logos and Chaos to do the work of the Logos, the Demiurge became personalized as God the Creative Spirit. Thus trinitarian theology was actually a product of Greek thought, rather than of Hebrew thought. Trinitarian theology was primarily the product of a theological dialogue between the proponents of rationality and the proponents of personality.

Now it is also important to appreciate the fact that an influential element among the Jewish intellectuals had accepted this Greek philosophical theology, believing that it was as much a product of divine guidance as their beloved scriptures. Philo, for example, the famous, influential Jewish thinker from Alexandria who was a contemporary of Jesus, speaks in his writings of the Logos as just such a personal being. For Philo the Logos is an intermediary who provides contact between the transcendent God and the created world. Philo designates this Logos as God's first born son, second only to God himself, and as God's own image and shadow and as man's high priest and advocate. For Philo, God is able to avoid a polluting contact with the world through the mediation of the Logos.

It is essentially this already partly Judaized view of things theological and christological that is assimilated and baptized by John A and Paul B in the Fourth Gospel and in the epistles to Colossae and to Ephesus. Therefore, when John A declares that "in the beginning was the Logos" and when Paul B states that the son of God is the "image of the invisible God, the first-born of all creation," in whom "all things were created," they are not talking about something unknown to their Hellenistic auditors. The people who received this Gospel and these letters were as well acquainted with the many forms that Logos thought had taken in their day as we are acquainted with modern political concepts of freedom or economic concepts of federal money management.

But John A and Paul B in their christology use more from the ancient Greek philosophical theology than the *nature* of the Logos. They also use some of the non-Hebrew ideas of the redeeming *activities* of the Logos.

A number of the Hellenistic religions that had been shaped according to Logos thought taught that the Logos was also the savior of the world which he had created. The ancient mythmakers of these religions developed liturgies which proclaimed how the Logos had once descended from the highest heaven disguised as a man and had slipped past the seven planets, which were thought to be spiritual powers that ruled a spiritually lost mankind in an oppressive and demonic manner. On earth the Logos had supposedly taught man the truth about God

113

and about life and had then carried all who believed in him back past the enemy planets and the other antagonistic spiritual powers in the lower heavens into paradise in the highest heaven. Many of these mythological liturgies were essentially allegorical and quite noble ethically.

John A and Paul B take this basic Logos redeemer idea, cut away much of the Hellenistic embellishment, and present Jesus Christ as God's redeeming Logos who descended to earth, gave light and truth, overcame the principalities and powers in the lower heavens by erasing the tragic gap between sinful men and God which had given those powers their chance to oppress us, and rose again to rule all things for the safety and nourishment of the church. John A and Paul B utilized these non-Hebrew christological concepts so extensively in presenting the mission of Jesus to the ancient world simply because they, too, evidently believed with Philo and other Jewish intellectuals that God had been active among all men—even among the Greek philosophers.

Paul declares as much in Acts 14:17 when he explains that God "did not leave himself without witness" in any nation, and also in Acts 17:27 when he assures the Athenians that God "is not far from each one of us." I agree with John and Paul. For I believe that the "fullness of time" when God sent his son was a time of completed divine preparation partly because God had prepared the non-Hebrew world with universally understood concepts and with great spiritual hungers that were essential if his Word in Jesus the Messiah was to be accepted far and wide.

But several questions naturally spring up at this point. What, for instance, can be the value of this high christology of John A and Paul B if they are drawing it from so-called pagan philosophy? Are we to take at face value their presentation of Jesus of Nazareth as such an exalted eternal portion of God, or as the first son of God generated before all things and once come incognito to earth? Did Jesus really make all the claims about himself that he is quoted as making in the Fourth Gospel? Or is John merely presenting the significance of God's Messiah in a poetic, dramatic manner in which he speaks for Jesus?

With respect to the letters to Colossae and to Ephesus, I agree with the great majority of scholars who believe that, while Paul B's Logos christology—just like the virgin birth story of Matthew and Luke—is a powerful testimony to the godly impact that Jesus made, nevertheless, Paul B went somewhat overboard in interpreting the messiahship

of Jesus too literally in terms of Greek philosophic theology and redeemer mythology. A number of respectable scholars believe that the
Logos christology of Ephesians and Colossians was due to the influence
which was exerted late in his ministry upon the apostle Paul himself and
his followers by the apostle John and his followers. There may be
much truth in this theory. But at any rate, the Gospel of John appears
to be the more original source of Christian Logos thinking.

There are also able scholars who believe that John A was none
other than the apostle John himself and that almost all the Greek-
sounding declarations of Jesus that John A reports were indeed Jesus'
own words. These scholars believe that Jesus was well acquainted with
the everywhere-present Greek thought of his day and that on proper
occasions, when Jesus was confronted with Greek-influenced audiences,
he used appropriate Greek terms and thought forms to convey his divine
mission and message.

I believe that the conclusions of these scholars are basically sound.
For when John A is carefully examined, minus John B, the christology
that is presented by the sayings of Jesus, although it is in a Greek
mold, is *the christology of the sonship of divine adoption.* The words
and thought forms are very Greek. But Jesus' message is very Hebrew.
Jesus speaks in typical Hebrew poetic symbolism in a Greek setting.
And the Messiah that John A portrays is essentially the same Messiah
that Mark presents following Jesus' baptism in the Jordan.

For example, when John A declares that "the Logos became flesh,"
he could just as easily have said in more literal language that "the
truth of God and the saving power of God have broken forth among
us in a manner that we can understand and appropriate in the life,
death, and resurrection of a man, Jesus of Nazareth." Jesus' statements
"I and the Father are one" (10:30), "I proceeded and came forth from
the Father" (8:42), "I am the living bread which came down from
heaven" (6:51), and so forth, are equally symbolic Hebrew statements
in Greek vocabulary and thought forms to the effect that Jesus is the
Messiah who comes to men with the liberating and eternal life-bestow-
ing truth of God.

We might be puzzled, however, by the apparently straightforward
exclamation of "doubting Thomas" in the upper room (20:28), when
he gazes upon the risen Christ and says "My Lord and my God!"
If this event is one of those events reported by John A, is he not taking
the Logos christology rather literally here rather than symbolically?

We must answer both "yes" and "no." For one of the most difficult ideas for people in Western Christendom to grasp is the mythical-philosophical concept of godhood that was held by the Greeks of Jesus' day and that is still held by the Eastern Orthodox Church to this day.

We Westerners hold to a very "materialistic" concept of godhood. For us God is God. And nothing, and no one else, is God. But in the more philosophic and symbolistic and mystic East, *people also* may in a sense be God.

An explanation of the mystical-philosophical view of godhood would go something like this: When God creates man in his own image, man's true spiritual shape is also of necessity God's true spiritual shape. To know what God is, then, is also to know what man is, and vice versa. True man, therefore, is in his spiritual structure simply God on a very small scale. Consequently, when a twisted man becomes converted into the shape of true spiritual manhood, he is simultaneously converted into the shape of true spiritual godhood. He has become God in a real sense—or deified—even as a man who conforms his life to any truth becomes part of that truth itself. Since God is omnipresent, or everywhere, the man whose soul has become reverently patterned on God's love and knowledge is joined into God and is become one with God in a mystical sense.

Now this philosophical, symbolical, mystical concept of godhood is used by John A in the Fourth Gospel. In a very important passage in chapter ten (vss. 31-38), for instance, Jesus tells his Jewish enemies, who look at godhood in the same materialistic, literalistic sense that we Westerners do today, that they have no right to kill him for claiming to be the Son of God, because the precedent for considering ourselves to be sons of God is set, Jesus says, in their own Psalm 82, which sings of men having a metaphorical, or figurative, kind of godhood and divine sonship.

So when Jesus calls himself the "Son of God," and when Thomas calls Jesus "My God!" and when modern Greek Orthodox theologians speak of Christians "becoming deified" or "becoming God," they all mean essentially the same thing, namely, that when men become like Christ Jesus who is the perfect mirror image of God, they take on the structural (or formal) pattern of God and become one with him. Therefore, we can all acknowledge that in this Eastern philosophical-mystical sense intended by Jesus and by John A, Jesus is indeed the Son of God, proceeding from the Father and one with the Father from all eternity. Or, as the Nicene Creed says, Jesus is true God and true man.

At the same time we declare that Jesus is God in this special sense, however, we must also make clear that in the Western pragmatic-materialistic sense Jesus is *not* God. In the Western sense we can say only that Jesus is an outstanding godly man who at a crucial point in human history had laid upon his shoulders by God a unique mission of worldwide redemption which involved him in a special closeness to God's counsel and powers, and which required a reappearance after death to his disciples.

And so we come to the end of our consideration of the divine sonship of Jesus. You can appreciate that I have saved this most sophisticated and also this most beautiful New Testament christology until the last. I have systematically proceeded from the most Hebrew of the New Testament christologies to the least Hebrew of the New Testament christologies, and from the most easily comprehended to the most difficult. In conclusion I want to sum up this chapter and also to show its significance for the Christian church.

First, the idea of the Eternal Word, or the Logos, and the idea of the transcendent Redeemer who descends to earth were ideas that began in Greek philosophical theology—not in Hebrew thought.

Second, John A and Paul B used these ideas because most of the rest of the ancient world to which they were commissioned by God to bear the gospel was brought up on Greek thought and also because John A and Paul B believed that God had been instrumental in much of the development of non-Hebrew thought.

Third, there is a very strong probability that Jesus could and did speak through the medium of Greek thought forms, as well as through the Hebrew thought forms of parables and epigrams that are found in the three Synoptic Gospels.

Fourth, Western Christians today who wish to understand the Gospel of John in any adequate manner must remember that the christology of John A is highly allegorical and mystical, and that while John A's wineskins of communication are primarily Greek, the wine of God's word which he pours into them is primarily Hebrew.

Fifth and finally, all of us must appreciate the Gospel of John as a great testimony to the mission of Jesus, a testimony awesome in its profundity, grand in its scope, breathtaking in its beauty, and almost irresistible in its appeal. This great testimony can arouse in our breast a deep hunger to become part of the eternal unity with Jesus in god-hood, a part of that divine unity which Jesus prays for when he longs for the day when "they may be one even as we are one, I in them and thou [Father] in me" (17:22-23), a part of that divine unity which John A proclaims was a reality in Jesus in whom "the Logos became flesh and dwelt among us, full of grace and truth."

Before ending this chapter, however, we must also briefly make note of another title that is often applied to Jesus, and also used by Jesus in the Gospels, the title "Son of man." This somewhat mysterious title is first found in the late Old Testament prophets. Ezekiel (33:10) and Daniel (8:17), two of the very late and quite normally human prophets, who are divinely commissioned to deliver their people from trouble by revealing to them God's guiding word, are addressed by God as "son of man." Such a usage makes "son of man" synonymous with "member of the human race" or just "man" or even "Hey there, you!"

But the original Old Testament ordinary-but-inspired-man concept of Messiah developed in much of the popular fancy during the intertestamental period into a concept of a demigod Messiah. This process was helped along by a popular literalizing of passages such as Daniel 7:13 in which a messianic political deliverer who is to come is poetized in a demigod manner, much as was done for King David of old (II Sam. 23:5, Ps. 45).

Consequently, since Ezekiel and Daniel who were a general type of messiah were addressed by God as "son of man," this quite normal address, under the impetus of the developing demigod Messiah concept, became stylized in the popular understanding as a messianic title for the expected divine deliverer. By Jesus' day, it seems, this quite general Old Testament address by God to his prophets had become for many of the Jews a very particular messianic title "Son of man," that is properly capitalized.

But what makes the title "Son of man" so confusing in the New Testament is that at least Jesus, and perhaps also some of his more sophisticated followers, seems to have been giving this phrase the meaning that it originally had for the prophets. For both the prophetic-revealer concept of the address "son of man" and the demigod ruler concept of the title "Son of man" are frequently used in all four Gospels. The messianic title "Son of man" seems, therefore, to have a contradictory usage in the Gospels. However, those scholars who believe that the dismal apocalyptic sayings of Jesus in the Gospels have been attached to Jesus' ministry by the haphazardly developing religious milieu of his day discount the demigod "Son of man" passages as inauthentic (Matt. 24:30; 26:64; John 5:27). This still leaves a sizable body of Gospel material in which Jesus' title for himself as "Son of man" seems to indicate underneath the stylizing that Jesus sees himself as God's chosen and adopted deliverer by virtue of his function of providing direly needed divine revelation (Luke 7:34; John 6:27, 53).

Thus it seems that the messianic title "Son of man" does not provide a valid or persuasive argument for viewing Jesus as a creature more than a man. Christian tradition, it is generally agreed, has been as wrong in its literalizing of the poetic Old Testament messianic passages and the general address "son of man" as it has been wrong in its literalizing of the poetically used Greek thought forms of John A. Despite the magnificence of his divine sonship, Jesus is still only a man.

Section IV: SALVATION

11. How Was Jesus Crucified for Us?

"And was crucified also for us under Pontius Pilate." The Nicene Creed

"If any man would come after me, let him deny himself and take up his cross and follow me. For whoever would save his life will lose it, and whoever loses his life for my sake will find it." Matthew 16:24-25

Christians have always believed, as the Nicene Creed states, that Jesus was "crucified also for us under Pontius Pilate." But precisely what do we mean, and what should we mean, by these words "crucified also for us"?

Throughout much of Christian history Jesus' crucifixion for us has been understood as a blood payment for the sins of man that was offered up as the penalty price to satisfy the offended righteousness of a holy God. But today the Christian churches are reexamining this understanding in the light of new biblical knowledge. And generally the churches are adopting another, and more valid, biblical viewpoint. This other biblical viewpoint understands Jesus' crucifixion for us as the climactic conclusion of a sacrificial life that was so filled with the revelation of God's love that Jesus was able thereby to persuade sinful men to return to their God and Father.

The modern view is basically a continuation of the outlook of the Old Testament prophets, while the traditional Christian position is

120

basically a continuation of the outlook of the Old Testament priests. And as the prophets and the priests in the Bible have something of a running battle between them in their disagreements with each other, so in Christian history their successors have continued the same battle. The significant thing about the present age in this matter is that biblical scholars and theologians are insisting more strongly every year that the school of the prophets is the *primary* biblical tradition, and also the school to which Jesus himself belonged, while the school of the priests is only *secondary* and, as the prophets often insist, is theologically misleading.

Now the first thing that we must do in this chapter is to examine the atonement ideas—that is, the forgiveness and reconciliation ideas—of the Old Testament prophets and priests. We must begin with an examination of the Old Testament because when Jesus' disciples tried to comprehend the meaning of his life and death, they naturally thought along the same lines that the leaders of their inherited religious traditions had been thinking along for hundreds of years.

The Old Testament prophets believed that when a man sinned he was forgiven by God without any kind of payment except that honest and sincere repentance which results in rededication. The only kind of material sacrifices, using animals and vegetable foodstuffs at an altar, that the prophets authorized were sacrifices that were intended only as a material way of thanking God for his goodness or of praising God and declaring personal devotion to him. But liturgical services where material sacrifices were viewed as a payment for sins that had been committed were never approved by the prophets.

David, for example, who is a unique Old Testament combination of prophet, priest, and king, confesses to God, supposedly after his adultery and murder:

You have no delight in sacrifice. Were I to give a burnt offering, you would not be pleased. The sacrifice acceptable to God is a broken spirit, a broken and contrite heart, O God, you will not despise. . . . Then [after such repentance on my part] you will delight in right sacrifices, in burnt offerings and whole burnt offering.

Thus we see that for David sin and guilt are entirely spiritual problems centered in the soul of man. He knows that the material blood of animals, or even of man, cannot cleanse away his guilt, because the two things are

121

not in the same realm of reality. He knows that material payments cannot erase spiritual deficits, any more than apples can be subtracted from oranges. Only making the heart spiritually right can work cleansing and forgiveness when the heart has been spiritually wrong.

We can also appreciate from this passage in Psalm 51 that the prophetic concept of righteousness and unrighteousness is not only spiritual but also personal. The prophets do not look at sin primarily as a formal legal offense against the righteousness of God which requires that a proportionate legal fine be paid to satisfy God's honor. Rather, the prophets look at sin primarily as a personal act that causes a fracture in the relationship between God and the man who has sinned. So, holding to this spiritual and personal concept of righteousness and sin, the Old Testament prophets always declare God's merciful forgiveness without any payment except a broken and contrite heart that is determined to rededicate itself. The prophets also give no indication that all forgiveness for the sins of the human race will be held in abeyance until later when Jesus dies on a cross to pay the accumulated price.

Listen to these prophetic passages which speak of free, complete, immediate, and unconditional divine forgiveness:

> The Lord is merciful and gracious,
>   slow to anger and abiding in steadfast love.
> He will not always chide,
>   nor will he keep his anger for ever.
> He does not deal with us according to our sins,
>   nor requite us according to our iniquities.
> For as the heavens are high above the earth,
>   so great is his steadfast love toward those who fear him;
> as far as the east is from the west,
>   so far does he remove our transgressions from us.
> As a father pities his children,
>   so the Lord pities those who fear him.
> For he knows our frame;
>   he remembers that we are dust. (Psalm 103:8-14.)

> Return, faithless Israel,
>   says the Lord.
> I will not look on you in anger,
>   for I am merciful,
>   says the Lord;

122

Only acknowledge your guilt,
    that you rebelled against the Lord your God. (Jeremiah 3:12-13.)

"Yet even now," says the Lord,
    "return to me with all your heart,
with fasting, with weeping, and with mourning;
    and rend your hearts and not your garments."
Return to the Lord, your God,
    for he is gracious and merciful,
slow to anger and abounding in steadfast love. (Joel 2:12-13.)

Thus, for the prophets guilt is a spiritual matter that is atoned for purely on the basis of sorrow for sin, because God is a loving and compassionate God who is more concerned with his human relationships than with his holy honor.

Now this atonement doctrine brought the prophets into conflict with the priests who seem to have believed—or at least they generally give the impression—that the correct animal or vegetable sacrifices were quite acceptable and sufficient payments for sin. One of the chief concerns of the priestly writers of the books of Genesis, Exodus, Leviticus, Numbers, and Deuteronomy is to establish the claim that they can trace the custom of offering material sacrifices for sin all the way back to divine, or Mosaic, commands during the wilderness wandering of the Israelites, and even back to father Abraham. God himself, these books declare, instituted the various traditions of material sacrifice so that men could accurately pay their penalties for infringing upon God's laws. These payments were viewed as actually propitiating, or appeasing, the divine wrath. (See Lev. 4:20, 31; 10:17; 16:32; also I Sam. 3:14; II Sam. 21:3-4.)

This priestly belief in acceptable reparations probably developed quite naturally. In every age men have attempted to placate with suitable gifts the anger that they have aroused in other men. Jacob, for example, in order to assuage the resentment of his brother Esau, whom he had tricked out of his birthright and blessing, sent droves of cattle and sheep ahead of his family caravan as a present for Esau. For the Bible says that he thought "I may appease him with the present that goes before me, and afterwards I shall see his face; perhaps he will accept me" (Gen. 32:20).

In the priestly writings basically this same method of appeasement

123

has been transferred from the man-to-man relationship to the man-to-God relationship without recognition that God is different from man, at least in the fact that since God already owns all things he surely lays less value on material gifts. This priestly belief that material gifts can affect God as they affect man can be seen, for instance, in Leviticus 4:20 where instructions are given for a proper animal sin-offering sacrifice, and the concluding words are "[Then] the priest shall make atonement for them, and they shall be forgiven."

But the prophets always reacted against this concept of sacrifice in a strongly negative manner. Amos, years before the priestly writers had compiled and edited the historical books of the Old Testament, challenges the priestly opinion that sacrifice had been divinely instituted during the wilderness wandering. Speaking for God, he asks rhetorically, "Did you bring to me sacrifices and offerings the forty years in the wilderness, O house of Israel?" (5:25). And Jeremiah, also speaking for God, sides with Amos strongly: "For in the day that I brought them out of the land of Egypt, I did not speak to your fathers or command them concerning burnt offerings and sacrifices. But this command I gave them, 'Obey my voice, and I will be your God' " (7:22-23).

The only Old Testament passage where there is any apparent cloudiness in the prophetic position is in Isaiah 53, which is the famous suffering servant passage. This suffering servant gives an amazing preview of the type of suffering ministry that was laid upon Jesus. The prophet is evidently referring to, and eulogizing, a man who had been a Christlike suffering servant in his day when he writes that this man "was wounded for our transgressions" and "bruised for our iniquities," that "upon him was the chastisement that made us whole," that "with his stripes we are healed," that "the Lord has laid on him the iniquity of us all," that "it was the will of the Lord to bruise him," that "he makes himself an offering for sin," and that "he bore the sin of many."

This passage has traditionally been interpreted by Christendom in a literal way to mean that by the death of this suffering servant sin has been paid for. But contemporary biblical scholars point out that such an interpretation does violence both to the poetic style in which the prophets wrote and to the prophets' clear rejections of such an atonement doctrine in all their appeals for repentance. What the prophet Isaiah is more likely doing in this passage is publicly eulogizing—or praising—a man of God who, in order to lead people back to their spiritual senses and back to their God, was forced so to speak and act that he caused himself to be resisted and eventually to be put to death. This view agrees with Isaiah's statement in the same passage that "By his knowledge shall the righteous one, my servant, make many to be accounted righteous" (53:11). For the words "by his knowledge" seem to indicate that the suffering servant's *method* had been to release the people of God from the miseries caused by their sins by *enlightening* and *inspiring* them, rather than by paying a punishment price for them.

And, lest there be any doubt that the prophets reject the theory that one man can suffer to pay for another man's sins, both Ezekiel (18:1-4) and Jeremiah (31:29-30) declare that such a practice is nothing less than ungodly and immoral. In those days there was a familiar proverb which many people were interpreting to mean that God often deliberately punished the children for the sins of their fathers. But Ezekiel announces that this proverb contains a doctrine that displeases God.

The word of the Lord came to me again. "What do you mean by repeating this proverb concerning the land of Israel: 'The fathers have eaten sour grapes and the children's teeth are set on edge.' As I live," says the Lord, "this proverb shall no more be used by you in Israel. Behold, . . . the soul that sins shall die. The son shall not suffer for the iniquities of the father, nor the father suffer for the iniquities of the son. The righteousness of the righteous shall be upon himself, and the wickedness of the wicked shall be upon himself."

Thus the biblical evidence is quite clear that the prophets placed the guilt of each man's sins plumply upon himself. Only a man who helped a sinner come to repentance and righteousness, and who got hurt in the process of helping, could, in a poetic sense, be bearing the transgressions of another. But a literal vicarious—or substitutionary—bearing of guilt for another person is an offense to the moral conscience of the prophets.

The contention of most biblical scholars and theologians today is that Jesus placed himself squarely in the fellowship of the prophets and that Jesus did not at all interpret his divine mission as a call to pay for the sins of all men in a bloody sacrifice of himself. Very importantly, the Gospel writers themselves know nothing of a divine payment plan. For the Gospel writers wrote about what Jesus did and said primarily because they believed that the greatest part of Jesus' saving mission was to sacrifice himself in a teaching and healing ministry in which he led the lost people of God back to their heavenly Father.

In Luke 1:30-55 the angel informs Mary that Jesus' work of salvation will be to restore the greatness of the Davidic kingdom of God and to crush the forces of oppression and evil in the world. The angel says nothing about paying for sin, nor does the angel speak of payment in Matthew 1:21 either. Aged Simeon, taking the infant Jesus in his withered arms, says nothing of a substitutionary atonement, only of revelation and inspiration: "Lord, now let your servant depart in peace. . . . for my eyes have seen your salvation, . . . a light for revelation to the nations, and for glory to your people Israel."

John also speaks throughout his Gospel not of a priestly sacrificial ministry of payment but of a prophetic sacrificial ministry of revelation. Jesus is the true *light*. In Jesus "the true light that enlightens every man was coming into the world. . . . [And] we have beheld his glory" (1:9, 14).

Jesus himself informs the congregation in his hometown of Nazareth that:

> The Spirit of the Lord . . . has anointed me to preach good news to
>   the poor.
> He has sent me to proclaim release to the captives
> and recovering of sight to the blind,
> to set at liberty those who are oppressed,
> to proclaim the acceptable year of the Lord. (Luke 4:18-19.)

Thus, reading directly from Isaiah 61 on that sabbath day, Jesus interprets his ministry as a prophetic sacrifice of preaching and healing and witnessing, rather than as a priestly sacrifice of payment and satisfaction.

Matthew, in a very significant passage (8:17), clearly interprets Jesus' work of miraculous healing during his ministry to be the fulfillment of what was believed to be Isaiah's "prophecy" of a coming suffering servant. Jesus, he says, is fulfilling the prophecy because he is taking the people's infirmities and bearing their griefs (or diseases) by taking time and effort to heal them. This sacrificing, according to Matthew, was taking place all during Jesus' ministry, not only upon a cross at the end.

Furthermore, in the Gospels Jesus boldly forgives the sins of the penitent all along throughout his ministry because, he declares, he has been given authority by God to do so (Matt. 9:2 ff.). There is no indication from him whatsoever of any priestly belief that this forgiveness is conditional upon his later dying on a cross. Toward the end he delegates to all his disciples the same authority to forgive sins. And, even then, he has nothing to say about a sacrificial deposit in a heavenly ledger that will cover all their forgiveness withdrawals (Matt. 16:19; 18:18; John 20:23).

Again, the fact that Jesus prophetically sees his sacrifice as the revelation of God's pattern for living is noticeable in his famous declaration: "If any man would come after me, let him deny himself and take up his cross and follow me. For whoever would save his life will lose it, and whoever loses his life for my sake will find it" (Matt. 16:24-25).

On several occasions when Jesus is criticized by his opponents for not observing the ritualistic rules of the Jews that forbade good people to companion with sinners or to behave normally on the sabbath, Jesus rebuts them by quoting God's words from the prophet Hosea (6:6): "I desire steadfast love and not sacrifice."

Jesus is not once quoted as making any kind of sacrifice in the temple or as urging his disciples to do so. Rather, he always talks like a prophet who knows that God has been freely and fully forgiving sins all along everywhere with no strings attached (Matt. 9:2; Mark 2:10). Jesus evidently had such a prophetic antagonism to the temple sacrifices that there was some discussion among him and his disciples as to whether they should even pay the temple tax (Matt. 17:24 ff.). Jesus' statements in Mark 2:17 that "I came to call not the righteous, but sinners" and that "those who are well have no need of a physician" imply that at least some people were even then right with God and in no need of a sacrifice in their behalf.

Jesus' driving of the money changers out of the temple is also the action of a prophet against the priests, reminiscent of Amos at Bethel. In that action Jesus seems to rebel not only at the commercial perversion of priestly sacrifice but also at the very doctrine that sacrificial animals are an adequate payment for spiritual sin. Jesus does not want priests standing between God and his people, as though sinners need a middleman in order to reach God. Jesus wants a direct relationship between the sinner and his God. " 'My house shall be called a house of prayer' [that is, of direct contact]; but you make it a den of robbers." (Matt. 21:12-13.)

One of the most important statements of Jesus which show that he identifies himself with the school of the prophets is his remark that he must go to Jerusalem to die: "For it cannot be," he says, "that a prophet should perish away from Jerusalem. O Jerusalem, Jerusalem, killing the prophets and stoning those who are sent to you!" (Luke 13: 33-34.)

The messianic conception of many of the disciples of Jesus appears to be the same as that of the two men on the road to Emmaus, who say that Jesus was "a prophet mighty in deed and word before God and all the people" (Luke 24:19). And the crowds that Jesus teaches reportedly assess him in the same way. For they inform strangers upon his triumphal entry into Jerusalem that this is "the prophet Jesus from Nazareth" (Matt. 21:11). (See also Matt. 21:46; Mark 4:24; 8:28; Luke 7:16, 26; 9:8, 19.)

Jesus' statement in Matthew 26:28 that the cup at the last supper in the upper room is the new covenant in his blood which is poured out for many for the forgiveness of sins, Jesus' statement in John 6:53 about eating his flesh and drinking his blood, and John the Baptizer's statement in John 1:29 that Jesus is the lamb of God who takes away the sins of the world—all are statements which are interpreted most satisfactorily when they are interpreted in the poetic way that Isaiah's suffering servant passage and all the rest of Jesus' and John's prophetic metaphors are interpreted.

At Jesus' death the only reasonable significance of the reported tearing of the veil that hid the holy of holies in the temple from view (Matt. 27:51) is that God is thereby indicating his displeasure at the priests. They had perverted the true spiritual worship into mere external sacrifices. They had crucified God's Messiah who had attempted to bring men back to true heart religion. They had claimed that they stood between God and sinful men as mediators. To the Gospel writer the tearing of the veil in the holy of holies probably represents God's final vindication of the prophets over the priests. For he will not have anything separating him from his people.

Luke's book of the Acts of the Apostles also knows only a prophetic type of sacrifice. Jesus is never declared to be our Savior on the basis of paying the price of sin. Rather, the preachers in Acts always call people to come and accept God's free love and forgiveness which he has revealed through his messianic representative. In a truly prophetic manner, also, forgiveness is never declared to a sinner until he has met the moral condition of repentance. Here are six prophetic-type passages:

Acts 2:38. "Repent, and be baptized every one of you in the name of Jesus Christ for the forgiveness of your sins."

Acts 3:26. "God . . . sent [Jesus] to you first, to bless you in turning every one of you from your wickedness."

Acts 15:9. "God . . . cleansed their [the Gentiles'] hearts by faith."

Acts 17:30. "The times of ignorance God overlooked, but now he commands all men everywhere to repent."

Acts 22:16. "Rise and be baptized, and wash away your sins, calling on his name."

Acts 26:22-23. Paul to King Agrippa: "I stand here . . . saying nothing but what the prophets and Moses said would come to pass: that the Christ must suffer, and that, by being the first to rise from the dead, he would proclaim light both to the people and to the Gentiles."

In this same manner the whole first half of the New Testament knows nothing of a priestly sacrifice of Jesus on the cross paying for our sins. It knows only of a prophetic sacrifice. (We shall not consider here the several dozen prophetic passages in the Gospels that indirectly imply that God forgives freely and gladly: e.g., Matt. 5:39 ff.; 5:44-45; 5:48; 6:12, 26, 28; 7:1, 11; 8:11; 9:36; 10:42; 11:9; 13:1 ff.; 15:22; 18:12, 21, 27, 35; 20:1 ff., 30; 25:30; Luke 6:35-36; 9:55; 11:9; 15:10; 17:3-4; Acts 14:17; 17:27-28; 18:9.)

Now the priests get back into the picture with Paul, a theologian who was not one of Jesus' precrucifixion disciples and hence could easily fail to appreciate how staunchly and thoroughly the prophet Messiah had opposed the priestly doctrine of atonement. There probably were two schools in the early church that differed on the extent to which Jesus was a priest and the extent to which Jesus was a prophet, because people from both traditions were part of the movement almost immediately after the resurrection (Acts 6:7; 11:27). Paul was a brilliant theologian who probably helped to prevent any great theological dissension over this issue by joining together, some time after he wrote his earliest letters, the prophetic and the priestly concepts of Jesus' sacrifice. In performing this systematic compromise, however, Paul opened the door to a priestly misunderstanding of Jesus' sacrifice which has plagued the Christian church until the present century, the Roman Catholic doctrine of the sacrifice of the Mass being the most extreme development of it.

How then does Paul go about this combining of prophet and priest in Jesus Christ when he knows that the Old Testament is full of divine declarations of free and unconditional forgiveness long before Jesus died on the cross? The key passage is Romans 3:25, where Paul declares that our redemption is in Jesus Christ "whom God put forward as an expiation by his blood, to be received by faith. This was to show God's righteousness, because in his divine forbearance he had passed over former sins." What Paul is saying here, it seems, is that, until Jesus' time, the sins of men were forgiven without a blood sacrifice. But now that Jesus has died, God, in order to impress upon men the seriousness of his righteousness and of our sinfulness, has arbitrarily decided to consider Jesus' death a universal payment for sin. So, from the time of Jesus on, unless men are covered by the blood of Jesus through faith, they cannot be forgiven.

Now this is quite an ingenious, creative way for Paul to merge the prophetic and priestly Old Testament traditions. But Paul provides us with no information about where he got the authority to propound such a sweeping change in God's established way of granting forgiveness. Rather, Paul, in his letters to Rome, Corinth, and Galatia (and Ephesus and Colossae, if he wrote them), simply proceeds without further explanation to speak numerous times of how Christ has been killed for us and how we have redemption and peace with God through his blood in a rather commercial accounting sense. (See Rom. 4:25; 5:1, 9, 10, 18, 19; 6:6; I Cor. 1:20; 15:22; II Cor. 5:14, 15, 19, 21; Gal. 1:4; 2:16, 20, 21; 3:13; 4:5; Eph. 1:7; 2:5, 13, 18; Col. 1:20, 22.)

Paul's sacrificial concept is taken to its most literal extreme by the writer of the epistle to the Hebrews, who believes that in the crucifixion Jesus spiritually entered once for all into Heaven's holy of holies as God's specially established high priest for man, taking his own blood. And when he had offered for all time this single sacrifice for sins, he sat down at the right hand of God as Lord of all (9:12 ff.; 10:12). The writer of I Peter follows Paul's lead also (1:18; 2:24), as the writers of I John and Revelation seem to do (I John 1:7; 2:2; Rev. 1:5; also II Pet. 3:16). The letter of James, however, is the letter of a prophet through and through, as are Paul's early letters to Thessalonica and to Timothy and Titus (II Thess. 2:13).

So if this is the true picture, as the Christian church today is becoming increasingly convinced, how then should Christians understand the creedal statement that Jesus Christ "was crucified also for us under

130

Pontius Pilate"? We should understand this as a prophetic type of sacrifice, not as a priestly type of sacrifice.

That Jesus was "crucified for us" means, therefore, first, that God appointed and empowered Jesus of Nazareth to testify for God to the humanity that God loved, even though this mission would result inevitably in Jesus' death. That Jesus was "crucified for us" means, second, that Jesus took the perfect godlike path of self-giving love, even though it led to a cross, and that we, his disciples, are to do likewise.

Thus we can appreciate that the prophetic sacrifice has always been harder for man to support than the priestly sacrifice. For the prophetic sacrifice puts the burden not upon a substitute but upon us. It is we who must offer the sacrifice of true repentance if we are to be forgiven. And we must surrender our selfish life totally to the love of God and our fellowman, if we are to remain in the Father's good graces.

For as Jesus declares: "If any man would come after me, let him deny himself and take up his cross and follow me. For whoever would save his life will lose it, and whoever loses his life for my sake will find it."

12. Is There Really a Hell?

"He descended into hell." The Apostles' Creed

"My God, my God, why hast thou forsaken me?" Matthew 27:46
"Father, into thy hands I commit my spirit!" Luke 23:46

Is there really a Hell? Or is the idea based only on ancient folklore? How are twentieth-century Christians to relate to this traditional doctrine which the early church preserved in the Apostles' Creed by affirming that after his death Jesus "descended into Hell"? To be quite forthright from the beginning, we must admit that the contemporary church is highly skeptical of the traditional doctrine of Hell when this doctrine is interpreted in any literal manner.

The Old Testament contains no formal doctrine of the nature of life after death or of the nature of any punishment after death. God simply does not reveal any such information in the clear manner in which he has said "I am the Lord your God," or "Walk in this way." The occasional Old Testament passages that deal with life after death are nothing more than a reflection of the common folklore of the ancient Semitic family of peoples, among whom the Hebrews were numbered. Almost every Old Testament detail on life after death can be paralleled from Mesopotamian and Canaanite literature. This folklore saw a four-stage development which I shall now sketch out roughly. The four stages overlapped in a complicated manner and were accepted to a different degree by different thinkers in the same era.

The first stage that is presently known to us was belief in a cavernous abode of the dead under the earth, a place called "Sheol" in Hebrew and "Hades" in the Greek. The term "the Pit" is also used (RSV) to designate Sheol in the Old Testament (Num. 16:33; Job 11:8; Prov. 5:5; Isa. 14:9). The ancient Semites believed that all men died and went to dwell in this Sheol as mere shades—or shadows—of themselves (Gen. 42:38; II Sam. 12:23; Job 3:11; Ps. 88:4), even though they retained their earthly rank and personality there (I Sam. 28:11-12; Isa. 14:9).

There was no joy in Sheol. There was only the sad remembering of the fuller life upon earth. There was also no hope for the dead of betterment in their condition (Job 16:22). Consequently those ancients who still lived on earth strove to live as long and as fully as possible. It was believed, furthermore, that if men or nations were righteous God would preserve them from premature death and give them a long, happy life on earth (Ps. 16:10; 86:13). But if an individual were wicked, God would cut off the life of that man in his prime and send him to Sheol. And if a nation were wicked, God would destroy that entire social order and send it to Sheol (Ps. 9:17).

The second stage of the development of the ancient folklore about the underworld was the addition of belief in rewards and punishments in the afterlife. This belief developed during the second and first centuries before Christ.

The Hebrews believed that God was a just God, that he rewarded good and punished evil. Yet even an ancient thinker such as Job had noticed that many times it is actually the evil men who live the long and prosperous lives, while the good men live the short and miserable lives. If belief in God's righteousness and goodness were not to be undermined by this observation, therefore, it was necessary to believe that the evil men received their punishment at least after death, while the good received their reward also after death. This fulfillment of justice, it was believed in the beginning, would take place following a resurrection of all the departed dead from Sheol for a great judgment.

It was probably this reasoning that caused general acceptance of the ancient Iranian idea that God had established a burning furnace in the bottom of the underworld where the wicked would someday receive the due reward of their sins. Part of Sheol, therefore, was now believed to be set aside for punishment, while the remainder of Sheol was now believed to be only a temporary hold for the spirits of the dead. After the great resurrection of all of the dead out of Sheol for the day of judgment, it was believed that the wicked would be consigned to this furnace of burning pitch and sulfur at the bottom, or at one side, of the pit of Sheol, while the righteous would be restored to a long, or even to an eternal, life on earth (Deut. 32:22; Isa. 42:21-22; II Pet. 2:4; Jude 6; Matt. 11:23).

The New Testament calls this furnace "Gehenna," which literally means "valley of Hinnom," a valley outside Jerusalem which had once been a site of Baal worship and which had been turned into a city dump in order to desecrate it. The Valley of Hinnom came to designate symbolically the eternal fires of the underworld because the refuse on the dump was always burning. It is only this furnace part of Sheol—or Hades—therefore, which may properly be called "Hell."

One of the unresolved questions in the intertestamental literature was the period of time that was to be spent by the wicked in this Hell of fire. The ancients had numerous opinions on the matter, some saying that the punishment lasted forever, others that it lasted only for a short time, such as a year, by which time the wicked would be annihilated in the fire.

This difference of opinion carries over into the New Testament itself. In Matthew 10:25, for example, Jesus is reported as saying that we should fear God "who can destroy [that is, annihilate] both soul and body in hell." Yet in Matthew 25:46 he is reported as saying that the wicked shall suffer "eternal punishment." In John 15:6 Jesus is reported to have said that the human branches which bear no fruit shall be cast into the fire and burned. And the Greek word for burned that is used here means "burned up" or "consumed totally." In Mark 9:48, however, Jesus is reported to have said that in Hell "their worm does not die, and the fire is not quenched." In Revelation 20:10, 15, also, the burning is to continue to all eternity. Thus, while much of the ancient Mediterranean world, including early Christianity, came to believe in the necessity of a just God who gives out rewards and punishments after death, they did not agree on the details.

The third stage of the development of the ancient folklore about the underworld was perhaps due to the influence of the Greek belief in the immortality of the soul and the disposability of the body. At this stage it was believed that the rewards and punishments would come immediately after death without an intervening wait in Sheol for resurrection to a great judgment. In what is reported to be Jesus' parable of the rich man and Lazarus, for instance, the rich man goes into the lake of fire immediately after his death (Luke 16:23). And on the cross Jesus promises the repentant thief that "Today [not after a long wait in Sheol, but today] you will be with me in Paradise" (Luke 23:43; see also Prov. 15:24; Ps. 49:15). Thus in the development of the ancient folklore the blessed dead are gradually moved from Sheol below into Heaven above, as is indicated also in Stephen's last words, as he looks heavenward and petitions, "Lord Jesus, receive my spirit" (Acts 7:59). This development of the idea of immediate entrance into Hell and Heaven makes the idea of a resurrection of dead bodies for a day of judgment quite unnecessary. And we may wonder, therefore, why the New Testament writers included it. But they seem here to have been more concerned to include everybody's ideas, rather than to exercise their critical faculties so as to present only those ideas that were fully consistent with each other.

The fourth stage of the development of the ancient folklore about the underworld was the addition of some legends about Jesus by the first- and second-generation Christians. These early Christians developed some imaginative notions of what Jesus did between the time of his crucifixion and the time of his resurrection appearances to his disciples. None of the New Testament books intimates that Jesus on any occasion informed his disciples where he had been and what he had been doing before his Easter appearances to them. But the subject appealed to the curiosity and imagination of many of those who were delighted to hear that Jesus was still alive.

Most of the people of that day believed that the condemned dead were gathered down in Sheol awaiting punishment or were already being punished. It seemed natural to these early Christians, therefore, that the spirit of Jesus the Messiah would yearn to carry redemption even down to Sheol at his death. And in Sheol, of course, he would do exactly what he had done on earth. He would teach and preach. Consequently the writer of I Peter declares the early Christian conviction that Christ was "put to death in the flesh but made alive in the spirit; in which he went and preached to the spirits in prison, who formerly did not obey" (3:18-19).

Then, of course, if Jesus preached down in Sheol he would surely get results, as he had always done. And if the dead who had refused their

135

heavenly Father on earth accepted this gospel of Jesus in the underworld, then surely the Father's mercy would be extended to them also.
So declares the writer of Ephesians, who finds a quite fantastic messianic meaning in Psalm 68: "Therefore it is said [in Ps. 68:18],

'When he ascended on high he led a host of captives,
and he gave gifts to men.'

(In saying, 'He ascended,' what does it mean but that he had also
descended into the lower parts of the earth?)" So, according to
Ephesians and I Peter, at his resurrection Jesus had led a great converted host of formerly disobedient souls out of Sheol into Paradise
above.

However, despite these opinions of several New Testament writers
that are scattered around in a few short passages, the first-generation
church in convention evidently never declared any formal doctrines
about Hell as matters of divine revelation. The subject seems to have
been ignored as quite incidental to the church's main task at hand.

This, then, is a rough systematic and historical outline of the biblical
material that deals with Hell. But what are Christians to make of
this ancient doctrine? We believe that Jesus' appearances to his disciples have a solid historical foundation and indeed are the very reason
that Christianity survived and increased. But when we consider the
subject of Hell, we are confronted with the absence of a formal deliberate divine revelation in either the Old Testament or the New
Testament and with the presence of nothing but unauthoritative folklore.

It is almost as though the heavenly Father did not want us to waste
time worrying about what happens to the wicked after death but rather
to concentrate on living righteously so as to escape whatever the destiny
of the wicked is. As Moses says, "The secret things belong to the Lord
our God, but the things that are revealed belong to us and to our children for ever, that we may do all the words of this law" (Deut. 29:29).
In the absence of any clear word from our heavenly Father on this
matter, therefore, twentieth-century Christians seem to have only two
choices: They can remain reverently agnostic, or they can use their
dedicated theological imagination and hope that the twentieth-century
folklore which results will show greater insight than the folklore of the
first century.

The intellectual leaders of the Christian church have always had
among them men who feel uncomfortable with many of the biblical

notions about Hell. Eternal Hell has simply not seemed to them to be consistent with the heavenly Father's nature of perfect love, which as Jesus says includes even its enemies. That a just heavenly Father would condemn a child of his to burn in agony for all eternity, which is trillions and trillions of years unending, because that child misused a mere seventy short years has always been appalling to many.

Surely the writer of Psalm 103 could not have believed in a God like this when he sang that

> The Lord is merciful and gracious,
> slow to anger and abounding in steadfast love.
> He will not always chide,
> nor will he keep his anger for ever.
> He does not deal with us according to our sins. . . .
> For he knows our frame;
> he remembers that we are dust. (Ps. 103 :8-10, 14.)

A heavenly Father who would fry his enemies to all eternity would seem to be infinitely worse than the monster Adolf Hitler who gassed and cremated at places like Buchenwald and Belsen some six million Jews whom he counted as his enemies.

Modern biblical scholars and theologians simply do not believe that Jesus said the things about Hell that are attributed to him in the Gospels, because these passages contradict everything that Jesus was and stood for. Jesus, for instance, exhorted us to love our enemies with a perfect—or complete—love such as the heavenly Father has. And the Father has a love, Jesus said, that sends the blessings of rain and sunshine upon the wicked as well as upon the good. Jesus also urged us to turn the other cheek and to go the second mile for our enemies. Could this same Jesus really have agreed with the common opinion of his day that God overpunished his enemies after death with an everlasting grudge that roasted them in an eternal oven? No! I do not believe that Jesus would have agreed with that. For such a vengeful God, rather than being the marvelous deity of love and mercy and forgiveness, is in my eyes a frankenstein of hatred and pitilessness and revenge who orders his children to be more moral than he is willing to be.

Again, could the same Jesus who prayed upon a cross "Father, forgive them, for they know not what they do" have told his disciples in Matthew 25 :31-46 that on the last day he would sit on his judgment throne and condemn all these human "goats" who had refused to feed and clothe him in the person of unfortunate people to eternal torture with the words "Depart from me, you cursed, into the eternal fire prepared for the devil and his angels"? No! I cannot believe that the same Jesus who prayed for his murderers with his last dying breath would have taught such a horrible and vengeful overpunishment of his enemies. (Even our ordinary human judges try to measure out a just punishment that fits the crime better than that! Furthermore, the fact that Jesus turned and rebuked those of his disciples who wanted to know if they should pray for fire to descend from Heaven to consume the Samaritan village which would not receive him seems to be a definite indication that Hell was a reality only in the imaginations of his disciples and that his concern was with tolerance and mercy (Luke 9:54).

Protestants often criticize unfavorably the fabulous nature of the Roman Catholic doctrine of Purgatory without realizing that to a large extent this doctrine came to appeal to Christian thinkers of a thousand years ago because it partially rescued God from this moral scandal of hating *his* enemies in an eternal Hell, while he claimed to be love and ordered us to love *our* enemies. According to the doctrine of Purgatory, the damned, by repenting of their evil and serving their deserved time of punishment, could eventually escape the torments of hellfire and rise to bliss in Heaven.

The great Protestant reformer John Calvin evidently was also one of those who are distressed at the biblical notions of Hell. For while he believed in God's absolute predestination of who would be saved and who would be lost, Calvin softened this doctrine by saying almost nothing about Hell. Indeed, from his great systematic work *The Institutes of the Christian Religion,* one gets the impression that if Calvin did believe in Hell he probably believed in only a brief burning spell there that resulted in the annihilation of the damned.

Calvin also doubted the late New Testament legends of Christ's descent into Sheol so much that he completely reinterpreted the phrase in the creed which says that Jesus "descended into Hell." For Calvin, Jesus was in Hell *figuratively* when he felt forsaken and without God in the agony of Gethsemane and later upon the cross. Jesus' cry of "My God, my God, why hast thou forsaken me?" was to Calvin a cry out of the Hell of spiritual loneliness that Jesus had descended into rather than some mythical flaming and smoking netherworld into which Jesus had entered after death.

The Methodist Church and other Protestant churches have always openly doubted the truth and foundation of the New Testament passages about Hell and about Jesus' descent into Hell, or into Sheol. For this reason the Apostles' Creed is repeated in some Protestant churches without the phrase "He descended into Hell."

Not that a literal Hell has been written off by all Christendom, however. Besides the uneducated sectarian groups and the fundamentalists of all varieties, there are some Christian thinkers from mainline churches who insist that there must be some kind of eternal Hell, even if it is not filled with pain, or else some kind of temporary Hell, with or without pain.

Those who believe in an eternal Hell—even a painless one—argue that if God did not have some place in which to segregate the wicked from the righteous, then the wicked with their wickedness would keep Heaven from being Heaven. Since God does not force man's free will, man has to choose to be righteous or unrighteous. So in Heaven why should God afflict these obedient children who have chosen him with the company of those stubborn and self-centered children who have made such a Hell out of this good earth? They would only make another Hell out of Heaven.

But the rebuttal can be made that if the rich man in Luke's parable could still change his mind in Hell's torments, how could a loving God not continue to work for the conversion of all his children even in Hell if he were keeping them alive there? Surely enough punishment, or merely enough aching loneliness, would in a short time change everybody there. And Hell could be emptied entirely. It simply does not seem consistent with God's loving nature that he would permit any of his children to remain eternally in any kind of Hell.

Those who argue for a short—even though painful—Hell sentence seem to have a slightly better case. These people are of two kinds. The first kind, the annihilationists, agree with Jesus' statement in John 15 that the wicked are thrown into the fire and consumed—that is, totally destroyed. Those of them who are concerned more with the physics of the matter see hellfire as a kind of spiritual reduction furnace where God breaks down into the original energy particles those spiritual personality structures that were self-centered and hence not suitably shaped for eternal life in Heaven's perfect love. This conception, of course, is based upon the unprovable assumption that spirit is a stable substance and upon the unprovable assumption that God does not love his children enough to use Hell redemptively.

139

The annihilationists who are concerned more with the *morality* of the matter believe that God subjects each wicked person to the exact amount of hellfire that he deserves so that he will pay for the sins that he has committed upon earth. Then, after payment, that damned soul is consumed in the fire and blotted out forever. But these moralists are thinking more like the persecuted Jews of old than like Christians.

For what purpose does punishment serve within the framework of God's perfect love? Even on earth a loving father punishes his child only in order to correct the boy for further and better fellowship and in order to protect the rest of us from him. That is why God, too, punishes us. An improved relationship and benefit for us all may come out of it.

But what loving purpose could punishment in Hell that would end in annihilation possibly serve? Merely punishing the dead man in Hell so that he would not get away with anything would be a reflection of the old Hebrew "eye for an eye" morality rather than a reflection of the Christian "turn the other cheek" morality. The Christian revelation is that our heavenly Father's justice serves his love rather than his love serving his justice. The Father's divine love, we proclaim, is the ultimate reality, not his divine justice. Surely, then, a loving heavenly Father would sadly say to a persistently rebellious child as he died, "All right, my child, since you insist, *your* will be done." Then, because that rebel would pollute Heaven, a loving God would perhaps permit him to lapse into nothingness without any futile, senseless chastisement. Or else a loving God would decree enough pain or lonesome self-examination to bring the rebel to repentance.

It is no wonder, therefore, that the second group of those who believe in a temporary Hell—whatever the nature of the punishment—are called "correctionists." Correctionists believe that the Heavenly Father punishes the wicked in Hell only until the rebellious souls see their errors and repent. For, they argue, if a man can still be saved on his earthly deathbed and be fitted into Heaven, then why cannot a man who is saved through the discipline in Hell be fitted by his repentance for Heaven also?

We must be clear about the fact that we have no way of knowing if any of these positions is correct. Therefore, while we may have a preference for one concept over another, we must maintain throughout our pondering that a reverent agnosticism is in order. But, if there is a Hell at all, the only kind that does not seem to contradict and embarrass the Christian gospel of the God of love is the temporary Hell of the correctionists.

Yes, from the point of view of historical and theological investigation the Christian church today is coming to the conclusion that the doctrine of a literal Hell for the eternal torment of souls cannot hold any more water than the literal eternal Hell itself was supposed to hold. But in a symbolic sense the doctrine of Hell is still as valid and useful as it was for Jonah of old, for whom it was a present experience (2:2).

Today Christian theologians and preachers usually speak of Hell symbolically as a this-worldly reality. Today Hell is described as the mess—either individual or social—that men make out of this life when they do not acknowledge the heavenly Father and walk in his way. Today Hell is defined as any place where the heavenly Father is not, or more precisely, where his blessing is absent. A battlefield, a prison cell, a hate-filled marriage, or a broken friendship is Hell.

Today we do not "frighten Hell out of" people, as Jonathan Edwards the Puritan divine did with his famous sermon "Sinners in the Hands of an Angry God." Many of Edwards' congregation, we read, became so terrified that they felt as though the floors of the church were giving way beneath them and as though they were sinking into the raging inferno below them. Some of the listeners even gripped the pillars of the church and cried out to Edwards to pray for them.

Today, instead, Christians affirm that Hell is right here in this life when our sins, the sins of other people, and even chance misfortunes overwhelm us with trouble. In this earthly Hell we too cry out with Jesus the dereliction words of the twenty-second psalm: "My God, my God, why hast thou forsaken me?" But we also experience that even this spiritual kind of Hell is not our conqueror whenever the heavenly Father draws near to us and rescues us. For we too are able to pray every day and at life's end, with relief and gratitude: "Father, into thy hands I commit my spirit!"

13. Why Are We So Sure That We Have Heard from God?

"The third day he rose again from the dead." The Apostles' Creed

"Paul, a servant of Jesus Christ, called to be an apostle, set apart for the gospel of God . . . concerning his Son, who was descended from David according to the flesh and designated Son of God . . . by his resurrection from the dead." Romans 1:1-4

Man has always been hungry to know the truths about himself and about God. Furthermore, man has always been hungry to know that he knows the truths about himself and God. That is, he has always hungered to be sure that his knowledge is knowledge of the truth and not mere human guesswork. This hunger for surety becomes the search for *authority*. For man senses that only God himself, or someone whom God has designated to speak for him, is qualified to know the truths about man and God.

This is why Christianity has made the resurrection of Jesus Christ the center pole that holds up the entire tent of the Christian message. For the resurrection of Jesus is that act in which God establishes once and for all the authority of Jesus of Nazareth to speak for him. Thus the resurrection of Jesus is the reason for our Christian surety that we have indeed heard from God the truth that we need.

Both the Apostles' and the Nicene creeds testify to Jesus' resurrec-

142

tion, the Apostles' Creed declaring that on "the third day he rose again from the dead." But the utter cruciality of this belief in Jesus' resurrection would have been better testified to if these early creeds of Christendom had begun instead something like this: *"Because* Jesus the Messiah was raised from the dead, therefore, I believe in God the Father Almighty, and so forth."

Today, unfortunately, there are various thinkers on the outer fringes of Christendom who wrongly believe that we can retain all the value of Christianity without insisting upon the historical resurrection of Jesus Christ. These thinkers have not studied deeply enough, I believe, the nature of Christianity's compelling power or the historical evidence upon which our claims for Jesus' resurrection are based. Rather, these men are simply drawn to the attractive ethical and theological teachings of Jesus and are repelled by the historical problems in any attempt to prove that the resurrection of Jesus took place. "We are not interested in whether he was raised or not," they assert. "We are quite satisfied to be blessed with the ethical and theological insights that Jesus taught."

But, we must retort, just because the ideas that Jesus taught happen to appeal to us, is that any indication that they are true ideas? If there is no more persuasiveness behind the ideas about God and man that Jesus taught, other than the fact that they strike our fancies, then Jesus' ideas carry no more weight than the ideas of any other philosopher who is speculating about life. Jesus' ideas about God and man, therefore, *must have had something special behind them* that gave them the persuasiveness of authority, or else Christianity would never have overwhelmed all the religions and philosophies of the ancient world.

This "something special," Christians believe, consisted of certain indispensable events called "miracles" or "signs" which took place in Jesus' life—events which were divine testimonies to Jesus' authority as the mouthpiece for truth. On these important occasions God did some mighty act to corroborate—to back up—Jesus' claim that he did not speak only on his own but for God himself.

In their turbulent history the people of Israel had had sufficient dealings with God to appreciate what a blessing divine authority was in guiding their daily living. But the authoritative voices of the prophets had been largely stilled for hundreds of years when Jesus came upon the scene. Consequently the people were desperately hungry at that time for a sure word from God. The cry of their hearts was "Is there any word from the Lord?"

In the absence of such a sure word from God the people of Israel had been attempting to meet their needs with their own mental efforts. The religion of Israel had produced the great Midrash and Mishna schools with their rabbis and scribes. These scholars had given birth to the world's most voluminous and useful store of religious tradition, much of which has been collected into a multivolume commentary called the Talmud. The scribes and rabbis were constantly busy criticizing, expanding, and preserving this huge and unwieldy body of tradition.

Now, although the people of Israel were benefiting greatly from the teachings of the Talmud, they were still being left unsatisfied with its wealth of brilliant opinions and debates. Quantity simply did not make up for lack of quality. Many even of the great rabbis were not satisfied with their labors and longed openly for the day of the Messiah who would speak with the trumpet tones of divine authority. Every honest rabbi could only declare, "It is my opinion that . . . ." But the people wanted to hear him say: "In *truth,* I say to you that . . . !"

When we turn to our New Testament, we discover that the single reason Jesus' influence spreads like wildfire is that in the midst of a great multitude of uncertain speculators he alone speaks out with the loud, clear voice of divine authority. The compelling power of Jesus' teachings about God and man is centered, we learn, not in the natural attractiveness of these teachings about the supremacy of holy love— attractive as they are—but rather in the fact that *Jesus is speaking authoritatively for God.* That is what grips the people! When Jesus speaks, he is not merely one brilliant man revealing the profundity of his insight in comparison with other men. When Jesus speaks, he speaks for God. The crowd that listens to his sermon on the mountain is stunned and delighted, Matthew reports, "for he taught them as one who had authority, and not as their scribes" (7:28-29; Mark 1:22; Luke 4:31-32). When Jesus teaches, people do not hear *him* make the unsure rabbinic-like statement: "It is my opinion that . . . ." Rather, men such as Professor Nicodemus hear Jesus declare *"Amaen! Amaen! Lego soi,"* or, "Truly, truly, I say to you . . ." (John 3:3).

Now when Jesus turns up speaking with such compelling authority, the religious leaders are forced to make an assessment of him. They have four options. He is a rascal, a fanatic, a demoniac, or the expected Messiah. But the choice very quickly narrows down to either demoniac or Messiah because of these miraculous signs that accompany Jesus' work.

At Capernaum, Jesus looks down penetratingly at a paralyzed man and declares, "My son, your sins are forgiven." This strikes the observing religious leaders as blasphemy. So Jesus asks them, "Which is easier, to say to the paralytic, 'Your sins are forgiven,' or to say, 'Rise, take up your pallet and walk'? But that you may know that the Son of man has authority on earth to forgive sins," he turns and says to the paralytic, "I say to you, rise, take up your pallet and go home" (Mark 2:1-12). Thus Jesus proves his God-given authority by a sign in which God backs up Jesus with his mighty power.

This seems to be the primary purpose of all the miraculous signs that occur throughout Jesus' ministry. They are God's certification, God's warranty, God's endorsement of Jesus' message as his own. This purpose the people understand clearly, and so join themselves to Jesus.

But the chief religious leaders, in jealousy for their positions, will not acknowledge that the power behind Jesus' miraculous signs is God himself. For if they do so, they will be forced to put themselves under the messianic command of Jesus. So they stick by their accusation that the power behind Jesus' signs is the power of Satan rather than the power of God. "He casts out demons by the prince of demons." (Matt. 9:34.)

Many of the so-called nature miracles, however, such as the feeding of the five thousand and the walking on the water, are almost certainly legends, or are less spectacular accomplishments given a legendary expansion. But the signs that are provided through Jesus' charismatic healing are not only acknowledged by Jesus' enemies (Matt. 9:34), but are quite sufficient in themselves to substantiate Jesus' divine authority, as he declares to a doubting John the Baptizer. Jesus is fulfilling, he says, Isaiah's prophecy that the blind see, the deaf hear, the lame walk, and the poor have good news preached to them (Luke 7:20).

Now the miraculous signs that accompanied Jesus' ministry are sufficient to convince his army of followers that Jesus is God's own representative and Messiah until near the end when Jesus is captured in Jerusalem and *no miraculous signs of deliverance occur* to show that God indeed supports him. According to the popular expectation, the Messiah of God is never supposed to be defeated. The people have joined Jesus because, one and all, they have been taught that the promised Messiah is to be invincible, that no earthly power is to be able to stand against him throughout his campaign for world dominion. And Jesus' signs of healing and demon expulsion have been their assurance that he is this promised undefeatable deliverer.

Jesus' arrest and crucifixion, consequently, utterly demoralize the multitude that follows Jesus—even his closest disciples. They completely lose their confidence in him as the Messiah because at the crucial moment he fails to be backed up by God. As that forlorn disciple explains on the road to Emmaus, "We had hoped that he was the one to redeem Israel" (Luke 24:21). Thus Jesus' authority, which he had exercised for perhaps three years, disappears entirely within a period of twenty-four hours. His whole movement falls to pieces because it has been built entirely upon the belief of the people in his divine authority.

So when Jesus' disciples begin to disband and demobilize immediately after the crucifixion, his influence upon their lives is also in the process of falling to practically zero. They can only reason from now on that they have been mistaken about him, that he was only a fanatic and impractical visionary with a good heart who was acting *on his own,* or else that he was a man of God who had gone beyond the boundaries of his divine commission. His ignominious end is incontestable proof to them that God has not authorized his messianic mission. Jesus' attractive ideas about God and man, therefore, were only the products of his own imagination. So there is really no compelling reason for them to prefer Jesus' ideas over the ideas of others.

In this manner *the influence of Jesus' teachings died along with Jesus himself.* For when God permitted Jesus to die, he was also permitting Jesus' authority, which alone had made Jesus' teachings influential, to die also. And the irrefutable historical point that the Christian church makes here is that *if Jesus had not been seen alive after his crucifixion, the crucifixion would have been so thoroughly the end of Jesus' influence that history would probably not have recorded even his name for us!* But the fact is that history has recorded the name of Jesus of Nazareth. The fact is that Jesus of Nazareth has had far more influence on human history than any other single man.

This is the church's strongest argument for the truth of the resurrection reports. For only the resurrection of Jesus is able to account for the return of Jesus' influence. When Jesus had died and his influence had died with him, God had to do something to restore Jesus' authority. And the only reliably attested historical action of God that could have restored Jesus' authority was Jesus' resurrection.

On Easter day, we read, Jesus' authority is suddenly and surprisingly restored with a permanence that can never be shaken. When his disciples first encounter their risen master that day, their first reaction is a near delirious joy that this loved one is alive, that his personality has survived beyond the grave. Their second reaction must have been delight at realizing that Jesus' survival means that when they die they will survive with God also.

But their third reaction—the one which later shook the world—must have been the realization that *Jesus is still the authority who speaks for God.* Jesus' claim to be the Messiah is established. Jesus' teachings about God and man are validated. Jesus' plan for spreading the knowledge and fellowship of God over all the earth is approved and vindicated. The vigor and the excitement have returned to their discipleship. They now have something to tell the whole world, and all because the resurrection appearances of Jesus have restored for them his divine authority. His authority is the basis of their mission.

In our text Paul too is making precisely this point. He has just set himself to the demanding task of writing a meaningful letter to the inadequately shepherded Christians in Rome. This is a city that he has not yet visited. And, except for a few recent immigrants, these are all brethren whom he does not yet know. So Paul is aware that the first reaction of these Roman Christians to the news that a Paul from Tarsus has written them a long sermonic letter will be "Oh? And who is this Paul? What is his authority for presuming to instruct us?"

So at the very beginning Paul lays his credentials as an authority before them. For only if he can convince them that he is a bona fide authority will they give serious attention to his words. He informs them that he has been called to be an apostle by none less than Jesus the Messiah, who was promised to Israel through the sacred writings of the prophets. Furthermore, Paul reminds them, this Jesus was the true authoritative Messiah because Jesus was *"set forth to be recognized as* son of God . . . by his resurrection from the dead." (The Greek is *horisthentos;* RSV has "designated.")

Jesus' authority, Paul is saying, resides in the fact that God has raised up Jesus for public appearances in order to prove to all men that Jesus is indeed Heaven's spokesman. The only reason that Paul dares, or cares, to write this letter to Rome is that Jesus' resurrection gives divine authority to the Christian mission. Thus, from this passage we can appreciate that if Jesus' disciples, such as Paul, had not been convinced that Jesus had been raised from the dead, there would surely have been only a few sadder but wiser friends up in Galilee who occasionally talked about a foolish and unfortunate messianic adventure of their young adulthood. There would have been no apostles, no missionaries, no church, no Christian civilization. But because there *were* apostles and missionaries and church and Christian civilization, Jesus' disciples—such as Paul—must indeed have believed that they had seen the risen Lord.

Today men are still searching for a sure word from God, still listening for the clear ring of divine authority. In the midst of an information explosion in the physical world men still find a baffling silence and mystery in the spiritual world. Men still stand unsatisfied and listen to the mumbling speculations of the philosophers of the world whose ideas about God and man have little more persuasiveness than their intrinsic attractiveness or expediency. And to this day the only place where the voice of God comes in clear and strong through the babel of human speculations is still in the words of Jesus that are shouted down the long corridor of time: *"Amaen! Amaen! Lego soi!"* "Truly, truly, I say to you!"

Yes, we Christians believe that we know with certainty the truths about God and man, which includes what to do with our lives and what to hope for in eternity, because the authority of the man who revealed them was vindicated by God on Easter day. Is it not understandable now why I asserted in the beginning that the resurrection of Jesus Christ is the center pole that holds up the entire tent of the Christian message? We cannot hold onto the truths that were taught by Jesus' tongue unless we also hold onto the truths about authority that were taught by Jesus' life, especially the truth that he was "set forth to be recognized as son of God . . . by his resurrection from the dead."

14. Is There Really a Heaven?

"He ascended into heaven." The Apostles' Creed

"Blessed be the God and Father of our Lord Jesus Christ! By his great mercy we have been born anew to a living hope through the resurrection of Jesus Christ from the dead, and to an inheritance which is imperishable, undefiled, and unfading, kept in heaven for you, who by God's power are guarded through faith for a salvation ready to be revealed in the last time." I Peter 1:3-5

The hope of Heaven has always been one of the fondest hopes that burn in the Christian heart. For Heaven has always meant to us the happy place where man will dwell in the glorious presence of his heavenly Father from everlasting to everlasting. Both the Nicene and the Apostles' creeds have committed Christianity to this hope by affirming that Jesus of Nazareth, after he rose from the dead on the third day, subsequently "ascended into Heaven."

Every Christian turns to a modern examination and evaluation of this doctrine of Heaven with a distressing dread in his heart. For this doctrine is so very precious to all of us that we can hardly bear to think of dying, or even, under many circumstances, of continuing to live, without it. The hope within us begs that this doctrine would still be true, regardless of how much else would be found in error.

So I am happy to put the reader's mind at ease by presenting at the very beginning of this chapter the twofold conclusion of nearly every comprehensive Christian investigation of the doctrine of Heaven today: First, nothing has been discovered through biblical scholarship, through theology or philosophy or the physical sciences, that rules out the existence of the Heaven that is spoken of in the Christian revelation. Second, much has been discovered, however, through biblical scholarship, through theology and philosophy and the physical sciences, that rules out many of the traditional ideas about Heaven that have been held by the people of God through the ages.

The universe, as the ancients imagined it, was but a very small fraction of the size of the awesomely immense universe of which astronomers have informed us today. The men of Jesus' day believed that they lived in a flat, rectangular universe that was only about three or four thousand miles across. This little universe was believed to have three layers, or stories. Heaven was the top story. Earth was the middle story. And Sheol was the bottom story. Earth was the abode of man and the animals. Sheol was a cave under the earth for the souls of the departed dead, and a portion of this cave was a burning furnace for the wicked. Heaven was the central headquarters and living quarters for God and his heavenly family (Ps. 11:4; I Kings 22:19; Job 1:6).

Because the ancients believed that Heaven was just out of reach over their heads, the Bible uses the same words for "sky" and "Heaven," which can sometimes be confusing (Luke 21:33; John 1:32). However, if the ancients would have made a distinction, they would have called the "sky" only that space of probably around fifty thousand feet which they believed existed between the ground and where "Heaven" began.

Furthermore, the fact that Heaven was directly over their heads in the air did not at all imply to the ancients that the furnishings of Heaven were composed of light, ethereal materials that could float up there in the air without support. Rather, the point at which the sky ended and heaven began was believed to be determined by a very hard and solid structure which in the Genesis creation story (1:7) is called the "firmament." The Hebrew word for firmament suggests that the firmament was constructed of beaten metal. From below, the firmament was looked up to men as the vault—or canopy, or roof—of the earth. From above, the firmament was looked down upon by God as the floor of his heavenly abode. Thus the firmament was the separation between the first and second stories of the universe.

The firmament was pictured by the ancients as a shallow bowl-shaped structure that was inverted, or turned upside down, over them, and that was held up at the four corners of the earth where it rested upon four tall mountains called the pillars of Heaven. Rain, snow, hail, frost, and dew were believed to be held in storehouses above the firmament (Job 38:22), from where they were released as God willed through sluices called the windows of Heaven (Gen. 7:11). The sun, moon, and stars were believed to be moving lights that God had installed just under the dome of the firmament to give light to the earth. Sometimes these lights were believed to have personalities (II Kings 17:16).

Above the firmament was the dwelling place of God, who was thought of as having a basically human shape. God was supposed to have built there a glorious palace for himself and his family of sons with his throne at the center of it. God is spoken of as sitting upon the throne and as walking about upon the floor of Heaven (Rev. 4:2; Job 22:14).

Occasionally God is thought of as coming to earth, as in the Genesis creation stories (3:8) where he walks in the garden with Adam and Eve and as in Job's hope (19:25) that on a last day of judgment that sets history right God will descend and stand upon the earth as Job's vindicator. As a rule, however, it was believed that God remained in Heaven. For there was no need for him to come to earth, since he could see and hear and control everything that took place on earth from the celestial height (Ps. 14:2; 18:6; 57:3). If his children were endangered, he could in anger hurl lightning bolts and hailstones down upon his enemies (Ps. 18:13).

According to the Bible stories, it is this Heaven of very solid, earth-like materials from which Jacob saw a ladder let down which angels descended and ascended (Gen. 28:12). It is this Heaven into which Elijah, and probably Enoch too, was carried by a whirlwind (II Kings 2:11; Gen. 5:24). It is this Heaven from which Jesus, the Holy Spirit as a dove, and Peter's sheet let down by four corners were supposed to have descended (John 3:13; Luke 3:22; Acts 10:11). It is this Heaven into which Jesus was supposed to have ascended until obscured by a cloud from the observers' vision (Acts 1:9). It is this Heaven in which Jesus is supposed to be sitting at the right hand of the Father's throne (Heb. 10:12), which is the position that ancient rulers gave to the

151

second in command in their kingdoms. It is this Heaven from which Jesus is supposed to come on the day of judgment, bringing with him the souls of the faithful departed (Acts 1:11; I Thess. 4:14). It is the firmament of this Heaven which on the day of judgment is supposed to roll back like a scroll (Isa. 34:4; Rev. 6:14) as the old sky and earth are dissolved in fire, and a new sky and earth are created in their place (Rev. 21:1). It is from this Heaven that the New Jerusalem built by God is to come down to earth, a walled city of dazzling splendor in which all the resurrected righteous live forever with God himself dwelling in the center of the city as in a second headquarters to give it light and joy and righteous government (Rev. 21, 22).

This biblical picture of Heaven, as simply a more magnificent edition of our material earth, has obviously been disproved by the scientific discoveries of modern man. The first Russian cosmonauts came back to earth as gleeful propagandists, scornfully reporting that they had been out in space and had not seen God or angels or any kind of heavenly furniture. Long before the Russian feat, of course, educated skeptics had been cynically referring to the traditional Christian doctrine of Heaven as mythical "pie in the sky by and by" that had been dreamed up to pacify those who were unhappy with their lot on this earth and those who lacked the courage to face the reality of extinction at death.

So the situation that faces us is that a material, earthlike Heaven which Christians have believed in quite literally is proved to be ancient myth and fable. The Bible which we have for centuries depended upon as the absolute Word of God has been demonstrated to contain a considerable amount of unreliable reports and opinions in this area. Our very confidence in divine revelation at this point appears to be threatened.

How then do we Christians set about salvaging and reconstructing our beloved doctrine of Heaven? Our modern doctrine of Heaven begins, of necessity, with the realization that we must depend upon those parts of the Bible that investigation has proved are reliable sources of divine revelation. Those parts of the Bible which are based merely upon pious human imagination must be acknowledged for what they are and set aside for use only as parables—when they are valid even for this end.

The most reliable biblical report upon which we then proceed to build a twentieth-century doctrine of Heaven is the central doctrine of the resurrection of Jesus of Nazareth. No report of spiritual experiences in the Bible has a more adequate basis than the multiple reports that Jesus' friends and disciples encountered him personally after his death. In fact, had the evidence not seemed powerfully persuasive to great numbers of people in Jesus' own era, the Christian church would not exist today; and history would probably not even have recorded for posterity the name of Jesus of Nazareth.

This report of Jesus' continuing alive after his death as a distinct personality is still just as valid and relevant today as it was two thousand years ago. No amount or type of investigation has been able to refute the reports of the first Christians in this matter as being unfortunate mistakes or deliberate untruths. So today we can declare as confidently as ever, "Jesus is alive!" And this means, of course, that he is alive somewhere, in some kind of special condition, a place and condition which Christians have traditionally designated as Heaven.

Ever since Christian thinkers first began dealing with the fact that the material three-story universe is ancient folklore, they have been thinking of Heaven as an unperceived dimension that is present in all reality. Length, of course, is traditionally considered to be the first dimension, width the second dimension, height the third dimension. And today time is spoken of as the fourth dimension. Heaven, or the realm of unascertainable, unapprehendable spiritual realities, is now frequently spoken of by Christian thinkers as the fifth dimension.

There is no reason today, of course, to locate this fifth dimension above our heads in a limited space in the sky. And we must acknowledge that because of what the heavenly Father has chosen not to reveal to us, we cannot know precisely "where" Heaven is until we arrive "there." But I suspect that, as the fourth dimension of time is present everywhere where the three-dimensional things are present which are involved in time, even so the fifth dimension is everywhere the other four-dimensional things are, which are created and guided from the fifth dimension. In other words, Heaven can be anywhere and even everywhere.

Some sense-bound people scoff immediately at the idea of a spiritual fifth dimension which none of our human senses can verify by any test based on sight, hearing, touch, taste, or smell. But these people can be forced into a more fitting humility by reminding them that even they believe in, and work with, realities such as infrared light, ultraviolet light, X rays, bacteria, protozoa, and chemical reactions which cannot be

153

investigated directly with our physical senses but which can be known only through laboratory instruments.

Our bodily senses are able to experience directly only a limited sector of the great circle of physical reality. We are able to see only certain wave lengths of light, to hear only certain wave lengths of sound, to feel only certain physical matter that presses upon our nerve endings, to taste and to smell only certain chemicals that react upon special oral and nasal nerve endings. The farther man's scientific investigations progress today, the more numerous are these realities in which he is being forced to believe by the aid of laboratory instruments and mathematical computers alone. Thus increasingly modern science is dealing with a dimension that lies beyond sense perception. This dimension many theologians and reverent scientists believe is nothing less than the narthex of Heaven itself.

The idea of a fifth dimension in which the heavenly Father and his self-conscious children live in fellowship is quite consistent with modern understandings of the human soul (or "spirit," "mind," "personality," or whatever we wish to call it). Today our soul is generally viewed as being essentially a complex pattern of electrical charges which in certain respects is different for each individual. This pattern of electrical charges grows in size and complexity throughout life, like the data in a giant electronic computer. Our beliefs, our desires, our habits, and our memories are all part of our pattern of electrical charges.

On earth this electrical soul is maintained by our body, which provides a protective container for it and which sustains it by chemically converting food into electrical energy for its operation. Thus our soul today is viewed—and I think quite reasonably—as an arrangement of physical energy, and not as some mysterious spiritual substance that is opposite to matter. Today everything that exists appears to be reducible to some form of energy. Many thinkers speculate that the heavenly Father's being must be the highest form and the most complex pattern of energy.

Now at death, it is reasoned, the heavenly Father can either transfer our soul—which is this individualized pattern of electrical charges—into another dimension where it continues to be held together and nourished; or the Father can permit our soul simply to disintegrate into its basic parts as a random discharge of electrical particles. Christian thinkers believe that Heaven is the dimension in which the heavenly Father sustains those loving souls that he desires to maintain throughout eternity.

The dimension of Heaven may be like an ocean in which our heavenly Father is the water that directly sustains the souls of his faithful children, much as animal or plant tissue is nurtured while suspended in a bath of chemical nutrients and as a fish is sustained by the sea. Or our heavenly Father may be concentrated in one or more localities in the heavenly dimension. And we may obtain the electrical energy to maintain our mental operations through the energy that radiates throughout Heaven from him, as a photoelectric cell gets its power from the sun even while being separated from the sun by ninety-three million miles.

In either kind of situation our soul might need some kind of container, or body, to hold it together and to provide for locomotion and activity within its environment. This heavenly body, which is what some modern Christian thinkers mean by the terms "resurrection body" and "spiritual body," would also be composed of appropriate energy particles.

This heavenly body would probably be capable of assuming any desired shape. And our personality would probably be active in every part of it. Our recognition of people whom we knew on earth would be through an ability to recognize their personality features rather than their physical features. And the recognition would be even more effective and deep, and our relationships more joyful, than on earth.

As all our present personality activities and earthly ecstasies are ultimately electrical actions and reactions, there is every reason to expect that the heavenly personality activities and ecstasies will be even more full and delightful electrical experiences. We will certainly stand to have greater joys in Heaven than on earth if our entire self, soul and body, is involved there in seeing, hearing, feeling, tasting, smelling, learning, laughing, communing, worshiping, and loving. The electrical basis of our heavenly being, furthermore, does not detract from the personal reality of it, any more than our physical body in this life detracts from our reality as a person.

Of course, we must appreciate that however reasonable and attractive such speculations as these may appear, we cannot place much weight upon them. All that the Christian can say about Heaven with any kind of spiritual certainty is first, that Heaven is where our heavenly Father is forever; second, that Heaven is where Jesus is forever; third, that

Heaven is where all of us who are patterning our lives on the perfect love for our heavenly Father and our brother man that was revealed and urged in Jesus will someday be forever; and fourth, that Heaven, in some foretasteful measure, is where the perfect love of the heavenly Father is present now in our lives and in the world around us.

Christian concern with Heaven is always only coincidentally with its nature and furnishings. Our chief interest in Heaven is that our loving Father is there and that we want to be with him. As an old rural minister two hundred years ago said to his dying parishioner, "Do you hear how the doorknob is being rattled? It's my little boy. He's never been in this room before. And he doesn't know what it's like. But he knows that I'm in here. And he wants to be with me. Heaven is like that. We don't know what it's like either. But we do know that our Father is in there. And we want to be with him."

But then what are we to do with the quite detailed biblical passages about Heaven that belong to the old disproved materialistic three-story universe? We use these passages symbolically whenever their symbolism is accurate. For they still contain much profound and beautiful and useful spiritual meaning.

For instance, if we wish, we may still speak of Heaven as "up" because psychologically we naturally think of something greater than us and our world as higher than ourselves. Certainly our heavenly Father made use of this human tendency in the visions and revelations that he gave to men in olden times. The message in the story of the ascension of Jesus—the "going up"—is precisely this. Whatever the historical accuracy of the story of the ascension, it communicates and proclaims the report that Jesus has gone ahead of us to a superior realm. If we wish, we may also still speak of Heaven as a celestial city with gates of glittering pearl and streets of shining gold, where the air is filled with the melodious music of harps and with the harmonious voices of uncountable choirs singing glory. For this constructing of an imaginary world, by arousing in us a feeling of mystical rapture and exaltation, may help to elevate our thoughts into our heavenly Father's presence in the fifth dimension.

Yes, Heaven has always been, and still is, the greatest Christian hope. And the more I read and reflect upon it, the more I agree with the first letter of Peter where it exults that for us, the heavenly Father's children, there is awaiting "an inheritance which is imperishable, undefiled, and unfading, kept in Heaven."

156

15. Will Jesus Return?

"And sitteth at the right hand of God the Father Almighty; From thence he shall come to judge the quick and the dead." The Apostles' Creed

"Jesus answered, 'My kingship is not of this world.'" John 18:36

One of the most picturesque and constant doctrines of Christianity since the first disciples began testifying about Jesus has been the claim that he will return in heavenly splendor to be the judge of the living and the dead in a great drama of resurrection and judgment. As the Nicene Creed declares it: "And he shall come again with glory, to judge both the quick and the dead; whose kingdom shall have no end." The Apostles' Creed affirms that Jesus now "sitteth at the right hand of God the Father Almighty, from thence he shall come to judge the quick and the dead."

But after two thousand years this claim has still not been fulfilled. And today Christian laymen, as well as Christian scholars, are increasingly concerned to study the earliest Christian documents and, by using the tools and findings of modern historical research, to re-evaluate this ancient dogma of the church.

In order to reduce what would amount to a seminary course in eschatology into one chapter, I shall present the subject of the return of Jesus and the final judgment in a summary outline of fifteen points.

Our beginning point must be located long before the time of Jesus in the history of the Hebrew people. And we must understand that this whole problem is wrapped up in this question: What kind of kingdom is the kingdom of God on earth supposed to be?

First, in dealing with God, Israel learned that God reigns over the world and is all-powerful. One of the main differences between Israel and the majority of the neighboring peoples was that Israel's neighbors felt that their national lives and destinies were merely a part of the natural world around them and that all life, including human life, moved in meaningless cycles. The Israelites, on the other hand, learned by experience, after God had introduced himself to them, that man is more than a part of a meaningless natural order. The Israelites learned that man is a child of the God who has created all things and who determines man's destiny. They saw how God dealt summarily with their enemies, how he raised men up and dashed men down as he saw fit. And whenever the Israelites decided to live as though this all-powerful Creator did not exist, he saw to it that they suffered dire consequences that restored their former awareness. "All the nations are as nothing before him," Isaiah declares (40:17).

Second, in dealing with God, Israel learned that God rewards the kind of human living that meets his requirements and punishes the kind of human living that fails to meet his requirements. Israel discovered not only that God reigned but that he required ethical living and that no man could escape chastisement for unrighteousness or lose the rewards of righteousness. Isaiah speaks for God:

> I make weal and create woe,
> I am the Lord, who do all these things.
> let the earth . . . cause righteousness to spring up. . . .
> Woe to him who strives with his Maker. (45:7-9.)

Third, in dealing with God, Israel learned that God usually acts through the leadership of some individual to deliver the righteous from trouble and to destroy the unrighteous who trouble his people. In a sense, the history of old Israel is the history of a line of heroes: Abraham, Joseph, Moses, Joshua, Barak, Gideon, Samson, Samuel, and David. The writer of Exodus, for instance, tells how God calls Moses: "I have seen the affliction of my people who are in Egypt, and have heard their cry because of their taskmasters; I know their sufferings, and I have come down to deliver them. . . . Come, I will send you to Pharaoh that you may bring forth my people . . . out of Egypt" (3:7-10). David, however, as a prophet, priest, and king, became the final and the highest type of human savior that Israel looked for.

Fourth, in dealing with God, Israel learned that God did not want to live separated from his people but that God desired to live closely in, with, and among his people. God established a special place signifying his presence among the wandering Israelites in that marvelous tent called the Tabernacle, which stood in the center of the camp and shielded the Ark of the Covenant. God also established a special place signifying his presence in the Temple in Jerusalem. God spoke with certain men and informed them that he wanted to dwell deep in the heart of every Israelite. In Leviticus, God says: "I will make my abode among you . . . . And I will walk among you, and will be your God, and you shall be my people" (26:11-12). In Isaiah, God says:

> I dwell in the high and holy place,
>   and also with him who is of a contrite and humble spirit. (57:15.)

Fifth, in dealing with God, the Israelites learned that God desired them to be a nation of priests who would bring a blessing to all nations by eventually bringing all these nations into the same relationship of religious loyalty and fellowship with him. It was only in the golden age prophets that the people of Israel seemed seriously to have realized how God's love longed to flow beyond the borders of their own little country. Isaiah proclaims,

> The Lord has bared his holy arm
>   before the eyes of all the nations;
> and all the ends of the earth shall see
>   the salvation of our God. (52:10.)

Sixth, in all these lessons Israel's prophets began to develop for the people the expectation of a future age when the human perfection that should exist on earth would indeed exist on earth. This future age, which in time became known as the kingdom of God, was to be an age when a particular individual from the family line of King David would lead Israel in a campaign of evangelizing through which all nations and individuals would be brought to know and to accept the lord-

159

ship of God, the laws of God, and the presence of God, in order to establish a universal society where utter peace and prosperity and piety would reign forever.

This future God-picked deliverer gradually became referred to as the Messiah, which means literally "anointed one," or "one appointed by God to do the job." Probably nowhere is this vision so eloquently expressed as in the hopeful words of Isaiah about a young prince in his day:

> For to us a child is born,
>   to us a son is given;
> and the government will be upon his shoulder,
>   and his name will be called
> "Wonderful Counselor, Mighty God,
>   Everlasting Father, Prince of Peace."
> Of the increase of his government and of peace
>   there will be no end,
> upon the throne of David, and over his kingdom,
>   to establish it, and to uphold it
> with justice and with righteousness
>   from this time forth and for evermore. (9:6-7.)

This deliverer, the Messiah, eventually gained as an alternate name the title "Son of man." This very late title seems to have come at least partly from a messianic vision of the prophet Daniel about a heavenly creature who, he says, looked "like a son of man." This human-appearing creature arrived upon the clouds of Heaven and was presented before the throne of God. "And," Daniel continues,

> To him was given dominion
>   and glory and kingdom,
> that all peoples, nations, and languages
>   should serve him;
> his dominion is an everlasting dominion,
>   which shall not pass away,
> and his kingdom one
>   that shall not be destroyed. (7:14.)

This lifted-out phrase "Son of man" becomes a boldly messianic title which, because it occurs in Daniel in such an exalted metaphorical

160

context, can be literalized to imply that the coming Messiah is to be a semidivine creature from Heaven above.

Seventh, in the latest books of the Old Testament this glorious vision of a universal kingdom of God in the hearts and societies of all men became blurred and twisted by lesser men and by terrible historical tragedies that followed the era of the golden age prophets. The great vision of an all-embracing kingdom of God on earth that was painted by the Isaiah school in beautiful poetic metaphors was often interpreted in a woodenly literal manner by the less sophisticated and educated generations that followed. Harsh invaders who devastated the land and its cultural institutions and who decimated and enslaved the population gradually turned the dream of the universal age of piety, peace, and prosperity to bitterness and gall in the minds of many sensitive souls who could only imagine God utterly destroying such oppressor nations.

Under persecution the vengeful imagination of these anguishing post-exilic Israelites often ran riot in a nationalistic reaction. They began to develop all kinds of cataclysmic notions of the form that their longed-for deliverance and the worldwide reign of God would take. Zechariah, for instance, foresees a great battle when all the godless nations would combine to fight against God himself on the hill called the Mount of Olives just east of Jerusalem. But God would descend and stand on the mountain and would split it in two. Then by his power he would destroy those evil kingdoms and armies and reign on earth himself from that day forth (14:1 ff.).

Eighth, with the exception of a brief period under the Maccabee brothers, Israel between the last of the Old Testament books and the time of Jesus was a conquered nation whose severe oppression caused the people to grasp at any hope of deliverance by God's promised anointed one with that desperation with which drowning men clutch for support even at straws. The literature of the intertestamental period, which includes books such as II Esdras, reveals to us that most of the people of Israel, from the very influential Pharisees down to the humble peasants, had a prayer burning in their hearts for God's deliverance— a prayer that often amounted to a national obsession and a pathological fanaticism. And it seems that only a minority of these longing souls thought at all in the metaphorical, poetic, figurative manner of the great golden age prophets. To the average man God's deliverance was to be a very physical, political, military affair in which the Messiah

161

would conquer the world in a bloody fashion by divine power, then judge all evil men and nations, and rule as king forever.

Ninth, when Jesus came on the scene, he was in the unfortunate position of being a leader whose movement had already decided what kind of deliverer he was supposed to be. The crowds who gathered to Jesus were not coming out of idle curiosity or because they had nothing better to do. They had heard that he was the expected deliverer, anointed by God by the hand of John the Baptizer to bring in the rule of God. When Jesus performed a divine sign by inspiring them to bring out their loaves and fishes, they excitedly tried to seize him on the spot and make him messianic king (John 6:15). Simon the Zealot was a disciple, most likely, because he was convinced that Jesus was God's irresistible commander-in-chief for whom the nation was looking (Luke 6:15).

The Jewish and Galilean populations were whipped up into such a fever pitch of messianic expectancy by Jesus' miracle-studded ministry that the result was that Jesus had forced upon him an eschatological "suit of clothes" that he had never wanted to wear. The crowds already had grandiose, earthly messianic interpretations of their own to put on everything that he said about the kingdom of God (Mark 8:31-32; John 4:25; 7:27; 12:34). Even his twelve disciples were sure that they had been chosen to be the new princes of the twelve tribes of Israel (Matt. 18:28). The impatience of some, such as his brothers and John the Baptizer, got out of bounds when they urged him to declare himself and get his program rolling (John 7:3 ff.; 7:19). At least a portion of his followers saw him as a semidivine Son of man (Matt. 13:31).

Tenth, the result was that Jesus' disciples and the early church largely succeeded in interpreting Jesus' messiahship and the kingdom of God in the external terms of what they wanted. The New Testament presents primarily such a concept of the Messiah's kingdom. We can outline the main features of the church's interpretation. However, the New Testament materials do not fit very neatly into the outline because the various strands of tradition differ somewhat in their messianic expectations.

(a) After his resurrection Jesus ascended to the right hand of God in Heaven, which is the position of first in command over all God's forces, so that he now has authority and power over all creation. In Heaven he intercedes for us and guides the church on earth (Luke

22:69; Acts 3:20-21; 7:56; 9:5; Rom. 8:34; Eph. 1:20; 2:18; I Pet. 3:22).

(b) As a prelude to Jesus' return the earth will see great troubles, with unusual happenings in the earth and sky. People will be afraid and will make predictions about Jesus' return. False messiahs will arise and do signs and wonders and lead many people astray (Matt. 24; Mark 13; Luke 17; Acts 2:19).

(c) One of the most significant signs that Jesus is soon to come will be that evil will reach its nadir—that is, its lowest point—with the Antichrist, who will claim to be God and who will collect great armies to rule the world (II Thess. 2:3).

(d) Then at some time known only to the heavenly Father, the sky will suddenly and unexpectedly roll back like a scroll. All the physical elements will melt with fiery heat. And Jesus will descend in dazzling glory with a cry of command, with the trumpet call of the archangel, and with the hosts of shining angels and his irresistible army (Matt. 16:27 ff.; 24; Mark 13:26; 14:62; Luke 17:24; 21:27; John 6:38 ff.; 14:3; Acts 1:11; I Cor. 1:7-8; 11:23 ff.; I Thess. 1:10; 3:13; Phil. 3:20; Col. 3:4; Titus 2:13; Rev. 1:7).

(e) At Jesus' shout the graves will be opened and the dead will rise, and the living will be transformed in the twinkling of an eye. The angels will then separate the evil from the good (Matt. 13:49; 24:31; John 5:25; I Thess. 4:14 ff.; Acts 24:15; I Cor. 15:51).

(f) Jesus will then sit on a throne and judge all men for God. The twelve apostles are somehow also supposed to be on twelve thrones judging the twelve tribes of Israel. Even the evil angels will be judged by men (Matt. 19:28; 25:31; Luke 22:28; John 5:22, 27; 12:40; Acts 10:42; 17:31; Rom. 2:16; 14:11; I Cor. 4:5; 6:2; II Cor. 5:10; II Tim. 4:1).

g) Those who have obeyed God will be caught up into the clouds to join the approaching Messiah. They will enjoy forever a glorious banquet hall and the rest of the Father's large house in a Heaven here on earth (Matt. 8:9; 19:29; 25:43-44; 26:28; Mark 10:29; 14:25; Luke 13:28; 14:14; 18:30 22:16 ff.; Eph. 6:8; I Pet. 5:4).

(h) Those who have not lived righteous, faithful lives will go to burn in unquenchable fire and to be eaten on forever by worms (Matt. 3:12; 10:15; 12:36; 13:30; 25:41 ff.; Luke 10:14 ff.; 12:49; Acts 2:5; II Thess. 1:7 ff.).

(*i*) When the judgment is over, Jesus will then turn all command back over to the heavenly Father (Luke 1:33; I Cor. 15:25).

Eleventh, a very crucial part of this dominant concept in the New Testament is the imminence—or closeness—of Jesus' return to rule and judge. John the Baptizer, for instance, excites the crowds by insisting that the kingdom of Heaven "is at hand"—which means "near enough in time to touch it" (Matt. 3:2). "Even now the ax [of God's judgment] is laid to the root of the [evil life] trees," he declares (Matt. 3:10; Luke 3:9).

Jesus is reported to have told his disciples that he is coming in glory so soon that "Truly, I say to you, there are some standing here who will not taste death before they see the Son of man coming in his kingdom" (Matt. 16:28; Mark 9:1). Again, Jesus is supposed to have described the coming of the Son of man after all the great tribulations and then to have declared: "Truly, I say to you, this generation will not pass away till all these things take place. Heaven and earth will pass away, but my words will not pass away" (Matt. 24:34; Mark 13:30; Luke 17:32). Jesus is supposed to have told his disciples that "In a little while you will see me no more; again a little while, and you will see me" (John 16:16). Jesus is supposed to have made the time of his return appear very short by his statement that "Truly, I say to you, you will not have gone through all the towns of Israel, before the Son of man comes" (Matt. 10:23).

The communistic sharing of goods by the early church, as described by Luke in Acts, was due to the fact that the whole church expected the end very soon. Paul gets the Thessalonian Christians so excited about the coming Day of the Lord in his first letter to them that he must calm them down in the second letter (2:1 ff.). Paul urges the Roman Christians to wake up, for salvation is nearer to them than when they first believed (13:4). He tells the Christian husbands of Corinth to live only in private prayer as though they had no wives at all. For "the appointed time has grown very short," and "the end of the ages has come" (I Cor. 7:29; 10:11). He exhorts the Philippians to discipline themselves. For "the Lord is at hand" (4:5). The writer to the Hebrews exhorts his readers to note that the Day is drawing near (10:25) and that Jesus will not tarry (10:37). James agrees that the coming of the Lord Jesus is at hand (5:8). And Peter warns "The end of all things is at hand" (I Pet. 4:7). John too says "Children, it is the last hour" (I John 2:18). And the writer of John's Revelation ends up with Jesus saying "Surely I am coming soon" (22:20).

Twelfth, the court of time has judged that the early church was wrong about this interpretation of the kingdom of God, simply because the soon-promised end never came at all. An undercurrent of perplexity with this failure of Jesus to return soon, according to expectations, may be noted in the New Testament itself. Paul had trouble with two independent theologians, Hymaneus and Philetus, who, evidently noting the delay of Jesus' return, had reappraised the eschatological expectations of the early church and had decided that the resurrection brought by Jesus was a spiritual and individual resurrection and that it had already begun for all believers (II Tim. 2:18).

The second letter of Peter is very late—about A.D. 130—and tries to counter the worried questions of the church people of that day about Jesus' delay. It was understood that Jesus would return before all the disciples should die and before they had even gone on evangelistic tours through all the towns of Israel. But all the first generation were now dead. And evangelism efforts had spread far and wide. The writer calls these honest doubters "scoffers." "First of all," he says, "you must understand this, that scoffers will come in the last days . . . saying, 'Where is the promise of his coming? For ever since the fathers fell asleep, all things have continued as they were from the beginning of creation.' . . . But do not ignore this one fact, beloved, that with the Lord one day is as a thousand years, and a thousand years as one day. The Lord is not slow about his promise as some count slowness, but is forbearing toward you, not wishing that any should perish" (3:3-4, 8-9). But this fancy act of arbitrarily reversing mathematics for God's own figuring does not satisfy the simple promises of the early church that Jesus was to come back soon.

A similar problem comes up in the Gospel of John where the writer labors to explain that Jesus did not say that John would remain alive until Jesus returned, but that if John were to live until Jesus returned, what business was that of Simon Peter? (21:22-23.) James, too, must counsel patience (5:7). And Matthew must use a parable of Jesus about foolish maidens and a delayed bridegroom with an eschatological interpretation to keep his readers, who are evidently wearied with waiting, expectant (25:1; 24:33).

Thirteenth, Jesus' failure to reappear in glory means that the entire doctrine must be reexamined. Traditionally the church has usually decided in its perplexity that the New Testament writers were correct about the *fact* of Jesus' return but wrong about the *nearness* of it. Or, the church has simply avoided the issue by labeling all the "coming soon" passages as unfathomable mysteries. But today we must more honestly admit that if the New Testament writers could be wrong about the fact of an early return of Jesus, they could also be wrong about the fact of the second coming of Jesus itself. So today there is generally a consensus among biblical scholars and theologians that the second coming of Jesus was an erroneous doctrine of the early church, that either Jesus or—much more likely—the disciples alone were very wrong about the kind of messiahship that Jesus was intended by the heavenly Father to have.

The four Gospels, as was explained earlier, are scrapbooks that were gathered together from various written and oral sources some thirty to sixty years after Jesus' death. A large part of the material is authentic words and deeds of Jesus. Some of it, however, is exaggeration, or even legend. And to distinguish when an item is an actual saying of Jesus rather than an interpretation by the first Christians of what Jesus said is the crucial problem.

Now in this matter of evaluating the eschatological materials in the Gospels, the scholars divide into two basic camps. One camp—following Albert Schweitzer—believes that Jesus himself accepted the popular messianic expectations of the day and hence believed in his glorious return. It was none other than Jesus himself, therefore, who so excited his disciples about it. Consequently, the blame for being wrong must be laid upon Jesus.

However, I—and a great host of other interpreters—cannot go along with this school because we believe that their interpretation is based on a rather hasty examination of the Gospels that overlooks a sizable number of New Testament passages where a different concept of the kingdom of God shines through, a different concept that is almost covered up by the popular ideas of the first century. This different eschatology, which breaks through only here and there, is more true to the depth of love and spirituality in Jesus' teachings and actions than is the other and is in essence quite contradictory to it.

In these occasional passages Jesus seems to prove that he alone in his day understood the true messianic insights of the golden age prophets, and hence that he alone was qualified to be God's anointed one. His concept of the kingdom of God can be quite clearly reconstructed,

I believe, from an analysis of these salient passages. Furthermore, the fact that Jesus could be quite independent in his biblical interpretation and that we should expect unusual insights from him is well demonstrated on two forensic occasions when he turns the literalistic Old Testament interpretations of the hot-blooded messianic scribes of his day into ridiculous contradictions (Matt. 22:43 ff.; John 10:34).

Fourteenth, an examination of the minor contradictory eschatological theme that runs through the Gospels reveals that Jesus promoted an inner spiritual kingdom of God that exists here and now, that Jesus believed judgment is taking place here and now, and that eternal life begins here and now and continues after physical death through all eternity. Let us look at some of these passages that bear witness to what appears most likely to have been Jesus' true doctrine of the kingdom of God.

(a) Jesus, standing before Pilate, says: "My kingship is not of this world; if my kingship were of this world, my servants would fight" (John 18:36). This statement directly contradicts the worldly expectations of the major New Testament concept.

(b) Jesus' refusal to permit the crowd to make him king shows that he does not intend worldly kingship (John 6:15).

(c) Jesus' declaration to the twelve disciples that the greatest person in the kingdom of Heaven was the one who became like a little child directly contradicted the proud self-images of these men who were convinced that they had been chosen to be judges of the twelve tribes of Israel in the triumphant messianic kingdom (Matt. 18:4).

(d) Jesus' announcement to the twelve that he must suffer and die went directly contrary to their idea of the Messiah who was to triumph irresistibly over all earthly opponents (Matt. 16:21 ff.).

(e) Jesus' promise to those who suffer persecution for the faith in this life that your reward "is great in heaven" contradicts the expected reward in this life that his supporters expected in the messianic kingdom (Matt. 5:12; Mark 10:29-30).

(f) Jesus' reply to the Sadducees that only some people are accounted worthy to attain resurrection from the dead contradicts the belief that there will be a resurrection of both the evil and the good and an eternal punishment for the wicked (Luke 20:35).

(g) Jesus' promise to the thief on the cross, "Today you will be with me in Paradise," contradicts the idea of a long wait in sleep or in a shadowy underworld until a great resurrection (Luke 23:43).

(*h*) Jesus' reply to the Sadducees that the resurrected souls are like the angels in Heaven who have no need of physical love and marriage contradicts the idea that after the resurrection there will be physical eating and drinking with the Messiah in an earthly banquet hall in the Father's house (Luke 20:36).

(*i*) Jesus' claim that the hour "now is, when the dead will hear the voice of the Son of God, and . . . live" contradicts the idea that there will be a spiritual resurrection only after the death of the body and also implies that when a man truly comes to believe in the Word of God that comes through Jesus, at that very moment he becomes spiritually resurrected (John 5:25).

(*j*) Jesus' assertion that the man who believes in him has eternal life now (John 6:47) and that he himself is the resurrection and the life and that the man who lives and believes in him shall never die (John 11:25-26) strengthens the idea that the resurrection is a spiritual rebirth that takes place in this life and that simply continues on in another state after bodily death.

(*k*) Jesus' reply to the Pharisees who wanted to know the signs that would herald the coming of God's kingdom is "The kingdom of God is not coming with signs to be observed; nor will they say, 'Lo, here it is!' or 'There!' for behold, the kingdom of God is in the midst of you" (Luke 17:20-21). The kingdom of God is a spiritual kingdom, Jesus is saying, invisible here and now wherever people acknowledge the rule of God in their hearts. This crucial passage contradicts all the involved sign information that is given about the supposed end of the world in the Gospels and the epistles. The fact that Matthew, Mark, and Luke all organize their end-of-the-world materials differently shows how confused even the Gospel writers were about much of their dominant theme messianic material (Matt. 21; Mark 13; Luke 17; 21).

(*l*) Jesus' claim that his healing of diseases by the power of God is testimony that the kingdom of God has come among the Hebrews is more evidence that the kingdom of God does not require the opening of Heaven and visible thrones and fires (Matt. 12:28).

(*m*) Jesus' encouragement "Lo, I am with you always, to the close of the age" is a claim to be able to guide his church in some invisible or symbolic way from the inner spiritual dimension and makes his visible presence here on earth unnecessary (Matt. 28:20).

(*n*) Jesus' commissioning of his church to spread the good news of God's love implies a long-range program that contradicts the statements that he is returning soon. He tells the twelve disciples in Matthew 28:19 and in Luke 24:47 to make disciples of all nations, which is a lot of people in a lot of far-off places. He orders the disciples in Acts 1:8 to be his witnesses in Jerusalem and Judea and Samaria and to the ends of the earth, which contradicts the statement that he would return before they finished preaching in all the towns of Israel. He sends Paul to the Gentiles (Acts 26:17) and urges Peter to go to them also (Acts 10:28). None of these commissions harmonizes with statements about a return of the Son of man in glory within one generation.

(o) Jesus' insistence (John 12:47) that he did not come to judge the world but to save the world contradicts his purported statement (Luke 12:49) that he came to cast fire on the earth and wished that it were already kindled.

(p) Jesus' statement that the wicked human branches are thrown into the fire and consumed—or burned up—by his Father the vinedresser contradicts the idea of an eternal burning in Hell, or of Jesus personally carrying out the judgment (John 15:1-2).

(q) Jesus' statement that his message itself will be the judge of man on the last day contradicts the idea that he will personally sit as the judge of all (John 12:48).

(r) Jesus' parable that the kingdom of Heaven is like yeast that slowly permeates dough implies that God's kingdom will grow and spread quietly until it has filled the earth (Matt. 13:33).

(s) And finally, John the Baptizer's doubt about Jesus being the promised Messiah that moved John to send some of his disciples to ask Jesus "Are you he who is to come, or shall we look for another?" is evidence that Jesus was not acting like the Messiah people were looking for. Jesus' reply to John's disciples that he was the Messiah because he was fulfilling Isaiah's prophecy that the blind see, the deaf hear, the lame walk, and the "poor have good news preached to them" demonstrates the spiritual and peaceful and inner nature of the kingdom of God that Jesus was anointed to advance (Luke 7:20).

These passages are sufficient to indicate to me and to many other interpreters that Jesus' true message about the kingdom of God and judgment was almost completely covered up by the fanatical force of the messianic theology that was on the scene when Jesus arrived. Jesus believed that he was commissioned to lead men and women into the kingdom of God that is being established in that on-moving dimension called the here and now. Jesus knew that wherever and whenever men and women give their hearts to the heavenly Father, that there and then is the kingdom of God.

Jesus believed that our every thought and word and deed are being judged right now, because our every action evokes a positive or negative divine reaction that leaves us changed emotionally, socially, and physically. Jesus believed that the great judgment is taking place right now and at every moment in history as the thousands of people who die every day pass in an unending stream before the eternal Father into the destination for which their kind of living with God and man has prepared them. Jesus believed that those who give their hearts to the God of love begin that eternal life right now and that those who persist in rebelling against God's rule of love which continues on beautifully forever will be punished at death in a destruction that ends in their nonexistence, or else will be punished at death in a measure necessary for their conversion and restoration.

Fifteenth, even in this internal concept of the kingdom of God that is a minor theme in the Gospels, the truth in the major theme of an external kingdom of God is still preserved symbolically. After his death Jesus has indeed returned among us in greater glory than ever. For every passing generation of history bears witness that the revelation of God's truth that he brought is the secret to noble and stable and fulfilled living. Jesus is also the great judge, in a symbolic sense, because we are all being judged according to our active acceptance of the truth of God that he revealed. And we too are assisting him in his judicial work. For the church in every age is to prove by its spiritual and moral pronouncements and by its rebukes and encouragements that it is the most valuable court for the guiding of human civilization. History always carries out the church's correct verdicts upon individuals and groups and nations and upon whole generations that resist the wise and loving rule of God.

Yes, the Nicene Creed is at least very correct in a metaphorical way when it declares that "he shall come again with glory to judge both the quick and the dead; whose kingdom shall have no end." And all of us Christians would be well advised to cease sitting around on our hands waiting for a kind of external kingdom of God that apparently never will come in this life. Rather, we should be up and about as diligent citizens of the present internal kingdom of God in which we are being prepared and judged for an eternity in fellowship with our Lord Jesus, who declared, "My kingship is not of this world."

Section V: SANCTIFICATION

16. What Is the Holy Spirit?

"I believe in the Holy Ghost." The Apostles' Creed

"Be aglow with the Spirit." Romans 12:11

All of us are familiar with the fact that the Christian church has declared its belief in the Holy Spirit in those words of the Apostles' Creed which say "I believe in the Holy Ghost." All of us are familiar, as well, with the church's traditional yearly observance of that first Christian Pentecost when the Holy Spirit reportedly broke out among the disciples of the risen Christ with a rushing mighty wind, with dancing tongues of fire, and with eloquent preaching in foreign languages. Today the Christian church believes just as strongly as ever in the Holy Spirit. This chapter is an effort to consider the Holy Spirit in the light of an ever growing doctrinal consensus on the matter.

We shall begin by asking "What is the Holy Spirit?" The term "Holy Spirit" or "Spirit of God" is used two ways in the Bible. One way is distinctly personal. The other way is comparatively impersonal. In the personal sense, the Holy Spirit is simply *God the Father at work in the world*. In the impersonal sense, the Holy Spirit is *the observed power of God at work in the world*. The term "Holy Spirit" whenever it is used always encompasses to some extent both the personal and the impersonal senses. But one sense or the other is always dominant.

171

Now regardless of which sense is used, biblical talk about the Holy Spirit is always talk about something that is *taking place in the world.* Not all our "God talk" is concerned with this area. For instance, when we Christians address the deity personally in prayer as his children, we call him "Father," just as Jesus taught us to do. And we do not imagine him doing anything but attentively listening to us while we talk with him. We Christians also like to discuss the deity in an abstract way, as theologians so often do. We like to talk about him, that is, about his nature. When we desire to talk about the deity in this manner, we call him "God."

But there are those other occasions when we do not want to talk about the deity either personally as children or only abstractly as theologians, but when we want to talk more concretely about him as historians do. We want to discuss what the deity has done in human history yesterday and today. We want to speak of what he has done in and around men in a down-to-earth, practical way. We want to speak in terms of our observations, of our sense perceptions, of how God has actually inspired and moved men. For this purpose we call the deity "Holy Spirit." If we are primarily concerned with the Holy Spirit as the One who is doing things in the world, we will speak of the Spirit as "he" or "him." But if we are primarily concerned with the Holy Spirit's powerful effects that we have observed among us, then we may refer to the Holy Spirit in the impersonal neuter gender as "it."

All these distinctions that we make in speaking to, or about, the deity each one of us makes in everyday life. When I converse with the wonderful lady I live with, for instance, I address her as "Rossina." When I discuss her abstractly with another person, I refer to her as "my wife." When I smell the aroma of cooking in the kitchen, I talk personally about "my cook," or I think impersonally about "the cooking." Thus I call out "Rossina," just as I pray "Father." I talk about "my wife," just as I talk about "God." I talk personally about "my cook," just as I talk personally about the "Holy Spirit" as "he." And I talk impersonally about "the cooking," just as I talk impersonally about the effects of the "Holy Spirit" upon man as "it." In each case these distinctions are being made about a single, unified subject.

The early children of God seem to have been thinking with just these distinctions when they labeled the work of God in the world the "Spirit of God" or the "Holy Spirit." For in both the Hebrew and the Greek

172

languages the word "spirit" (*ruach, pneuma*) is the same word as the word for wind and the word for breath (Gen. 2:7). To the early Israelites wind, breath, and spirit were all the same thing. They thought of the wind as literally the breath of God, a thought that still has great poetic beauty today.

Now the wind, which was viewed of old as God's very breath or spirit, is certainly something that is very much at work in the world around us. We can see the wind tossing the trees and lining up the waves on the sea. We can feel the wind cooling our brow or blinding our eyes with dust. And so, since the early children of God believed that the wind was God's spirit or breath, when they spoke of the Spirit of God, they always were referring to something that was happening right here in the world.

In accord with the ancient outlook, Jesus and his disciples also thought of the Spirit of God in either the personal or impersonal sense as God active in the world of man. If we compare Matthew 12:28 and Luke 11:20, for instance, we discover that in one passage Jesus is reported as saying that he was casting out demons by the "Spirit of God," while in the other passage he is reported as saying that he was casting out demons by the "finger of God." This interchange of the synonymous terms "Spirit of God" and "finger of God" shows that the evangelists were thinking here of the Spirit of God primarily in the impersonal sense of the power of God that is at work in the world, since it is with our hands and fingers that we do work (Exod. 8:14, 31:18).

In the Gospel of John, however, the Holy Spirit is called "Counselor." And this Counselor is referred to as "he" (14:16-17). The Fourth Evangelist is obviously thinking of the Holy Spirit in the personal sense of God himself at work in the world. (See also Isa. 40:3; John 4:24, Eph. 4:30.)

The chief historical problem in Christian theology with regard to understanding the Holy Spirit has been a failure to remember that the personality of the Holy Spirit is the personality of God the Father himself, and not another different and distinct personality. Many early Christian thinkers could perceive the Holy Spirit in action around them and knew that it was the power of God. They also heard this powerful action credited to a personal being called the "Holy Spirit of God." They also were familiar with the Gospel of John in which

173

poetic passages spoke about the "Counselor" who would be sent to the followers of Jesus (14:26).

It seems, consequently, that the early Christians reasoned that since "sending" requires one person directing another person to go somewhere, the Holy Spirit must be a separate personality from God the Father who sends "him." And if this is true, then God is not really one simple being at all. Rather, in a sense two god personalities are operating in a holy kind of eternal Siamese-twin corporation. Then when we add in the personified Logos as the eternal Son of God, we have the complete Siamese-triplets deity of traditional trinitarian theology. This structure parallels the Greek philosophical theology with its trinity composed of the Realm of Ideas, the Logos, and the Demiurge. Together they constitute the biblical and secular background of the interpretation in the Nicene Creed which says that the Holy Spirit is the "Lord and Giver of life, who proceedeth from the Father and the Son, Who with the Father and the Son together is worshiped and glorified, Who spake by the prophets." For the Holy Spirit to proceed from the Father and the Son means, in its effect, that the Spirit stands out from them so as to be close to us in the world.

The mistake here seems to have been that many of the delegates to the Council of Nicaea in A.D. 325 did not understand the degree to which the Gospel of John had been cast in poetic metaphors and altered by later editors. Also, if they had questioned the Greek philosophical theology of their day and been guided by the other New Testament books, which are all more literal and less poetical than the Gospel of John, they probably would not have considered the personality of the Holy Spirit as something other than the personality of God the Father himself. Paul seems to anticipate this problem of deciding whether the personality of the Holy Spirit is a distinct personality or not when he asserts in II Corinthians 3:17 that "the Lord is the Spirit." He is answering this question in the negative.

As the contemporary Christian church comes increasingly to understand that the Holy Spirit is not a separate personality, we are realizing that we must be careful how we use some of the most beloved hymns and prayers of the church which address God as "O Holy Spirit" or as "Spirit of God." God is always most fully and adequately addressed as "Father," as Jesus taught us to do. Addresses such as "O Holy Spirit" are not quite as adequate and can be misleading if we fail to remember that we are not praying to a third god, or divine personality, who is distinct from the Father, but that we are praying to the Father himself in a special poetic manner. For the Holy Spirit is simply God the Father at work in the world.

We want to ask second, "What precisely does the Holy Spirit of the Father do? What is the nature of God's work in the world?" Certainly the on-going creating and sustaining of the physical universe is part of the Holy Spirit activity of God. But the part of the Holy Spirit activity of God that most concerns us is God's personal dealings with the human race.

Throughout the Bible we hear of God's work with men and in men. In the Old Testament, for instance, the Spirit of God comes upon Samson and fills him with irresistible strength (Judg. 14:6, 19; 15:14). The Spirit of God gives wisdom to the judges and the kings (Judg. 3:10; 6:34; 11:29; II Sam. 11:6; 16:13). The Spirit of God gives the prophets the ability to foretell the future and to know God's way and God's will for individuals and for the nation (Gen. 41:38; II Sam. 23:2; Mic. 3:8; Isa. 48:16; 61:1; Ezek. 11:5). In the New Testament the Spirit of God descends upon Jesus after his baptism (Mark 1:10). Jesus casts out demons by the Spirit of God (Mark 5:1 ff.). The Holy Spirit breaks out with ecstatic power on the day of Pentecost and frequently afterward (Acts 2:1 ff.; 10:44). The Holy Spirit continually inspires and encourages individuals, such as Peter and Stephen, Paul and Barnabas (Acts 4:8; 7:55; 11:24). Thus the entire Bible testifies to the action of the Holy Spirit upon men.

But what is the nature of this divine action? Does God flood into a man's soul and take him over, as we put a bit and bridle on a horse and take over control of the horse, or as we manipulate gears in the operation of a machine? Is man spiritually, as Luther so graphically described it, a docile donkey ridden either by God or by the devil?

Many Christians have believed that this is the case. They have believed that man's will is enslaved either to the will of God or to the will of evil forces. These Christians have believed that all men are spiritually helpless. They have believed that if a man is to be saved as God's child, God must decide to take over totally that man's personality and then give him a new soul and heart. The man is supposed to be able to do nothing in the process. He is simply acted upon, as lifeless, passive clay is molded into a form by the sculptor. It is no wonder that Christians who believe in such a conception of the Holy Spirit tend to excuse their small faith and their trifling good works in a fatalistic manner as all directly God's fault. They spiritually just stand around waiting for God to do everything. And God just does *not* do everything!

There are, we must observe, a few portions of the Bible that encourage this fatalistic kind of thinking, which was generally accepted by the theologians of the Pharisees (Exod. 7:3 versus 8:15; Matt. 13:11; Eph. 1:4 ff.). But the overwhelming proportion of biblical testimony always speaks to man as though he were a free moral and spiritual agent who may call upon God or not call upon God as he desires, and who always keeps full control of his own willpower in his experiences with God's Spirit.

The personal title "Counselor," for instance, which the evangelist John gives to the Holy Spirit, is important evidence of the fact that man does retain control over his own willpower. The Greek word which is translated "Counselor" is *paraclete,* which literally means "one who is called alongside." Certainly one who is called alongside would be a helper of our willpower in some manner rather than a ruler of our willpower. For a ruler would be one who is called down upon us, instead of alongside us.

The other biblical reports of the Holy Spirit activities of God are quite consistent with John's idea of one who is called alongside us. Paul, for instance, thinks of the Holy Spirit as a divine assistant to human effort when he declares that "the Spirit helps us in our weakness" to pray "with sighs too deep for words" (Rom. 8:26). Again, Paul desires that God would augment the natural strength of the Ephesians when he prays that God "may grant you to be strengthened . . . through his Spirit in the inner man" (3:16). In these two instances Paul is not quite consistent with his belief in divine determinism.

Jesus himself never cast out demons or healed anyone by the Spirit of God unless faith was present, that is, unless the proper responsible person had made a personal decision for God on his own. Thus the help of God's Spirit was always conditional upon the correct action of a human will.

The father of the epileptic boy, for example, wanted Jesus to heal his son. And he cast all responsibility upon God's representative Jesus, by saying: "If you can do anything, have pity on us and help us." But Jesus knew that the boy's father had to be spiritually involved in the work of healing. Jesus knew that God did not want to do everything

176

for the man by himself, but that God wanted to work in cooperation with the effort of that human soul to believe and pray and hope. So Jesus retorted "If you can! All things are possible to him who believes." The father then realized that God was forcing him to do his part and to take the leap of faith before God would act to heal. So the anguished man summoned up his spiritual will and jumped Godward, blurting out: "I believe; help my unbelief!" (Mark 9:22 ff.).

Again, Jesus is reported to have been unable to do any mighty works in Nazareth "because of their unbelief" (Matt. 13:58). And there is nowhere a report that he miraculously healed a single person by the Spirit of God who held to a wicked or unbelieving will.

In the Bible man simply is required to do his part before God's Holy Spirit will assist him. What Christians call "God's unmerited grace" is God's coming to us sinful men with the good news that we can be forgiven and accepted into the power-filled, transforming, joy-bringing family of God—if we want it. But God's grace stops there, unless we believe his messengers, unless we decide to change our manner of living, unless we give our hearts and lives to him, and unless we petition him for help and guidance. This is our required part, and the condition laid upon us for receiving the Holy Spirit activity of God in meeting our needs. If God were to overpower our self-conscious free will, which is the very essence and core of our personhood, by manipulating us as psychological robots who are required to take no independent action, we would cease to exist as true persons.

We must not be misled, furthermore, by those special occasions when the Spirit of God possesses a man ecstatically in the biblical accounts, as when the Spirit of God sweeps up King Saul into a prophesying frenzy (I Sam. 10:10) and when the Holy Spirit breaks out on Pentecost in the speaking of foreign languages. Those disciples of Jesus in the upper room were not surprised by the coming of the Holy Spirit, as though some alien power had sneaked up on them and captured them unawares. Those disciples had been gathering daily and devoting themselves to prayer, Luke reports, ever since Jesus had first appeared after his crucifixion (Acts 1:14). Part of what they had possibly been praying for was the great outpouring of the Holy Spirit that had been promised for hundreds of years, and of which Jesus had likely spoken (Acts 1:8; John 12:28-32). Thus the Pentecost outpouring of the spirit was simply God "coming alongside" his people to uplift them

177

as he had promised, since they were doing their part to qualify for this ecstasy by believing, desiring, and seeking.

Furthermore, even ecstatic Spirit possession does not necessarily mean that we are any less ourselves or that we are transformed momentarily into some kind of holy maniac. People who have experienced Holy Spirit possession in its various forms will tell you that they have never felt so gloriously themselves as on those occasions. They are more in contact with reality than ever—not less.

By way of illustration, on a purely physical level alcohol has the same effect upon many singers as the Holy Spirit has upon the soul of the Christian. Some great singers, such as Caruso, have often been unable to sing superbly until their vocal cords have been "loosened," or stimulated, with a small amount of alcohol. The alcohol on these occasions does not diminish them as persons or as singers. Rather, they can only really become their famous selves by its assistance.

The fact that true Holy Spirit possession makes people more sane rather than less sane is the biblical test for whether the spirit that possesses a person is the Holy Spirit or an unholy spirit. Paul reminds the Corinthians, who had gone overboard on wanting ecstatic experiences of the Holy Spirit, that God is not a God of confusion but of peace (I Cor. 14:33), that he does not want visitors to think the Christian congregation has gone mad (14:23), and that they can indeed control themselves because "the spirits of prophets are subject to prophets" (14:32; I Thess. 5:19 ff.).

Even the case of mighty Samson was probably not different. Samson was brought up by godly Israelite parents (Judg. 13:22). He had been trained as a Nazarite, a member of a special group of religious ascetics (13:7). That his will was obedient to God is evidenced by the fact that he did not want his hair to be cut, since this would be breaking his Nazarite vow, and by the fact that at the end he prayed to God for the return of his strength for just one more time (16:4 ff., 28 ff.). That Samson was rational under the influence of the Spirit is shown in his having the presence of mind to strip the Philistines he had killed to pay off a lost bet (14:19).

When the Spirit of God came upon Samson so that he became so phenomally strong, what evidently took place was that somehow God reached into that primitive recess of the brain where the controls lie for our great prehuman physical powers and released those powers.

These powers still lie dormant in all of us, as anyone knows who has had contact with hypnotism or who has seen someone go berserk.

Yes, the Holy Spirit guides our efforts, augments our efforts, inspires our efforts, develops our efforts, makes way in the situation for our efforts to be successful. But the Holy Spirit does not make our decision for us and does not take from us the control of our own person.

Finally, each Christian wants to ask himself: "What does the doctrine of the Holy Spirit mean to me personally?" First of all, the doctrine of the Holy Spirit means to us that *God is not far from each one of us*. The fact that God has been so close to us in the world that men have spoken of his activities as happenings as close to them as the wind is a comfort to us who often feel so alone in the world.

Second, the doctrine of the Holy Spirit means to us that *there is eternal life only for those who have close fellowship with the Father*. Contact with the Holy Spirit is essential to salvation. Jesus says in the Gospel of John that "unless one is born of water [that is, of the repentance signified in baptism] and the Spirit, he cannot enter the kingdom of God" (John 3:5). By being "born of the Spirit," Jesus means setting out on a new path in life in a fellowship with God in which we constantly depend upon him and receive his spiritual aid in such a manner that we become ever more godlike. If we cannot find the Holy Spirit's sanctifying (that is, "holy-fying") effects in our lives, perhaps we had better change our ways before life's day is done! The life of faith is the life that is lived in dependence upon, and in cooperation with, God's spiritual aid, in order to meet his goals and demands. God does not seem to have offered anyone a solo salvation!

Third, the doctrine of the Holy Spirit means to us that *human initiative is necessary if we are to be saved*. God's Spirit constantly stands ready to instruct, to guide, to command, to encourage, to comfort, to inspire, to plead, to cajole, even to throw down barriers in front of us. But after we hear about God's offering of his fellowship, he does not draw near to us in power until we make our decision for him and draw near to him in earnest supplication for his presence and power (James 4:8). The Spirit of God does not operate in a vacuum. He is active only in the man who is actively doing his part in prayer, in Bible study, in worship, in spiritual meditation and discussion, and in holy works in the world around him.

Yes, the doctrine of the Holy Spirit means to Christians that God is near, that there is salvation only for those who live in close fellowship with him, and that the responsibility for initiating that fellowship is ours, after we have heard his gracious invitation and promises. Is this not why Paul could exhort us—as though it were indeed within our own power—to "Be aglow with the Spirit"?

17. What Is the Value of the Church?

"And I believe one Holy Catholic and Apostolic Church." The Nicene Creed

"And let us consider how to stir up one another to love and good works, not neglecting to meet together, as is the habit of some, but encouraging one another." Hebrews 10:24-25

There has never been any complete Christianity without the church. For without the church there cannot be any complete Christianity. It is this conviction that underlies the declaration about the church in the two chief creeds of Christendom. In the more original wording the Apostles' Creed affirms: "I believe in . . . the Holy Catholic Church." The Nicene Creed declares somewhat more fully, "I believe [in] one Holy Catholic and Apostolic Church."

Today, however, there are a number of critics within and without the church who assert that the church is not essential to Christianity but that Christianity should be individualized and unorganized. These critics attempt to demonstrate that the church is a burden rather than a blessing to Christianity by reading off a long catalog of blunders that have been made by the churches in the name of Christ. Some of these critics even assert that Jesus probably never intended to set up any kind of institution and that the church was entirely the idea of his followers.

But I—and many other churchmen—do believe that Jesus himself was the prime mover behind the organization of the church. I believe, for instance, that there is a true historical core of organizational interest on Jesus' part in his declaration to Simon Peter (Matt. 16:18): "I tell you, you are Peter, and on this rock I will build my church, and the gates of Hades shall not prevail against it." I believe also that there is a true historical core of organizational interest on Jesus' part in the Gospel reports of his calling and sending forth the apostles (Matt. 4:18 ff.; 10:1 ff.; 28:16 ff.; Luke 24:46 ff.; John 20:21 ff.). It is simply not reasonable to suppose that a man who believed himself to be God's Messiah, with God's own message for all the world, would fail to set up some social machinery to ensure the propagation of God's message.

But even if the improbable were true and Jesus had not been the one responsible for establishing the church, it would still make no great difference. For, if Jesus' mission were to fulfill its God-ordained purposes, then Jesus' very first disciples would have had to organize the church if he had not already done so. They would have had to organize the church simply because it is a practical necessity in the fulfillment of Jesus' mission.

In this chapter I shall deal with the essentiality of the Church under five points, the first point being the most important and the following points being largely subpoints of the first one.

First, *the church as an institution is essential because it is the earthly goal of the divinely given ideal of the family of God which Jesus proclaimed.* Historians have observed that great ideals become social realities only when they succeed in becoming embodied in an institution.

Consider, for example, patriotism and knowledge. The ideal of patriotism becomes a social reality only when men who wish to protect their country bind themselves together in a military organization. Patriotism without organization means defeat at the hands of the enemy. This is the reason we have military institutions such as the Army, the Navy, the Marine Corps, and the Air Force. The ideal of knowledge also becomes a social reality when men who wish to preserve and expand human knowledge set up educational and research organizations. Except for the practical knowledge for primitive living, knowledge that is not supported by an organization is lost almost as soon as it is discovered, and hence cannot lead on to greater knowledge. This is the reason that our civilization has established institutions such as the school systems, libraries, research institutes, and professional associations.

The same is true of the divinely revealed ideal of the family of God which it was Jesus' mission to make a social reality. For until Jesus organized the church, the ideal of the family of God on earth was nothing more than a desirable possibility. The ideal of the family of God took "flesh and blood" reality only when the ideal had given birth to this institution which we call the church. Thus the church is not something incidental and troublesome that occurred merely because Jesus and his disciples were the children of a culture with an institutional mentality. Rather, the church is nothing less than the message of Jesus about the family of God put into social practice.

We can understand this fact more fully when we examine Jesus' central ideal of the family of God. The three Synoptic Gospels report that, when Jesus went forth preaching at the beginning of his ministry, he went forth preaching the "kingdom of God" or the "kingdom of Heaven" (Matt. 4:17; Mark 1:15; Luke 4:43). Jesus' announcement that "the kingdom of Heaven is nearby" or that "the kingdom of God is nearby" is exactly the same announcement that had been used by his forerunner John the Baptizer. But Jesus in his ministry gradually filled these words with a meaning that was quite different from John's.

When John the Baptizer pictured the kingdom of God in which the Messiah was God's commissioned leader, John pictured God exactly as Isaiah had done and exactly as all the other religious leaders had pictured God during the second stage of Israel's theological development. For John the Baptizer, as for Isaiah, God was not a close and comfortable person with whom to consort. Rather, God was the Holy and Glorious One who sat upon a throne, high and lifted up, and before whom even the archangels hid their feet and their faces (Isa. 6:1 ff.). To the mind of Jesus' forerunner, therefore, men should quake in fear at the possibility of the presence or imminent appearance of this God.

But as we read the Gospels, we find that Jesus pictured God quite differently. Jesus saw not righteousness but love as the proper category in which to describe the central reality in God. Jesus saw God's creation, preservation, and deliverance of man purely as products of God's love. Love so utterly filled up the picture frame of reality for Jesus that he could define the perfect life for man, who is created in

183

the image of God, only as a life of perfect love that reflects God's perfect love. "You . . . must be perfect [in your love]," he declared, "even as your heavenly Father is perfect" (Matt. 5:48). The two greatest commandments, and actually, because of their inclusiveness, the only two commandments for man, Jesus asserted, were "You shall love the Lord your God with all your being," and "you shall love your neighbor as yourself." Jesus' understanding of the love of God transformed the Old Testament's divine exalted King into the most loving and caring and close of all fathers. Jesus taught his disciples to address God in prayer neither as "O King," nor even as "O God," but warmly and affectionately as "Our Father," or simply as "Father" (Matt. 6:9; Luke 11:2).

Yes, Jesus so thoroughly transformed the Old Testament concept of God that the phrase "kingdom of God," which is often used to sum up his message, would better be changed to "family of God" in order to communicate his meaning more accurately. This family of God, like our human families, includes both parent and siblings. Our heavenly Father is the parent. Our fellow men and fellow women are the siblings, that is, the brothers and sisters. In the last century or so the parenthood of God and siblinghood of man have generally been expressed in the phrase "the Fatherhood of God and the brotherhood of man." This phrase is quite good in that it sums up the two great commandments together with Jesus' teaching about the love of the heavenly Father. But the phrase is also seriously handicapped because it does not adequately signify the *family* relationship between God and his people—which is the very essence of the church.

I have heard men speak in glowing terms about the Fatherhood of God and the brotherhood of man who are not even members of the Christian church. These men believe that they have adequately accepted the truth in the message of Jesus purely on the basis of their childlike trust in the Father and their compassion toward all the people they meet. Their religiosity is an individualistic piety that they nurture between themselves and God alone, and perhaps also with a few other persons who share their thoughts. They see no need for any formal religious organization. But these individualists, I feel, have not completely comprehended the message of Jesus. The Fatherhood of God and the brotherhood of man are not truly realized until they are enjoyed simultaneously in the family of God.

In a sense, we could say that parenthood is not really parenthood except when the parents are in contact with their children. In the same sense childhood is not really childhood except when the children are in contact with the parents. And siblinghood is not really siblinghood except when the brothers and sisters are in contact with each other and when the parents who make their sibling relationship possible are also present. Furthermore, parenthood, childhood, and siblinghood are always the strongest where the whole family, which makes these relationships possible, comes together frequently and does things together.

So it is with the family of God. The heavenly Father knows that his parenthood and our siblinghood are completed realities only within the family of God. He knows also that these realities are preserved only through fellowship that maintains family ties. Hence he is not satisfied to fellowship with his children only separately, or with one or two at a time in isolation from the others. He desires, rather, to fellowship also with his whole family together. And I am confident that our loving heavenly Father enjoys a family reunion with his children just as much as our loving earthly fathers do.

In addition, we Christians have experienced in our own spiritual life that the family desires of us, God's children, correspond with his family desire for total family fellowship. We too do not wish to fellowship with our heavenly Father only when alone. We too do not desire fellowship with only one, or a few, of our spiritual brothers and sisters at a time. For we too enjoy a periodic family reunion of the family of God. There is always something more full and complete and exciting and uplifting about a divine family gathering where the heavenly Father and all the brothers and sisters are joined together in fellowship. Much of the inexpressible ecstasy of Christian church worship, for instance, is due to the joyous impact of this realization that, because the whole family of God is meeting together in love, everything is somehow now raised to completeness and overflowing.

The family of God also brings to us, in a spiritual manner, all the advantages of family life. Our weaknesses are helped by the strengths of the others, as our brothers and sisters teach us and warn us and encourage us and forgive us and comfort us and delight us. And our strengths help the others as we find happiness in serving them in like manner.

Thus we see that the nature of divine love makes the family of God indispensable. Love is not an abstract virtue that can exist off somewhere in isolation. Love, rather, is always that personal attitude that

185

enters into relationships of self-giving with other persons. And those who love perfectly, as God loves, are irresistibly drawn together in a great network of divine and human relationships. Thus divine love is the most integrative and collective of all realities.

These are some of the reasons why the Fatherhood of God and the brotherhood of man become completed social realities only where there is an appreciation for the familyhood of the church. Yes, the church as an institution is indeed essential because it is the goal of the divinely given ideal of the family of God which Jesus proclaimed.

Second, *the church as an institution is essential in order to preserve the divinely given ideal of the family of God.* An appreciation of the family of God is not something instinctual to our human nature like hunger and fear. Rather, this knowledge is a historical treasure that was given to man by God through Jesus the Messiah at a carefully prepared time in human history. And it is a knowledge that can be lost if it is not preserved and passed on. Without the institution of the church which keeps the Bible in print and which carries out continual scholarly research and which maintains schools in the church, most of the revelation of God which came through Jesus would be lost to man within two generations, and that which survived would be increasingly perverted by the limitations of oral transmission.

Third, the church as an institution is essential in order to exemplify the divinely given ideal of the family of God. How can those who believe in Jesus' revelation about the family of God have real confidence in his message until they see that family of God become a living reality? As we prove what kind of tree a tree is by its fruit, even so by the kind of fruit that an ideal produces we prove the worth of that ideal. And Christians must prove that the ideal of the family of God is a realistic ideal by organizing all believers into a reasonable approximation of the family of God.

Fourth, the church as an institution is essential in order to promote the divinely given ideal of the family of God. If those who preach the divine ideal of the family of God expect to be taken seriously, must they not practice what they preach? Unless we Christians can demonstrate to prospective Christians that the family of God is not only an ideal in our dreams but also a practical reality in our midst, they will dismiss us as fanatic and unrealistic visionaries. Furthermore, the message of the perfect love of God and man that Jesus brought is a message that is more caught from other love-inflamed personalities than it is taught as mere facts. It is the man who is brought into the midst of the Christian fellowship where he finds his soul bathed in the warm love of God's family who is most intensely drawn to the way of Christ. People can be won to the family of God only through contact with both the ideal and the reality.

Fifth, the church as an institution is essential in order to fulfill the divinely given ideal of the family of God. The heavenly Father has only a functional interest in any ideal. For he gives ideals to men only for the practical purpose of shaping the human soul and human society in the manner that he wants them shaped. Thus the creation of the church is not only instrumental in preserving and exemplifying and promoting the ideal of the family of God. The creation of the church is nothing less than the very goal, or intention, of the ideal.

This means that the members of the church can never be satisfied to let the church assume a minority role in society. God's perfect love wants everyone in the church. The church is not to see itself as a small, especially devoted religious minority that exists in order to be a guiding banner to the less religious majority of mankind. If the church truly appreciates that it has no validity except as the earthly manifestation of the family of God, then the church can never be satisfied with its membership as long as any human being remains outside the church. Rather, the church must constantly be seeking to enlarge and to improve the fellowship of the family of God in the hope that in some future year it will encompass every person on this earth. The deepest fulfillment for society and for the individual can be found only within this institution the church. Jesus' parable of the yeast that permeates and encompasses and transforms the whole loaf of bread is a graphic illustration of this all-inclusive goal of the family of God (Matt. 13:33).

When we turn to examine the affirmations about the church that are found in the historic ecumenical creeds, we can appreciate that the church was well aware in those early centuries of the family of God which we have been considering. The church, according to the creeds, is "One, Holy, Catholic, and Apostolic."

The church is "One" because the family of God can be only one family. The church is "Holy" because it is not an organization that has been set up by arbitrary human decision but rather an organization which has been given deliberate birth by the holy God. The church is

"Catholic," which literally means "universal," because it is spread, and is supposed to be spread, everywhere on earth where humanity dwells. The church is "Apostolic" because it is still essentially the same church that was begun by Christ-ordained emissaries two thousand years ago. The church is called "the church" because the Greek word for church (*ekklesia*) means "popular assembly," or literally, "those who have been called out." The One, Holy, Catholic, and Apostolic Church, therefore, is those people all over the world who have been called by God into his family through Jesus the Messiah and who have obediently and gladly come out of their spiritual isolation and gathered together with their eternal Father and with each other.

Christians are all aware, of course, that the flaws in the institutional edifice of the church are obvious and many and that they must continually be pointed out and corrected. But, despite its flaws, we believe that this institution is still nothing less than the divinely established family of God and the body in which God hopes that all mankind will eventually find the true humanity that leads to fullness of life here and hereafter. Those who would reject and destroy the church of God, therefore, would disastrously reject and destroy the very humanity and the highest fulfillment of man.

Only God knows, Christians acknowledge, just who is truly a member of his family in eternal good standing. Many members of his family are within the official church. Many members of his family, although they are seriously deprived by their lack, are outside the official church. But, Christians believe, it is absolutely essential that a person be a member of God's family, however God may determine that membership, if that person is to find eternal life here and hereafter. This is the truth behind Luke's report that God added to the church daily "those who were being saved" (Acts 2:47).

And this is also the motivation behind this exhortation of the writer to the Hebrews: "Let us consider how to stir up one another to love and good works, not neglecting to meet together, as is the habit of some, but encouraging one another."

18. What Is the Meaning of the Lord's Supper?

"The Communion of Saints." The Apostles' Creed

"Do this . . . in remembrance of me." I Corinthians 11:25

The sacred meal of Christendom, which is variously known as the Lord's Supper, the Eucharist, the Sacrament of the Altar, or the Holy Communion, is very precious to all Christians, even though we are frequently quite vague about what it is supposed to mean to us. It is appropriate, I believe, for us to consider the Lord's Supper under this second phrase of the Apostles' Creed which deals with the church, the phrase which declares belief in the "Communion of Saints." For at no point in our mutual life as the family of God are we so aware of the presence of our heavenly Father and of our earthly brother and of the Lord Jesus, through whom this blessed awareness has come to us, as at the Lord's Supper. We shall consider in this rather brief chapter three now discarded ideas of the meaning of the Lord's Supper, and a fourth idea of the meaning of this sacred rite that most modern biblical scholars and theologians will attest is the meaning that Jesus intended it to have.

One unacceptable idea of the meaning of the Lord's Supper views this meal as an act of magical transformation which results in a debt-paying sacrifice for us. The Roman Catholic Church still officially teaches that during the daily worship service called the Mass the priest by his words actually causes the bread and wine to turn into the fleshly body and blood of Jesus, although our physical senses of sight, smell, taste, and touch cannot note the change, and that when the priest offers up this amazing new substance to God he is offering up once more the sacrifice of Jesus Christ so as to pay anew each day on the Calvary of every Roman altar for the sins of believing people.

Most modern theologians agree that when the concept of Jesus Christ as a sacrifice for sin is taken literally like this rather than poetically, as Isaiah interpreted the sin-bearing of his suffering servant (53:3 ff.), the result is that a grave insult is heaped upon a most merciful God. For even in the Old Testament, God continually forgives freely whenever people sincerely repent and return to the right way. His forgiveness is never something that must be bought with a price. On this point the psalms and the prophets are very clear (Ps. 32:5; 51:16; Prov. 15:8; 21:3; Isa. 1:11; Jer. 6:20; 7:22; Hos. 6:6; Amos 5:25; 7:2-3). And, biblical scholars agree, the minute sacrificial instructions in Leviticus and Numbers were rules established not by God but by the priests themselves.

Furthermore, in the New Testament, Jesus never calls himself a payment for sin, as though God were a cold-blooded accountant who runs a harsh credit bureau, or as though God were an implacable and merciless judge who exacts a pound of punishment for a pound of guilt, even if his own son must pay the price for us. The heavenly Father whom Jesus speaks for is always a God of pure love, who desires from his sinful children only a change of heart and life as conditions for forgivenesss (Luke 15:20 ff.). Consequently Jesus could only look upon his messianic death as a divine sacrifice in the sense that he lovingly gave up his life as a free gift, in order that all men could learn the full truth about God and subsequently desire to become reconciled to him. Jesus' sacrifice, therefore, was certainly not a legal payment for sin two thousand years ago. Consequently, it cannot be so again at any repetition of the Lord's Supper.

A second unacceptable understanding of the meaning of the Lord's Supper views this meal as an occasion when miraculous food is produced that in some literal manner feeds our souls with a kind of spiritual glucose. This view is based on a literal interpretation of the instituting words of Jesus which emphasizes the verb "is" in his declaration that "This is my body. . . . This is my blood" (Matt. 26:26 ff.). Also, the symbolic statement of Jesus that "He who eats my flesh and drinks my blood abides in me, and I in him" is understood literally, and understood in conjunction with the Lord's Supper (John 6:56). In this century my own Lutheran denomination and other right-wing Protestant denominations are having to acknowledge that, even though we have often taught differently, these words of Jesus are actually Jewish metaphors, or illustrative figures, as many of our left-wing Protestant brethren have perceived from the beginning.

A third unacceptable understanding of the meaning of the Lord's Supper views this meal as an encouraging reminder to us that our sins are forgiven because of Jesus' death which has "paid away" our guilt. The bread and wine are looked upon here as tokens of the blood sacrifice which has been made in order to erase our divine debit. Modern scholars agree that the Lord's Supper does indeed assure us of God's forgiveness, but not through the idea of a substitute payment for our sins. Our confidence in God's forgiveness is based on something infinitely more noble and uplifting than supernatural blood barter at an executioner's cross. Our confidence in God's forgiveness is based rather on Jesus' revelation to us of the inexpressible fatherly love of God who gladly forgives the penitent without any repayment.

What then is the Lord's Supper supposed to mean to us if it is not to be another sacrifice for our sins, or the eating of supernatural manna, or the proof of the forgiveness of our sins by repayment? The only true meaning that remains is the meaning that Jesus himself seems to have given it, namely, that in this table rite *we may be made to remember him again.* He says quite clearly "Do this in remembrance of me," that is, "in memory of me" (I Cor. 11:25).

But what did Jesus mean by remembering him? Did he mean to remember the color of his eyes and hair, the outline of his face, the timbre of his voice, the powerful muscles in his arms? Not likely. From the second generation of Christians onward his disciples have not had any idea what Jesus looked like. Certainly he did not mean that we are to remember him as a physical being.

Rather, when Jesus says "Do this in order to remember me," he means for us to remember his divine mission which was fulfilled by what he taught and by what he lived. By using the metaphors of broken body and spilled blood, Jesus is drawing the attention of his disciples to what he has done and what it means to them forever. So in the upper room he is saying "Break this bread as though it were my body. And pass around this wine among yourselves as though it were my

191

outpoured blood. Do this in order to call again to mind compellingly how by divine instruction I lived and died in holy love for you and for many, and what my life and death in such love has meant to the quality of your lives."

When a Christian thus remembers Jesus' loving mission, through the symbolic bread and wine of the Lord's Supper, he should always remember in appreciation again at least four divine truths which Jesus revealed that now shape the Christian life.

First, in his life and death Jesus has revealed to me how much God loves me. Jesus taught that God is a loving Father who loves all men —the righteous synagogue-goer and the sinning prodigal son alike. "Pray then like this," he directed. "Our Father, . . ." (Matt. 6:9.) "For the Father himself loves you." (John 16:27.) Jesus also believed that God's love is so great that the man who loves as God loves must be willing to surrender even his life for those whom he loves. "Greater love has no man than this, that a man lay down his life for his friends." (John 15:13.)

It is this information that God's love is the love of the perfect Father that gives us our assurance that our sins are forgiven. For purely out of his tender suffering mercies the Father of a world of prodigals is eager to forgive guilt freely and to receive back fully every son who sincerely repents and returns (Luke 15:11 ff.). A desire for God's forgiveness is one of the things that Jesus wished to encourage when he coaxed: "Ask, and it will be given you" (Matt: 7:7). Just ask!

Second, in his life and death Jesus has revealed to my fellow Christians how much they are to love me, and also how much I am to love them. Jesus was not satisfied to let the children of God remain scattered individuals. It was his mission to create a family fellowship of God in the midst of a world of broken relationships, a family in which all of us are designated "saints," that is literally, "holy ones," because we are now spiritually related to him who is the holy God. Jesus reached out to shattered, lonely people who were estranged from their brothers and made them one with each other. He showed shallow, self-centered men through his own words and deeds how to love others deeply as God loves others. He created a continuing fellowship called the church whose members love me, a fellowship that is interested in me, that sustains and guides and encourages and corrects and companies with me.

But Jesus also revealed to me the love that I must have for my fellow

192

Christians. He created a fellowship in which I must reciprocate: As I am loved, so must I love. Many times I must love even more than I am loved. Jesus showed the way to ensure the permanence of this fellowship by his willingness to give the ultimate gift of his own life for the ones that he loved. So the pattern is set for me and my brethren to follow in each other's behalf. "This is my commandment, that you love one another as I have loved you" (John 15:12). Thus the love of the brethren for each other means fellowship, or communion, the close sharing of our lives in the love of God.

Third, in his life and death Jesus has revealed to me the love that I am to have for my fellow man outside the church. Jesus lived and died also for the man in need—good or bad—who may never officially become a Christian, for the nameless Jew whose past and future is unknown but who lies helpless on the Jericho road, for our neighbor who is suffering silently or with rage or with weeping in the steel trap of trouble. Jesus showed us how to be the salt of the earth by the manner in which he went about doing good and thus making the world a better place for everyone to live in. By casting out the demons of disease and despair and doubt and distress he showed us how to flavor the world with that salty flavor of helpful love that suits the taste of our heavenly Father. Thus Jesus has revealed to me that only Christian love which bears social responsibility—that only that Christian love which is active out in the world—is truly Christian love. "You are the salt of the earth; but if salt has lost its taste, . . . it is no longer good for anything." (Matt. 5:13.)

And fourth, in his life and death Jesus has revealed to me the everlasting nature of God's love, which brings to me hope for Heaven in fellowship with him and with all his faithful children. Jesus had to die in order to be revealed alive after death to his disciples. And he is encouraging them in the hope of Heaven when he declares in poetic metaphor in the upper room: "I shall not drink again of the fruit of the vine until that day when I drink it new in the kingdom of God." Thus that last supper was a foretaste of the joy of family communion in the unseen dimension of eternity with a loving Father who can never bear to let his children cease to exist. "I am the resurrection and the life. . . . Whoever lives and believes in me shall never die." (John 11:25-26.) "No one is able to snatch [my sheep] out of the Father's hand." (John 10:29.)

Yes, in Jesus' life and death I have revealed to me first, that God's love for me is a kindhearted fatherliness that freely forgives me and accepts me back whenever I sincerely repent; second, that God's love has created a special spiritual family called the church to love me as Jesus loved his followers, and in which I must love my fellow Christians likewise; third, that godlike love in my life cannot be limited to this gathered group that is filled with mutual love, but that godlike love must also move out into society as salt is mixed into food; and fourth, that God's love is so permanent that his loved ones can confidently hope to rejoice in his love and in the love of one another forever. Thinking through all this joyous truth of loving fellowship is involved in re-enacting the Lord's Supper in memory of Jesus.

Therefore, whenever we believers come to the sacred table of Christendom, our hearts in deep and loving communion should crowd close to God, close to each other, and close to these truths that our Lord Jesus desired us to keep before us when he urged his disciples in that upper room to "Do this in remembrance of me."

19. What Is the Meaning of Baptism?

"I acknowledge one Baptism for the remission of sins." The Nicene Creed

"Go therefore and make disciples of all nations, baptizing them." Matthew 28:18

Water baptism has always been the rite of formal entrance into the Christian church. So highly esteemed has this sacred ceremony been that the resolving of a doctrinal disagreement concerning baptism was memorialized in the famous Creed of Nicaea by the inclusion of the affirmation "I acknowledge one Baptism for the remission of sins."

But unfortunately, the rite of baptism, like the rite of the Lord's Supper, has been a divisive doctrine in much of Christian history, especially in the first centuries and in the most recent centuries of the Christian era. We Protestant Christians are most painfully conscious of the history of baptismal controversy. For most of it has occurred within our own Reformation movement. Throughout the past four hundred years this rite has often been an act that has divided and weakened us as much as it has unified and empowered us.

But today the scars of this tragic dissension are slowly being erased. For in the past half century Christian scholars, operating according to scientific principles of investigation, have uncovered the roots of Christian baptism enough that increasingly Christians are seeing that the baptismal doctrines which have caused separations are based on mis-understandings of the Bible, or are largely invalid "arguments from silence."

In the light of these many scholarly researches, nearly every denomi-nation of Christendom is finding it necessary to eat a few slices of "humble pie." Lutherans, for instance, have been among those who have taught that at baptism a miraculous rebirth takes place in the infant's soul. Some Lutherans have even taught that, if a child dies without this miraculous rebirth in the water of baptism, that child is eternally condemned. These doctrines are now seen to be without bibli-cal or historical support. Baptists, on the other hand, have taught that baptism was only for mature believers and that immersion was the method that must be used. These doctrines too are now seen to be with-out biblical or historical support.

In this chapter—hoping to help make baptism more a power than a problem in Christian lives—I shall present a modern outline of the doctrine of baptism in three main sections: the significance of baptism, the subjects of baptism, and the style of baptism. Since the subjects and the style of baptism are determined by—and also partly determine—the significance of baptism, the meaning and value of this rite is clear-ly set forth only after an examination of all three aspects.

A. Our first concern is with the Significance of baptism, or What does baptism mean? Christian baptism has at least three beneficial meanings: rinsing, rebirth, and registration.

Baptism signifies the *rinsing away of sin*. Water has been used in nearly every religion of man to symbolize cleansing from a wrong manner of life. In the God-ordained covenant religion of ancient Israel, water was continually used to cleanse. According to the biblical account, before God would speak to the children of Israel from Sinai, everyone in the nation was ordered to wash his body and clothing in order to be clean before the Lord (Exod. 19:10). Later God commanded Moses to make a huge laver—or public tub—of bronze, in which Aaron and his sons should wash their hands and their feet before they went in to minister before the altar (Exod. 30:17 ff.). In the Tabernacle and in the Temple the priests and Levites had lengthy and involved rules con-cerning the washing of their bodies, their garments, and the bowls and furnishings of the worship area. Before persons or things could be considered holy—or fit for a holy purpose—they had to be washed.

The prophets of Israel were concerned, furthermore, to ensure that the cleanliness of God's people would not be limited merely to an outward ceremonial act. They stressed the cleanliness of the inner man (Ps. 51:2; Isa. 1:16). To the degree that the prophets were successful, therefore, all this ceremonial water cleansing effectively symbolized the spiritual fact that, whenever men become God's and whenever men come into God's presence, they must be repentant for all the ungodliness that fouls up their lives and must desire henceforth to be righteous and godly.

Since the entire Hebrew nation was supposedly heeding God's requirements for cleanliness, the people of Israel were considered a "clean nation," while all the neighboring peoples who did not acknowledge God were considered "unclean nations." Hence, when the Jews of Jesus' day made a convert from a pagan nation—or a "proselyte," as converts were called—they insisted still that the converts be baptized in order symbolically to rinse away the uncleanliness of their physical and spiritual sinfulness.

John the Baptizer, therefore, was following established Jewish custom when he exhorted the people who wanted to be included in the Messiah's heavenly kingdom to become baptized. John, who probably had been decisively influenced by an ascetic prophetic sect called the Essenes in the wilderness, believed that his task, following a special spiritual experience, was to call a spiritually fallen people of God back to true cleanliness of soul. He rinsed them with water as a symbol that their true repentance had won them divine forgiveness. As Mark reports, "John the Baptizer appeared in the wilderness, preaching a baptism of repentance for the forgiveness of sins" (1:4).

According to the Gospels, when Jesus began his ministry he fell right in with John's understanding that baptism symbolized a spiritual cleansing by repentance. Mark reports: "Now after John was arrested, Jesus came into Galilee, preaching the gospel of God, and saying, '. . . the kingdom of God is at hand; repent, and believe in the gospel'" (1:14-15). Jesus' message at that time was, in essence, the same as John's. And his disciples by his authority baptized people, just as John did (John 3:22; 4:1-2).

There is no indication in any of Jesus' reported words that he ever rejected the cleansing element in baptism. And the rest of the New Testament seems to leave no doubt that Jesus' disciples believed they were following in Jesus' footsteps when they urged baptism as a symbol of the rinsing away of the sins of the penitent. Peter cries aloud on the day of Pentecost to the assembled thousands: "Repent, and be baptized every one of you in the name of Jesus Christ for the forgiveness of your sins" (Acts 2:38). And Ananias, speaking to the blinded Saul, also believed that baptism cleansed from sin. For he says to Saul: "And now why do you wait? Rise and be baptized, and wash away your sins, calling on [Jesus'] name" (Acts 22:16).

Thus from the beginning Christian baptism has been viewed as an official symbol of spiritual cleansing of the heart. The Nicene Creed is referring to this cleansing when it speaks of baptism "for the remission [that is, forgiveness] of sins." Our one precaution here must be to understand baptism only as a useful symbol of Christian repentance and of the forgiveness that has been granted at the very moment of repentance. We must not attribute to the rite of baptism a magical worth, as though it were somehow indispensable to divine forgiveness. For to do this—as Christians have often done in their extreme reverence for "sacraments"—is to impose a priestly obstruction, as a kind of mediator, between God and his people, which is to assert the antithesis of Jesus' good news of God's unconditioned love.

Baptism also signifies *spiritual rebirth*. John reports Jesus as declaring "Truly, truly, I say to you, unless one is born of water and the Spirit, he cannot enter the kingdom of God. That which is born of the flesh is flesh, and that which is born of the Spirit is spirit" (3:5-6). Such spiritual rebirth is not the magical implanting of a new soul substance, as many Christians who were accustomed to Greek philosophical thought forms once believed. Instead, spiritual rebirth is now recognized as a beautiful Jewish metaphor for a largely understandable phenomenon.

To say that a man has been spiritually reborn is to declare symbolically that he had once had a self-centered, and perhaps also very hateful, heart and life, but that he has now converted to a God-centered, loving heart and life in which he tries to be a true son of the heavenly Father by thinking his thoughts after him. A man is "born again" by God's Spirit, therefore, when he permits God's truth to come into his own spirit and reconstruct him in the loving image of God. Consequently, Christian baptism has always symbolized that the man who is baptized is declaring that he is now a new man with new goals and new ideals and new principles, who intends to live a new life.

Paul is speaking of this same rebirth into new life when he questions the Romans: "How can we who died to sin still live in it? Do you not know that all of us who have been baptized into Christ Jesus were baptized into his death? We were buried therefore with him by baptism into death, so that as Christ was raised from the dead by the glory of the Father, we too might walk in newness of life" (6:2-4). By saying "We were buried with Christ by baptism into death," Paul is not necessarily referring to immersion, any more than to the price of camels in Cairo. Rather, he is taking the death and resurrection of Jesus as a parable of our death to godless sin and our rebirth or resurrection to a new life of godly righteousness when we become Christians.

Paul is referring to essentially the same rebirth in our manner and goals of living when he declares: "For as many of you as were baptized into Christ have put on Christ" (Gal. 3:27). In other words, our baptism is not only a divine symbol of forgiveness. It is also a symbol of the new kind of life that we must live up to. Yes, baptism signifies the necessity of spiritual rebirth.

Baptism also signifies *registration* into the covenant of salvation. It is only natural that an act in which God officially forgives a man and urges him to live like his son is also going to change that man's official status before God. And so it is no surprise to find that Jewish proselyte baptism had initiation overtones. It was to be expected that after his baptism the once "unclean" gentile convert would from then on be listed with the "clean" Jews.

The baptism of John the Baptizer, in like manner, had an initiation—or registration—aspect. And Jesus very likely had this registration on the new covenant membership list in mind when he came to be baptized by John. According to the New Testament, Jesus did not need to declare that from then on he was going to change his ways and live like a son of God. Jesus' primary purpose seems to have been to become registered.

But John, in his concern with repentance and rededication, had difficulty seeing the registration aspect of his own baptism. With pain in his voice he tried to dissuade Jesus from baptism: "I need to be baptized by you, and do you come to me?" (Matt. 3:14). But Jesus evidently looked upon the people that John was baptizing as people who by this act were also setting themselves apart as a new spiritual people of God. Jesus evidently saw another element in John's baptism that John himself could not see—the element of being registered in a new covenant. So Jesus urged John to proceed with his baptism: "Let

199

it be so now. For thus it is fitting for us to participate in every righteous act" (Matt. 3:15, paraphrase).

Perhaps the most noticeable place where Christian baptism becomes a sign of registration into the new covenant is in the letter to the Colossians where the writer explains that in Christ "you were circumcised with a circumcision made without hands, by putting off the body of flesh in the circumcision of Christ; and you were buried with him in baptism, in which you were also raised with him through faith in the working of God, who raised him from the dead" (2:11-12). The writer here seems to be declaring that baptism is the New Testament parallel of Old Testament circumcision. For the conjunction "and" seems to imply that baptism signified both the initiation of circumcision and the rebirth of the new spiritual man.

Thus very early in Christian history baptism had apparently become the act of registration in the new covenant which takes the place of circumcision under the old covenant. Since baptism is such a covenant seal, therefore, no one ever needs to be baptized but once—even as husband and wife need not repeat their marriage vows, despite occasional rows, or adopt their child but once, despite his worst behavior.

These, therefore, are the three main benefits that appear to be the purpose of New Testament baptism: (1) rinsing from sins after true repentance, (2) rebirth into a new and godly life, and (3) registration, or enrollment in the new covenant. These are spiritual benefits that every man needs. Yet there is no biblical justification for any worry that lack of the physical act of baptism will make eternal life impossible. Baptism was planned by a loving heavenly Father to benefit mankind. And there are no scriptural reasons to suppose that those who could not be baptized before their death are necessarily lost. Only those who have refused to be baptized out of a basic rebellion against God have any just cause to be afraid.

B. Our second concern in our study of baptism is with the subjects of baptism, or Who is to be baptized? It is normal that every newly converted believer should desire to have the assuring covenant symbol of baptism. Furthermore, a sizable number of Christian interpreters still believe that it is a good practice to baptize as well all children for whom Christians are parents or guardians. The New Testament does not state directly that the first Christians baptized infants. But it does seem to state indirectly in several places that infants were baptized. The practice would be quite consistent with the ancient traditions of the Jews. Let us scan the evidence at this point for these assertions.

The old covenant seal of circumcision included infants eight days old. So the apostles would naturally include infants in the new covenant seal of baptism. The Hebrew boy was never permitted to wait until he had reached the so-called age of accountability before being registered as a child of the covenant. God made the decision for him through his parents by a clan covenant which was to cover every generation that followed the first one. The Hebrews consequently thought in, and were surrounded by, a covenant atmosphere. That Jesus' disciples did not reject this covenant atmosphere is witnessed to by Peter's statement on the day of Pentecost that "the promise is to you and to your children" (Acts 2:39).

Jewish proselyte baptism included the infants of adult converts to Judaism. The whole family coming from paganism had to be made clean. Even if the baptism did not mean anything to the babies until maturity, it certainly reminded the parents continually that these little ones were now God's spiritually clean children and should be brought up in a spiritually clean atmosphere. There was every reason for the first Christians to see the healthy symbolic meanings of this early Jewish infant baptism.

Jesus apparently never indicated that the tradition of including infants was to be broken. We have no evidence that he ever indicated that children were somehow to be second-class citizens of the kingdom of Heaven (Mark 10:14-15). Furthermore, so deeply imbedded in Jewish society was the understanding that babies had equal standing with adults in the covenant, that it would have required a definite and remembered word from Jesus for his disciples to have broken with one thousand years of Hebrew religious tradition by not including infants in the covenant ceremony. But since Jesus is silent on this point, the only obvious conclusion is that in this matter Jesus made no changes in Jewish custom.

The New Testament reports that the apostles baptized whole households. And this Greek word for "household" (*oikos*) definitely includes everybody under the roof—adults, infants, and even the slaves. Luke writes that Paul baptized Lydia "with her household" (Acts 16:15), and the Philippian jailor "with all his family" (Acts 16:33). Paul himself states: "I did baptize also the household of Stephanus" (I Cor. 1:16).

Paul includes infants in the Old Testament baptism of the sea crossing. He declares: "I want you to know, brethren, that our fathers were all under the cloud, and all passed through the sea, and all were baptized into Moses in the cloud and in the sea" (I Cor. 10:1-2). Paul interprets the dividing of the Reed Sea and the walking of the Israelites through it, and the water cloud of God over their heads, as a kind of baptism. Since the babes in arms were carried through the bed of the sea, and under the cloud, along with the adults, this passage is important evidence that the apostles automatically included infants in their baptisms without questioning the practice.

There is the logical a fortiori argument that if the circumcision seal of the *imperfect* old covenant could be applied even to infants, then it is necessary that the baptismal covenant seal of the *perfect* new covenant can be applied to infants also.

These points seem to be sufficient evidence for determining just who is a qualified subject for Christian baptism. Since this rite may be viewed as a covenant seal, every believer and all the children for whom believers are parents or guardians should be eligible for baptism.

C. Our third concern is with the style of baptism, or How is baptism to be administered? For several hundred years some churchmen, whose knowledge of Greek has been somewhat insufficient, have claimed that the word *bapto*, which is the Greek root for the English word "baptism," means simply "to dip." But more adequate study of ancient Greek literature has revealed that *bapto* had a primary meaning and several very significant secondary meanings. The secondary meanings of *bapto* could be "to wash," "to bathe," "to purify," or even "to dye [cloth]." Mark reports that the Pharisees always "baptized" themselves after returning from the marketplace (7:4). The RSV translates "baptize" in this verse as "purify." And Luke reports that one of Jesus' Pharisee hosts "was astonished to see that [Jesus] did not first baptize before dinner" (11:38). The RSV translates "baptize" here as "wash." Obviously the Pharisees did not require even the members of their own strict sect to immerse themselves completely in water before a meal or after buying a loaf of bread. The original meaning of the Greek word *bapto*, we see, simply cannot cover, or take the place of, all its later meanings.

We must turn elsewhere to find the preferred method of baptism. But when we search the Bible, we can find no direct evidence at all that tells us whether Christian baptism is to be by sprinkling, by pouring, or by immersion. And the only conclusion that we can reach in view of this silence is that the method in baptizing—or the amount of water that is used—is not important. However, if we look further, the indirect evidence in the New Testament seems to indicate that sprinkling or pouring was the usual biblical method.

New Testament baptism grew out of the soil of Old Testament ceremonies. And the Old Testament covenantal ceremonies never stressed completely covering the person with anything. A mere sprinkling with water was believed to purify sufficiently. In Numbers 8:7 God tells Moses how to cleanse the Levites for holy service: "Sprinkle the water of expiation upon them." And in Ezekiel 36:25, which is considered a messianic prophecy, God says: "I will sprinkle clean water upon you, and you shall be clean from all your uncleannesses."

Most importantly, Jesus ended once and for all the argument about how much water it takes to cleanse a person spiritually when he washed only the feet of his disciples in the upper room (John 13:1 ff.). Simon Peter wanted to be the first immersionist when he heard Jesus say: "If I do not wash you, you have no part in me." "Lord," Peter blurted out, "not my feet only but also my hands and my head!" But Jesus refused, and thus settled once and for all the question of whether the amount of water or the meaning of the water is most important.

Old Testament prophecy speaks of the "pouring out" of the Holy Spirit in the age of the Messiah (Joel 2:28 ff.). And Peter at Pentecost speaks of the Holy Spirit as now being "poured out" as promised (Acts 2:33). Then, since John the Baptizer says that Jesus will "baptize you with the Holy Spirit" (Matt. 3:11), Pentecost may also be viewed as the baptism of the disciples with the Holy Spirit. If so, then this Pentecost baptism is one of pouring—not of immersion. Very consistent with this is the fact that on that signal occasion God placed only tongues of fire on the heads of the disciples. He did not immerse them in fire.

The phrase "they went down into the water" does not indicate immersion. Except during floods, the water in every river and creek is lower than the banks. And one must go down even to stand in the water. Certainly the phrase "to go down into the water" means "to go down in order to get to the water." Otherwise, Philip's baptism of the Ethiopian eunuch was a most remarkable affair. For when they alighted from the chariot, Luke says, "They both went down into the water" (Acts 8:38). Certainly no baptizer ever tried to immerse himself while he was immersing someone else!

Even Christian archaeology indicates that the earliest Christian baptism was by pouring or sprinkling. The reputedly oldest picture in existence that shows Jesus being baptized is painted on a wall of one of the catacombs in Rome. In this picture Jesus and John are standing ankle-deep in the Jordan. And John is emptying a ram's horn of water on Jesus' head. Furthermore, there is the practical problem to immersion, such as how the disciples would have found enough water in high and dry Jerusalem to have baptized three thousand souls on the day of Pentecost without polluting the water supply.

And so, because of items like these, modern scholars can only conclude that, while immersion was certainly practiced occasionally in the early centuries, there is little doubt that some form of sprinkling or pouring was the most traditional and universal method. However, scholars just as readily agree that the amount of water is of no importance to the effectiveness of baptism.

At this point, after having considered the three main biblical aspects of baptism, Christians must be careful to acknowledge that, regardless of biblical precedents, not only the style but also the subjects and the significance of baptism are, in the final analysis, a matter of Christian freedom. Even though this presentation of key incidental New Testament passages seems to indicate that the apostles included a traditional posterity-wide covenantal significance in their baptizing, nevertheless, the covenantal aspect was evidently not a matter of great importance to them.

The absence of specific ceremonial instructions for baptism seems to imply that, however the apostles and their disciples viewed baptism, still they must have held to a certain ceremonial freedom in their practice that was consistent with their overall pragmatic attitude toward religious ceremony past and present. Paul's de-emphasizing of baptism for the Corinthians, and his statement that "Christ did not send me to baptize but to preach the gospel" (I Cor. 1:17) certainly seems to reduce the importance of this sacred rite, despite the special nature of the local problem.

Since the New Testament does not attempt any formal decision on the traditional covenantal aspect of baptism, and since the Christian gospel is rich enough to support several meaningful and valid interpretations of this ancient ceremony, the contemporary church, therefore, is certainly obligated to manifest the same freedom and to permit Christian choice in this matter. That "what is both practical and edifying shall be done" seems to be the only definite, though unarticulated, biblical rule which Christians are to follow. I can well imagine that the day of compromise will come when a special service of blessing—that has good scriptural precedent (Mark 10:16)—will replace infant baptism, and when adult baptism, administered but once by pouring or sprinkling, will replace the odd, detractive, and biblically ungrounded rite of confirmation.

And so we come to the end of this outline of Christian baptism with the affirmation that modern insights make it possible for Christian baptism to be no longer a problem but a power. We can forget the misunderstandings that have formerly divided Christians by accepting the good in every position and by allowing larger choice and personal preference in the significance, style, and subjects of baptism. Today we can lay aside wasteful and hurtful argumentation and instead concentrate for our spiritual welfare upon the rich significance that baptism has for all of us.

Our baptism should strengthen those of us who were baptized as adults because this completed act continually assures us that we have been officially cleansed of our former godlessness. Our baptism should strengthen those of us who were baptized as infants because we believe that this act was an official symbol of God's promise to forgive us throughout our lives whenever we truly repent. Furthermore, our baptism should strengthen us all because it reminds each of us that he is to live a resurrected, reborn life of total and responsible love as one of the heavenly Father's children. And finally, our baptism should strengthen us all because whenever we are anxious about our unworthiness, this act is like a wedding ring that reminds us of God's faithful love which has bound us with him in an unbreakable covenant of life.

It is to this beneficial end that our Lord Jesus was reported as commanding: "Go therefore and make disciples of all nations, baptizing them."

Section VI: DESTINY

20. Is Our Earthly Body Finished at Death?

"The Resurrection of the body." The Apostles' Creed

"Last of all, as to one untimely born, he appeared also to me."
I Corinthians 15:8

Just what did Paul see when Jesus "as to one untimely born" appeared to him? And just what did the disciples of Jesus see when he appeared to them after his crucifixion? We Christians ask these questions because we are convinced with Paul and John that Jesus is the "first fruits" of those who rise from the dead and that someday "we shall be like him" (I Cor. 15:20; I John 3:2). We ask these questions about Jesus' resurrection also because we are naturally interested in knowing if our earthly bodies will play any part in the plan of eternal life. That is, we wish to know if our resurrection bodies will use any of the materials that now compose our earthly bodies, or any of their present shape. These and other questions arise whenever we ponder the traditional Christian understanding of life after death which is expressed in the Apostles' Creed as belief in the "resurrection of the body."

In this chapter we shall first examine how this Christian belief in the resurrection of the body developed and precisely what was meant by it. Then we shall evaluate the traditional understanding in the light of current research and thought.

Old Testament studies have proved beyond a reasonable doubt that a belief in life after death was not part of the faith of the early Israelites. Rather, the early Israelites believed that only God was eternal, that man was but temporal, that God's blessings were only for this one life, and that they were given in order to make it bearable and enjoyable. The only kind of immortality for which the old patriarchs seemed to have been able to hope was for sons who would carry their family line on through time indefinitely.

Even in Jesus' day the Sadducees did not believe in life after death because they were extreme right-wing biblical conservatives who accepted only the first five books of the Old Testament—that is, the Pentateuch—as the authentic and therefore authoritative Word of God. The Sadducees could find no doctrine of an afterlife from Genesis to Deuteronomy, although Jesus insisted to them that they simply had not looked carefully enough (Mark 12:26). The Sadducees were also members of the well-to-do classes who were favorably enough situated to enjoy this life. Consequently, they were willing, without too much distress, to settle for one good, long life in the flesh.

Belief in the afterlife seems only gradually to have entered into the theology of Israel. The sources appear to have been the nations around about Israel who held to various doctrines of eternal life long before the Israelites did. Here, I believe, is one of these instances when we must not automatically condemn every non-Hebrew and non-Christian religion as totally "pagan"—that is, as false and worthless. God has not left himself without witness in any nation, Paul reminds us (Acts 14:17). And this almost universal belief in an afterlife may very well have been present in those other religions because God had been active in revealing his truth among them.

Precisely when the Israelites began to accept the common oriental belief in a cavernous abode for the souls of the departed dead under the earth is not known. But many portions of the psalms and prophets and even the historical books such as I Samuel (28:11-12) speak of this dark underworld, called Sheol, where all that remains of the dead is a bare spiritual minimum that, poetically put, is their "shadow." So they are called "shades." Here in Sheol is no happiness or hope for new life. The shades have only their memory of the joys and sorrows of the full life that they once had above on the earth (Isa. 14:9-10; 57:9).

But the later psalms and prophets begin to intimate that at least some of the departed dead can hope for a return to life, even though the primary purpose of such passages is to be poetic encouragement to the oppressed in this life that their fortunes will improve. The psalmist sings:

> Thou who hast made me see many sore troubles
>> wilt revive me again;
> from the depths of the earth
>> thou wilt bring me up again. (71:20.)

Isaiah also prophesies:

> Thy dead shall live, their bodies shall rise.
>> O dwellers in the dust, awake and sing for joy!
> For thy dew is a dew of light,
>> and on the land of the shades thou wilt let it fall. (26:19.)

Ezekiel, in ministering to a despairing people, tells of a vision in which God commands him to preach to a valley of sun-bleached bones. Under the power of Ezekiel's exhortations the bones join back together and grow nerves and flesh. Then when God breathes upon the restored bodies they stand up again, a mighty army of living men (37:1 ff.). (See also Gen. 3:22; 5:24; Job 19:26; Ps. 49:15; 73:24; 139:8.)

By the time of the latest books of the Old Testament, the resurrection of the dead is a well-established belief. An angel informs Daniel that "many of those who sleep in the dust of the earth shall awake, some to everlasting life, and some to shame and everlasting contempt. And those who are wise shall shine like the brightness of the firmament; . . . like the stars for ever and ever" (12:2-3).

During the period between the end of the Old Testament and the beginning of the New Testament, and on into the New Testament era, Jewish resurrection thought produced a great and colorful variety of opinions. The experience of visions of angels, for instance, had produced a strong belief in a world of spiritual beings who surrounded God in Heaven. Consequently, the belief of many people was that at death the souls of men went immediately to Heaven, there to exist among the angels forever as one of them, or as beings similar to them, while their bodies were discarded forever on earth. This belief in immediate translation of the soul into Heaven after death is more accurately labeled belief in "immortality" rather than belief in "resurrection." The proverb writer encourages belief in such immortality when he declares:

> The wise man's path leads upward to life,
>   that he may avoid Sheol beneath. (15:24.)

Other theologians of the intertestamental period thought in terms of a brief, or lengthy, sleep of the soul at death until some last day when the soul would be awakened for eternal life on earth or in Heaven.

Still others believed that the earthly body was involved in the afterlife. Some of these thinkers believed that the human body was intended only for this earth and that at some unknown future time God would destroy all the wicked, resurrect the bodies of all the righteous, and reunite their bodies with their spiritual shadows from Sheol, so that they could live on a purified earth forever. This is essentially the "new sky and new earth" concept of the writer of John's Revelation. The literalistic belief that God had created Adam and Eve almost instantaneously out of earth and bone assisted people to believe that this resurrection of the body was credible.

Others of those who believed that the earthly body was to be involved believed that the resurrection body would not be such a fleshly body but would be a spiritual body that somehow would be formed from our earthly remains. They believed that the resurrection body would have new qualities and capabilities and would be structured for life in Heaven forever. This is Paul's position in I Corinthians 15 when he distinguishes between the fleshly body of this life and the spiritual body of the next life and declares that on the day of judgment our fleshly bodies will be changed in the twinkling of an eye into spiritual bodies. This was also the understanding of the Gospel writers (Matthew 28, Luke 24, John 20).

But how did the New Testament writers arrive at this belief in the transformation of the physical body into a spiritual body at the resurrection to judgment? They came to this conclusion because it was the only way they could harmonize the two chief Easter facts: first, the appearance of the living Jesus, and second, the empty tomb.

The early church believed that it could put these two facts together only by assuming that on the third day God had transformed Jesus' dead fleshly body into a living spiritual body with new capabilities and that it was this new spiritual body in which Jesus appeared again to his disciples. Otherwise how could they honorably explain the absence of Jesus' body from the tomb? This assumption is the basis of the traditional Christian belief in the "resurrection of the body" that stands in the Apostles' Creed. For in the fifth and sixth and seventh centuries when the Apostles' Creed was being developed, the church accepted the New Testament documents uncritically and hence could only accept *in toto* the position of Paul and the Gospel writers.

In the last two centuries, however, with the development of the discipline of scientific biblical study, the whole subject of the nature of the resurrection has been reopened. Opinions of all kinds have been considered, some extreme, some reasonable. Testing of every lead and every notion has gradually eliminated many early questions. And today there is a growing consensus of a broad sort among biblical theologians and literary scholars about the nature of the resurrection and the part that the body plays in it. I shall list fifteen points of agreement.

First, there is general agreement that the testimony of Paul about the resurrection appearances of Jesus to the disciples and to Paul himself is our most significant information. The fifteenth chapter of Paul's first letter to Corinth and the first chapter of his letter to Galatia are considered to be the most authoritative portions of the New Testament for information about the resurrection of Jesus. Here as proof of the resurrection Paul mentions only the appearances of Jesus. There is not a word about an empty tomb.

The letter of I Corinthians was written in the spring of A.D. 56 or 57 at Ephesus. But Paul is speaking therein of experiences that had happened no later than A.D. 33, or only three years after Jesus' death. Thus we definitely know who this man Paul is. And he insists that he has met the risen Christ. We know that Paul talked with at least Peter and James among the original disciples at the Jerusalem conference no later than six years after the crucifixion. This means that in Paul we have a definite firsthand report of the resurrection.

Second, there is general agreement that the appearances to the disciples and Paul were not merely hallucinations. If the appearances had been only the pathological visions of disturbed minds, they would not have continued to take place over a period of time that was probably several years, because these temporarily disturbed persons would most likely have settled down in several months. Especially Paul, who was originally angry about Jesus, rather than grieving for him, would not have experienced hallucinations at all.

Third, there is general agreement that the tomb was empty on Easter morning. Various explanations, many of them rather wild and without any historical basis whatsoever, have been made as to why the tomb was empty. But there seems to have been no doubt that Jesus' body was not there that morning. The Jewish leaders never used the argument that the location of Jesus' grave had been confused by them or others. And they never produced his body either. The evidence appears quite incontrovertible that on Easter Day Jesus' body was not in the grave where it had been laid even though Paul is strangely silent about this fact.

Fourth, there is general agreement that the Gospel stories of angels and of the nature of Jesus' appearances show a legendary tendency to assert that Jesus' resurrection appearances were nothing less than the real presence of Jesus' supernatural body. The dynamic observed in all legends is their inexorable tendency toward embellishment in the telling. This development may be easily noted in the expansion of the experience of the women at the tomb that takes place in the years between the writing of Mark and Matthew. Even those elements in the Gospel reports that correspond to something in Paul's reports show that they have been progressively shaped by a strong legendary tendency to emphasize the bodily appearances of Jesus.

Fifth, there is general agreement that Jesus' appearance to Paul on the road to Damascus was in the form of a blinding light without any discernible earthly shape. Thus Jesus appeared to Paul out of Heaven rather than on earth. This agrees with the earliest Christian testimonies which speak of Jesus' resurrection and ascension as one and the same event (Phil. 2:9; Acts 2:36; 5:30-31; 9; Mark 14:62).

Sixth, there is general agreement that Paul nowhere implies that Jesus appeared in an earthly human form to the other disciples. Paul gives no indication that his experience of the risen Christ, as the flashing of a brilliant light and the speaking of an authoritative voice, was any different from the experience of the others who encountered the risen Christ.

However, Paul's explanation of the nature of the resurrection body in I Corinthians 15 does appear to be purposely vague. He insists that the body of flesh dies and is finished, that "flesh and blood cannot inherit the kingdom of God" (vs. 50). So he stands against that particular concept of the resurrection of the body. But Paul has perhaps heard other resurrection accounts by disciples who have recognized Jesus in an earthly human form. So this may be the reason that he does not go into the question of whether the light and voice that he has experienced is the true resurrection body of Jesus in contact with him, while the earthly human appearances to others are only divine visions— or whether Jesus has indeed sometimes resumed an earthly form but has not deigned to reveal himself in this powerless form to Paul the persecutor.

Seventh, there is general agreement that, while Paul does not mention the empty tomb, he does assume that the tomb was empty, and that he believed that Jesus' resurrection body had been formed by God out of Jesus' dead earthly body. Paul's statement about a judgment day when the dead would be raised imperishable can only be interpreted to mean that God did something to transform Jesus' corpse and thus caused it to "put on immortality" (I Cor. 15:62-63).

Eighth, therefore, there is general agreement that, while the *fact* that Jesus arose depends entirely upon the testimonies of those to whom he appeared, the *nature* of Jesus' resurrection body depends entirely upon conclusions drawn from the fact that the tomb was empty. Every biblical statement about a transformation of Jesus' dead fleshly body into a living spiritual body is only pious theorizing that is based on the fact of the empty tomb.

Ninth, there is general agreement that this theory of the early church that God transformed Jesus' corpse into a heavenly body in the tomb, in view of the scanty historical data, will probably remain nothing more than a more or less venerated theory. The Jewish leaders insisted from the beginning that the disciples had stolen Jesus' body. The Gospel of Matthew, written about A.D. 85, insists in retort that this is a bald lie. But there is no more historical evidence that Matthew is correct than there is evidence that the Jewish leaders were correct.

Nobody has reported the whereabouts of all Jesus' hundreds of disciples and thousands of sympathizers those two nights that his body was interred. Nobody can prove that at least some of them did not overpower or buy out the guards. Some defenders of the Gospel account insist that defeated men do not organize a body snatch when the cause is lost. Maybe we would not have done so. But zealous Orientals, who can be very passionate about the dead bodies of their loved ones and who in this case had given up everything to follow a religious leader, are certainly capable of enough emotional comeback to effect the retrieving of Jesus' body. And how can we be sure that the disciples were utterly demoralized as an organization simply because they intelligently fled the garden before superior military forces?

There are some scholars who theorize that Jesus' disciples did indeed steal his body and that they could not believe the women on Easter Day had really seen Jesus because these disciples knew where the body was. These men could believe that Jesus was still alive only when he had appeared to them personally. And they never revealed the whereabouts of the body because the average Jew, who thought of resurrection only in terms of transformation of the earthly body, would believe that their message of encounter with the risen Jesus was a deliberate falsehood.

Then there is also the theory that Pilate, in a peevish mood of revenge, sent soldiers dressed in civilian clothing, to steal the body and thus embarrass the Jewish leaders. These soldiers naturally would be identified by the tomb guards as disciples of Jesus, while the disciples would just as vigorously deny involvement.

But these too are just theories, and no more authoritative than the theory of the early church about a transformation of the corpse. Who, after all, would have been there to observe such an event? We simply do not have sufficient reliable historical information in the Bible, or elsewhere, to settle the matter of whether it was God or man that moved the body in the tomb. And there is little hope that we will ever have this information.

Tenth, there is general agreement that, since we do not know whether it was God or man who moved Jesus' body, we can never be sure about the nature of those reported Gospel appearances in which Jesus appeared to look like his former self, showing his hands and his feet and his side to his disciples.

Eleventh, there is general agreement that if Jesus in his appearances to his disciples did appear to look like his former self—despite evident legendary additions—then there are only three strong possibilities as to what the disciples saw.

Possibility A: If the dead physical body of Jesus had really been transformed by God into a living spiritual body in the grave, then what the disciples saw could have been Jesus' spiritual body assuming the shape that Jesus wanted it to assume as he reappeared and disappeared before them. Our knowledge of the atomic, or electrical, makeup of matter today would be readily consistent with this event.

Possibility B: If the disciples or someone else (such as Pilate) had removed the body, then Jesus' reappearance in which he looked like his former self would be a divinely caused apparition—or vision—in which the brain functions of the "viewers" were manipulated so that they "saw" something that was not really there and "heard" something that really did not make a physical sound. There is nothing extraordinary about this phenomenon at all, since it occurs in dreams and in hypnotism continually. The unique thing here would be that it was Jesus performing the mechanics of this vision in order to communicate his continuing existence in another dimension, or else God doing the work in order to communicate the same information.

Possibility C: If the body of Jesus had been removed, what the disciples saw could have been a vision of the new "electrical" spiritual body of Jesus, which was present around them, and which, while essentially amorphous, could "appear" to their brain functions in any form that would establish Jesus' identity.

These are the three chief options. And there is little hope here, too, that Christians will ever uncover sufficient new data in this life to prove one possibility and disprove the others. The only problem that it presents to Christian doctrine is that we do not know whether we should speak of the Easter *resurrection* of Jesus Christ or of the Easter *translation* of Jesus Christ. The doubtfulness of the disciples' transformation theory causes many modern scholars to put the word "resurrection" in quotation marks when referring to what happened to Jesus. The term "reappearance" is often preferred as a more precise description of what is most reliable in the "resurrection" accounts.

Twelfth, there is general agreement that either bodily resurrection or spiritual translation makes very little difference in our Christian hope. We will likely live in a spiritual dimension after death in which we never will reassume our former earthly physical form. And God certainly has at his command all the energy that is necessary to provide splendid spiritual bodies for us. So whether Jesus' earthly body was transformed into his spiritual body or whether that body still lies in dust in an unknown grave to this day means nothing to the quality of Jesus' heavenly existence.

As for our physical bodies, many people are eaten by animals, or their ashes are dumped in the sea. How would such remains be recollected? Throughout life, furthermore, we are continually replacing the molecules of our body, enjoying a complete change—a completely new body—every three to seven years. Our bodies are much like rivers that remain even though the waters constantly change. Which molecules in the great pile of molecules that have temporarily been in the structure of our body would be part of us in a bodily transformation? These are some of the problems that arise whenever we insist that the resurrection of the body means the resurrection, or transformation, of our physical corpse on a last day.

Thirteenth, there is general agreement that the creedal affirmation of faith in the "resurrection of the body," if it is used today, should be interpreted to mean that after death the individuality of each one of us remains a distinct entity. This creedal statement about the resurrection of the body has at least prevented Christians from imagining that at death our spirits will be absorbed into the great All of God's Spirit, as a drop of water is absorbed into the ocean and loses its individuality. The reappearance after death of the individual named Jesus testifies, rather, that our individual personality also will continue to be something distinct and separate after death and that when we go to be with God and his spiritual host in the unseen dimension we will have both perfect bliss in unity with others and perfect bliss as fulfilled and distinct persons.

Fourteenth, there is general agreement that the creedal assertion of belief in the resurrection of the body has preserved the church from falling into that ancient false understanding which viewed spirit and matter as entirely opposite realities. Today spirit and matter are appreciated as different organizations of the same basic energy of the universe. Modern man knows of no mind (or spirit) that does not require a body—especially that part known as the "brain"—in order to operate. Human thought requires electricity. And electricity is energy. So spirit today is not conceived of by theologians as a weak, empty, weightless, shining something that is opposite to matter. Spirit, rather, is viewed as some type of basic energy that is organized on a very high level.

Our heavenly self, therefore, modern theologians reason, must have some kind of stuff in it, some definite amount of organizable energy, if it is to maintain our personalities. This energy allotment will be sufficient to provide for our heavenly body and our heavenly soul— if the body and the soul will even be distinguishable entities in eternity.

Modern theologians go on to theorize that this body-soul will not have the shape of our earthly body, which is shaped to fulfill relatively crude earthly functions. On earth we are limited to seeing only with our eyes, to hearing only with our ears, to tasting only with our tongue, to smelling only with our nose, to touching only with our nerve endings, to acting only with our hands. In Heaven we will likely be able to see, hear, taste, smell, touch, and act with every part of our being.

So finally there is general agreement that the Christian resurrection emphasis should not be placed on the body of Jesus at all or on our own bodies, but on the continuance of our personal life after death in the blessed Presence of God forever. That Jesus appeared to his disciples from Heaven and that someday we too shall be in Heaven should be the chief emphasis of our resurrection testimony.

And so, on Easter day and every day we Christians sing "Christ is risen! Alleluia!" in joy and confidence that Jesus is alive and that because he lives we shall live also. This is a faith and hope glorious enough and reliable enough to live for and to die for. Yes, there is spiritual exhilaration for us in Paul's announcement that "Last of all, as to one untimely born, he appeared also to me."

21. Will We Have an End Without Life or a Life Without End?

"And the Life everlasting." The Apostles' Creed

"If a man die, shall he live again?" Job 14:14

Every Sunday morning as a pastor scans the congregation from the pulpit, he sees before him people in every stage of physical life. He sees small children who are just developing their basic humanity. He sees boys and girls at the impish age of giggle and wiggle. He sees adolescents whose maturity is just beginning to bud. He sees young men and women in the first bloom of adulthood. He sees men and women in their fruitful prime. He sees middle-aged adults whose brows are beginning to be crowned with grey and whose bodies are not quite as strong as once they were. He sees the ancient ones, hoary-headed and feeble, who are reverenced for their wisdom and experience. He sees before him every stage of physical life—on its way into physical death and decay.

This fact—that we are all irresistibly on our way to death—is one of the deepest and most powerful motivations that bring crowds of people to hear the Christian message every Sunday. They sing the hymns and listen to the Scriptures and turn toward the pulpit with a look on their faces that says: "Pastor, reassure us through whatever you say that we will not have an end without life but a life without end! Reassure us that the words of the Nicene Creed, which affirms belief in 'the life of the world to come,' and the words of the Apostles' Creed, which affirms belief in 'the life everlasting,' are words of truth. Reassure us that life has an eternal meaning that is woven into the very fabric of God's universe. For we must soon go out and face another week in which things that seem so meaningless by themselves will try to tear down our feeling that life has meaning and that we are more than dust. Pastor, reassure us of the truth of the Christian message that God has given human life too much meaning to let it end!"

From the beginning of time men have wondered and worried about what happens to their essential selfhood—the soul—at death. Do they still live on? Or do they cease to exist like a snuffed candlelight? And if they do live on, in what form do they exist? Does each soul merge into the great All of God's soul, as a drop of water merges into the ocean? Does the soul go to sleep when the body dies and remain asleep until a general resurrection or until it is reincarnated into another physical creature? Does the soul at death become immediately transferred into a different dimension where people remain distinct individuals who fellowship with God and their fellow immortals?

This central concern of man in all ages and places evokes from suffering Job of old the famous question that he asks for everyman: "If a man die, shall he live again?" Job's question was being asked with much seriousness in Jesus' day. Yet despite their relentless pursuit of an answer, the Jews could arrive at nothing that was conclusively persuasive. In fact, the Jewish religion in the year A.D. 30 was split right down the middle on this question of an afterlife, with the Sadducees rejecting life after death and the Pharisees accepting it.

The Sadducee party was composed of most of the very wealthy and powerful people in the land, including the chief priests, and based its doctrines on the first five books of the Old Testament. The Sadducees taught that God gave only one life to man, even as he gave only one life to all living things, and that when this one life was ended, the spirit—or breath—of man returned to God who had given it. The Sadducees could claim most of the Old Testament—even the psalms and the prophets—in support of their position. God's promises to the early Hebrew fathers were clearly for this life. And the value of obedience to God was that God blessed with a long life, peace, and prosperity those who obeyed his commandments. Since the Sadducees were the materially better-off people of Israel, this theology of death without afterlife was satisfying enough. For, after all, *they* had obeyed

God, and he had made *them* rich and happy. So it was relatively easier for them to accept the idea of one long, wealthy, pleasure-filled life. The rich have always been less disturbed than the poor at the prospect of having but one life to live.

The Pharisee party was primarily middle-class and was much more influenced by the writings of the prophets and by the writings of the intertestamental period. The Pharisees very stoutly believed in an afterlife, although there were many conflicting theories about the nature of the afterlife among them. The Pharisees pointed to passages in the psalms and prophets which they interpreted to refer to life after death, especially the "valley of dry bones" passage in Ezekiel 37 and the prophetic words in Isaiah 24–26 and in Daniel 12.

The Pharisees could not be as happy as the Sadducees with the thought that perhaps there was only one life. Through a blood-soaked history the party of the Pharisees had fought and died for the sake of the religion of the living God. And somehow it seemed unjust that a just God would encourage a man to die for him early in life or to live a life of misery and deprivation in order to sacrifice for him and subsequently that God would simply let such a zealous follower be extinguished without receiving any benefits for his faithfulness.

The Pharisees could also note the fact that a lot of rascals had lived rich, enjoyable lives, while a lot of saints had lived thoroughly miserable and tragic lives. The earthly life, they could perceive, is frequently not a just accounting at all. And since God is absolutely just, there simply must be another life in which to balance the sadly tilting scales of justice.

The common people—the poorer folk of the land—split on the issue of an afterlife. Some of them agreed with the Sadducees and consequently lived lives of total moral abandon. "If you have only one life to live," they reasoned, "then get all you can, any way you can, no matter who suffers." A sizable proportion of the common people, however, seems to have sided with the Pharisees, which is no great wonder, since the poor have often been more spiritually perceptive than the rich. Not having the riches of this world, the poor are more apt to desire the riches of the next world.

Furthermore, their hope of an afterlife is not merely a dream of "pie in the sky by and by" in order to keep from being emotionally crushed by the harsh realities of this one life. Rather, because the poor have always been the ones who have most deeply experienced the tragedies of life, they have also been the ones who have most deeply experienced the deliverance of God. They are the ones who, out of necessity, have developed through petitionary prayer a relationship with God that assures them that he is indeed a powerful and just God. They are the ones who have called to him for help in time of need and who have experienced the miracles of his deliverance. And something deep down inside these people simply rebels at the thought that this powerful and just God who delivers them would not thoroughly vindicate their poverty and pain in another life.

So this lack of agreement was the situation in Jesus' day. Everyone had his opinions on the afterlife. Many people had hopes. Most people lived according to their opinions and their hopes. But when all the arguments were heard, the truth was still that no one really knew the answer.

Our modern age is strikingly parallel to Jesus' day. For our age also is divided down the middle on the matter of the afterlife. The modern Sadducees are everywhere about us, believing that God has given only one life, and living accordingly. Most of the Sadducees of our age go even further than doubting that there is an afterlife, however. For most of today's Sadducees are also theological atheists or agnostics. They believe that there is no Creator God, that life evolved purely by chance, that there is nothing of real value or meaning in life, that there are no absolute rights or wrongs.

But the modern Sadducees can also be pressed into the confession that actually they do not really know that there is no afterlife. They too are still just guessing. They too are only living by their faith. But it is a "black faith." And they have no evidence at all for their position, except for one negative fact, which is that no one has ever reported back *to them* from the other side of the grave. The puzzling illogicality in their "black faith," therefore, is that they should be holding on so very, very firmly to something which has such little support and that they should not be more open to a faith that claims to be built on valid positive data.

But puzzling or not, the atheistic Sadducees of today cling passionately to their faith in the meaninglessness of life. They believe that we human beings are simply animals that suffer and play and fear and worry for a short life-span. And then we are no more. Everything, in the final weighing, is really nothing.

Consequently, the modern Sadducees, like their counterparts of old, approach their one life with the desperate attitude: "Eat, drink, and be merry, for tomorrow we die!" It makes no difference whether these people are rich or poor, "cool" or "gone," schooled or unschooled. Their outlook on life is essentially the same.

We see these "one life" people in our international communist enemies. "If you are a man without power or wealth and have but one life to live," the communist asks, "then why should you work patiently for a gradual improvement in your situation that will benefit only your children? Change things now!" he exhorts. "And use any effective method, including wholesale slaughter. Your enemy is merely another animal that is pursuing its pleasures and just happens to be standing in the way of your pleasures."

We see these "one life" people in our own communities today. They are the people who never participate in a good community work without being forced. They are the people whose after-work and weekend schedules are organized totally around entertainment—never around service. They are the people who will not do a lick of work if others will support them with taxes. They are the people behind bars in the jailhouse. They are the people who will lie and steal in a business arrangement. They are the people to whom marital and family loyalty means nothing. They are the people who will not go to the assistance of another person in danger or sacrifice to help another person out of hardship. They are the people whose names are not on church rolls because they see no sense in the existence of the church. They are the inactive members whose names are on the church rolls because they see no sense in making someone think less of them by asking that their names be taken off.

The biggest reason for the many millions of narrow and shallow lives that are purposely lived for the self and the present moment is this basic "one life" despair. These people believe that there is no God. Or they believe that, if there is a God, he gives us but one short life. And the opportunities therein are brutally unequal and apparently by chance. So why not be selfish and godless under these circumstances? What value can there be for us in living any other way? This being the situation, is it not true that to a crucial extent the whole success of God's dealings with man, and the very humanity of the human race in this life, has been determined and is being determined by whether there is or is not a blessed afterlife?

How thrilled we Christians are, therefore, to be able to announce to an anxious and despairing world the good news that because the crucified Jesus of Nazareth appeared alive to his followers on the third day after his death, there is to be a blessed life for us beyond this life! As Paul reports in I Corinthians 15: "He appeared to Cephas, then to the twelve. Then he appeared to more than five hundred brethren at one time, most of whom are still alive, though some have fallen asleep. . . . Last of all, as to one untimely born, he appeared also to me" (vss. 5-8). Because Jesus manifested himself from the fifth dimension of Heaven, mankind is no longer limited to mere guesses and hopes about survival of the soul! Here a historical person has reported back from the dead!

And what is so very, very significant about Jesus' return is that this man is no ordinary person. This man is acknowledged to have lived an especially righteous life on earth. He claimed to have had a special divine mission to reveal the heavenly Father to all men and to win back all men to the Father through the testimony of the church that he organized. He is reported to have been blessed with special divine powers to heal. Even inanimate nature was reportedly made flexible to his wishes in order to signify that this man indeed represented the living God.

Thus Jesus' reappearance was no accidental hole opened in the fence of death through which one man by chance slipped back momentarily. Nor was Jesus' reappearance an occult occurrence in which some medium or wizard or mentally deranged person claimed to have conjured up a soul from another dimension. Rather, Jesus' reappearance was evidently a deliberate action from God's side in the unseen heavenly dimension. God deliberately sent his representative—his ambassador—back from the other side to give us once and for all an authoritative word on the afterlife.

Of course, for us who live two thousand years later it is all still a matter of faith. The reappearance of Jesus was a matter of factual surety only to those to whom Jesus revealed himself. But our faith in the reappearance reports has solid historical foundations nevertheless.

The most solid historical fact is the existence of the Christian church. Something had to happen to change a group of scattered, demoralized followers into the core of a dynamic organization that converted the whole ancient world on the basis of its message of God's love and man's resurrection—a dynamic organization that is still spreading out today. The Christian church is much like the ever-widening ripples on the surface of a quiet pond—ripples that bear testimony that some time ago something heavy dropped into the pond. Other historical facts are gleaned from the New Testament documents. There is just enough disagreement between the accounts of what took place after the crucifixion to make the reappearance of Jesus sound authentic. There is just enough legendary addition to signify that a truly amazing historical core is being added to.

Another strong piece of historical evidence is the nature of the Christian church. This organization, which is based on the message of Jesus' reappearance, has benefited and ennobled the human race more than any other movement in history. And it just does not seem plausible that such a preeminently uplifting and effective enterprise as the church would be based on a dishonesty or an illusion.

Yes, we have the information for which a whole world is anxious. Many people will challenge our good news because they have not really investigated the matter, and simply hold the prejudiced opinion that Jesus' reappearance is all superstition and fable. Many people will challenge our good news because they are so spiritually dulled by selfish dissipation that they cannot bear to turn loose this dissipation. Many people will challenge our good news because it seems to them simply too good to be true.

But we are of the firm conviction that it *is* true that Jesus the Messiah has appeared alive to his disciples and that the evidence is as strong as ever. So on every Sunday, which we label "the Lord's day" in commemoration of Jesus' reappearance on that day, we gather again in God's house of worship and teaching—we who are keenly aware that we are scattered along every stage of life's way into death. We gather to hear anew the ancient but ever modern good news that the Messiah is alive, that God's official ambassador has brought us the sure knowledge that at the end of life we shall enter life without end. We gather to hear, and to give, an affirmative answer to Job's question: "If a man die, shall he live again?" Yes! If he is truly the child of the Father, he shall live again. Yes! Because Jesus lives on still, man shall live again.

APPENDIX A

The Nicene Creed

I believe in one God the Father Almighty, Maker of heaven and earth, And of all things visible and invisible.

And in one Lord Jesus Christ, the only-begotten Son of God; Begotten of his Father before all worlds, God of God, Light of Light, Very God of very God, Begotten, not made; Being of one substance with the Father; By whom all things were made: Who for us men and for our salvation came down from heaven, And was incarnate by the Holy Ghost of the Virgin Mary, And was made man; And was crucified also for us under Pontius Pilate; He suffered and was buried; And the third day he rose again according to the Scriptures, And ascended into heaven, And sitteth on the right hand of the Father. And he shall come again with glory, to judge both the quick and the dead: Whose kingdom shall have no end.

And I believe in the Holy Ghost, the Lord and Giver of Life, Who proceedeth from the Father and the Son; Who with the Father and the Son together is worshiped and glorified; Who spake by the prophets. And I believe one Holy Catholic and Apostolic Church. I acknowledge one Baptism for the remission of sins. And I look for the Resurrection of the dead, And the Life of the world to come. Amen.

APPENDIX B

The Apostles' Creed

I believe in God the Father Almighty, Maker of heaven and earth:
And in Jesus Christ his only Son our Lord: Who was conceived by
the Holy Ghost, Born of the Virgin Mary, Suffered under Pontius Pilate,
Was crucified, dead, and buried: He descended into hell; The third day he
rose again from the dead; He ascended into heaven, And sitteth at the right
hand of God the Father Almighty; From thence he shall come to judge
the quick and the dead.

I believe in the Holy Ghost; The holy Catholic Church; The Communion
of Saints; The Forgiveness of sins; The Resurrection of the body, And
the Life everlasting. Amen.

APPENDIX C

United Church of Christ 1959 Statement of Faith

We believe in God, the Eternal Spirit, Father of our Lord Jesus Christ and our Father, and to his deeds we testify:

He calls the worlds into being, creates man in his own image, and sets before him the ways of life and death.

He seeks in holy love to save all people from aimlessness and sin.

He judges men and nations by his righteous will declared through prophets and apostles.

In Jesus Christ, the man of Nazareth, our crucified and risen Lord, he has come to us and shared our common lot, conquering sin and death, and reconciling the world to himself.

He bestows upon us his Holy Spirit, creating and renewing the church of Jesus Christ, binding in covenant faithful people of all ages, tongues, and races.

He calls us into his church to accept the cost and joy of discipleship, to be his servants in the service of men, to proclaim the gospel to all the world, and to resist the powers of evil, to share in Christ's baptism and eat at his table, to join him in his passion and victory.

He promises to all who trust him forgiveness of sins and fullness of grace, courage in the struggle for justice and peace, his presence in trial and rejoicing, and eternal life in his kingdom which has no end.

Blessing and honor, glory and power be unto him. Amen.

APPENDIX D

The Author's Creed

(from experimental liturgy of 1966)

We believe that the everlasting God is our loving Father, who has created us and all things that exist, and who sustains us and all things, as he wills, and as we obey, through all eternity.

We believe that at the crucial time God sent a chosen son, Jesus Christ, from Nazareth of Galilee, to reveal to mortal man God's eternal love. We believe that God acknowledged Jesus' mission with mighty signs called miracles. We believe that in the person of Jesus we have seen the nature of God himself, that in the ministry of Jesus we have seen that true life is loving sacrifice, and that in the resurrection of Jesus we have seen the power and permanence of God's love.

We believe that God our Father is everywhere present, in a spiritual form, to enlighten, to encourage, and to empower us in every moment of our lives. We believe that he wishes us to gather as his family in the church of Jesus Christ and that we have fully found ourselves only when we have been found together in him. Amen.

INDEX